Six Sigma For Dummies®

W9-BUY-230

The Six Sigma Tools-Methods Landscape

DEFINE

- Project Selection
- Problem Statement
- Objective Statement

- Data Audit
- Attribute Measurement Analysis
- Gauge Repeatability & Reproducibility (R & R)

MEASURE

- Measurement System Analysis (MSA)
- As-Is Performance Baseline
- Process Flowcharting / Mapping
- Input (X) Identification
- Input (X) Funneling

- SIPOC Diagram
- Affinity Diagram
- Fishbone Diagram
- Value Add / Non-Value Add Analysis
- Cause-Effect (C-E) / X-Y Matrix Analysis
- Failure Mode Effects Analysis (FMEA)

ANALYZE

- Basic Statistics
- Graphical Analysis
- Observational Studies
- Capability Analysis
- Confidence Intervals

- Mean (average), Mode, Median
- Range (R), Standard Deviation (σ)
- Dot Plots / Histograms
- Box & Whisker Plots
- Scatter (X-Y) Plots
- Run / Behavior Charts

IMPROVE

- Correlation
- Curve Fitting / Simple Linear Regression
- Design of Experiments (DOE)
- Process Management Summary

- Yield Metrics (Y, FTY, RTY)
- Defect Rate Metrics (DPU, DPO, DPMO, DPPM)
- Sigma Score (Z)
- C_p, C_{pk}, P_p, P_{pk}
- 2^k Factorial Experiments

CONTROL

- Process Control Plan
- Control Charts / Statistical Process Control (SPC)
- Poka-Yoke

- Continuous Data: $I\text{-}\overline{MR}$, $\overline{X}\text{-}R$, $\overline{X}\text{-}S$ Charts
- Attribute Data: p, u Charts

Six Sigma For Dummies®

Cheat Sheet

What Is Six Sigma?

You can define Six Sigma in a variety of ways:

- A quality level of 3.4 defects per million opportunities
- A rate of improvement of 70 percent or better
- A data-driven, problem-solving methodology of Define-Measure-Analyze-Improve-Control
- An initiative taken on by organizations to create bottom-line breakthrough change

The Principles of Six Sigma

Sum up Six Sigma with the following simple principles:

- $Y = f(X) + \varepsilon$: All outcomes and results (the Y) are determined by inputs (the Xs) with some degree of uncertainty (ε).
- To change or improve results (the Y), you have to focus on the inputs (the Xs), modify them, and control them.
- Variation is everywhere, and it degrades consistent, good performance. Your job is to find it and minimize it!
- Valid measurements and data are required foundations for consistent, breakthrough improvement.
- Only a critical few inputs have significant effect on the output. Concentrate on the critical few.

The DMAIC Problem-Solving Method

The DMAIC problem-solving method consists of five clear-cut steps:

- **Define:** Set the context and objectives for your improvement project.
- **Measure:** Determine the baseline performance and capability of the process or system you're improving.
- **Analyze:** Use data and tools to understand the cause-and-effect relationships in your process or system.
- **Improve:** Develop the modifications that lead to a validated improvement in your process or system.
- **Control:** Establish plans and procedures to ensure that your improvements are sustained.

The Sigma Scale

Sigma Level (Z)	Defects per Million Opportunities (DPMO)	Percent Defects (%)	Percent Success (Yield %)	Capability (C_P)
1	691,462	69	31	0.33
2	308,538	31	69	0.67
3	66,807	6.7	93.3	1.00
4	6,210	0.62	99.38	1.33
5	233	0.023	99.977	1.67
6	3.4	0.00034	99.99966	2.00

Copyright © 2005 Wiley Publishing, Inc. All rights reserved.
Item 6798-5.
For more information about Wiley Publishing, call 1-800-762-2974.

For Dummies: Bestselling Book Series for Beginners

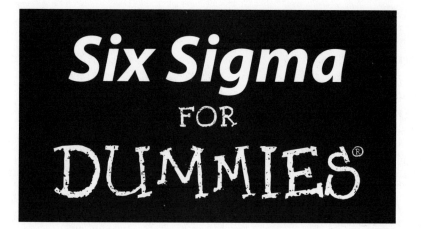

Six Sigma FOR DUMMIES®

by Craig Gygi, Neil DeCarlo, Bruce Williams

Foreword by Stephen R. Covey
Author, *The 7 Habits of Highly Effective People* and *The 8th Habit*

Wiley Publishing, Inc.

Six Sigma For Dummies®

Published by
Wiley Publishing, Inc.
111 River St.
Hoboken, NJ 07030-5774
www.wiley.com

Copyright © 2005 by Wiley Publishing, Inc., Indianapolis, Indiana

Published by Wiley Publishing, Inc., Indianapolis, Indiana

Published simultaneously in Canada

For general information on our other products and services, please contact our Customer Care Department within the U.S. at 800-762-2974, outside the U.S. at 317-572-3993, or fax 317-572-4002.

For technical support, please visit www.wiley.com/techsupport.

Wiley also publishes its books in a variety of electronic formats. Some content that appears in print may not be available in electronic books.

Library of Congress Control Number: 2005920302

ISBN: 0-7645-6798-5

Manufactured in the United States of America

10 9 8 7 6 5

1B/RY/QS/QV/IN

WILEY

About the Authors

Craig Kent Gygi began studying and applying the elements of Six Sigma well before they were formalized into today's renowned breakthrough methodology. As a graduate student in mechanical engineering at Brigham Young University in the early 1990s, he integrated these cutting-edge improvement techniques into his coaching of student product development teams. Upon beginning his career in 1994 at Motorola's Advanced Manufacturing Research Lab in Florida, he was formally introduced to the maturing Six Sigma method. It resonated deeply with his previous findings. From that time, Craig has applied, taught, and led Six Sigma in all his endeavors, including management and technical capacities at Motorola, Iomega, and General Atomics.

In 1998, Craig founded and led a software company to develop computational tools for Six Sigma practitioners. For several years, he also worked as a technical colleague of Dr. Mikel J. Harry, the original consultant of Six Sigma, co-developing and teaching new advances in its theory and application. Most recently, Craig has traded his mountain home in Utah for the Sonoran desert of Arizona to co-found Savvi International and direct and manage its Six Sigma products, services, and tools.

A Master Black Belt, Craig has wielded Six Sigma techniques now for over 12 years, spanning projects from design to manufacturing to business process management. He is also an expert teacher, having instructed and mentored at all levels of Six Sigma, from executives to White Belts.

Neil John DeCarlo has been a professional communicator in the continuous improvement and Six Sigma fields for more than 15 years, beginning with his work at Florida Power & Light company when it won the coveted Deming Prize for quality. Since that time, he has authored, ghostwritten, or edited more than 150 articles and six books in association with such companies as General Electric, Dupont, Bose Corporation, McKinsey consulting, UPS, AT&T, the Six Sigma Academy, and many others.

As a prolific author and writer, Neil's past work has covered a range of subject matter, including Six Sigma, information technology, e-learning, knowledge management, change management, business integration, TQM, ISO, lean management, and other disciplines. He has also worked with several CEOs and consultants, including Japanese quality expert Dr. Noriaki Kano, and worked extensively with original co-architect of Six Sigma, Dr. Mikel Harry.

In addition to his writing pedigree, Neil has managed communication and publishing campaigns for a variety of companies and consulting firms, most notably, the Breakthrough Management Group, a Six Sigma, lean enterprise, and performance-improvement industry leader. While not working, Neil avidly practices Bikram yoga and contributes to that community through his advocacy and writing.

Bruce David Williams has been fascinated with complex systems since the launch of Sputnik on his third birthday. With undergraduate degrees from the University of Colorado in Physics and Astrophysics, he entered a career in aerospace systems, where he first encountered Six Sigma after Motorola won the inaugural Baldridge Award in 1988. Later, with graduate degrees in technical management and computer science from Johns Hopkins University and the University of Colorado, and as a member of the Hubble Telescope development team, he was intrigued by how breakdowns in the smallest components could lead to colossal system failures. He entered the Six Sigma industry in the mid-1990s, when he founded a software company to pursue product life-cycle traceability.

Bruce has since been founder and CEO of two Six Sigma research and technology firms, and is now Chairman and CEO of Savvi International, a provider of solutions for business performance improvement using Six Sigma, lean, and business process management techniques. He resides in the desert foothills of North Scottsdale, Arizona, with his wife, two children, and assortment of dogs, cats, birds, and horses.

Dedication

Craig Gygi: To Jill, Ivan, and Gordon. Being part of their lives is my greatest success.

Neil DeCarlo: To Wanda Texon, who helped me believe in myself a long time ago, and who has been a constant source of support and intellectual stimulation for many years.

Bruce Williams: To Barbi, my spectacular wife of 22 years, and my amazing children, Hannah and Evan. Their tireless devotion, artful humor, and limitless thirst for knowledge truly make anything possible.

Authors' Acknowledgments

Six Sigma per se didn't exist twenty years ago. Miraculously, a single individual working for a large corporation in a cubicle at a nondescript office building saw something, and now — tens of thousands of individual practitioners, thousands of corporations, and hundreds of billions of dollars in savings later — we have a fully evolved system. On behalf of the entire Six Sigma movement, we'd like to acknowledge that individual: the late Bill Smith, a reliability engineer at Motorola in Arizona, who in the mid-1980s recognized a statistical correlation between product complexity, process capability, and system failure. We'd also like to acknowledge Dr. Mikel Harry, another Motorola Six Sigma pioneer, who has helped make the industry what it is today.

We'd like to thank Don L. Redinius, who contributed significant portions of this book. We're extremely fortunate to have had his contribution. Don is an internationally recognized business performance improvement consultant with more than 25 years of experience who has dedicated much of his career to Six Sigma.

In addition to writing Chapters 4 and 10, Don supplied extensive subject matter expertise, materials, guidance, and comments in reviewing, and in improving, nearly every page and figure.

Our deepest thanks to Dr. Stephen R. Covey, who honored us by writing the Foreword for this book.

We also thank Ms. Roxanne O'Brasky, president of the International Society of Six Sigma Professionals, for her Afterword. Roxanne is a singular tour de force in Six Sigma and she is making the world a better place through the work of the society.

We owe the very existence of this book to acquisitions editor Kathy Cox and project editor Tere Stouffer Drenth, who masterfully guided the ship through the storm, avoided the reefs, and sailed us gently into port.

We'd also like to acknowledge those tens of thousands of practitioners: the Black Belts, Green Belts, and Yellow Belts; the Champions; the Master Black Belts; and the deployment leaders. Their collective work has defined Six Sigma. They did it without a Six Sigma textbook, government study contracts, ISO standards bodies, or enterprise information systems. They made Six Sigma happen and evolved it to the point where this book became possible.

Publisher's Acknowledgments

We're proud of this book; please send us your comments through our Dummies online registration form located at www.dummies.com/register/.

Some of the people who helped bring this book to market include the following:

Acquisitions, Editorial, and Media Development

Project Editor: Tere Stouffer Drenth

Acquisitions Editor: Kathy Cox

Technical Editor: Lean Works, Inc. (www.leanworks.com): Tom Greenwood, Martin McGregor, Eric Lockhart

General Reviewer: Tom Pearson

Editorial Manager: Michelle Hacker

Editorial Supervisor: Carmen Krikorian

Editorial Assistant: Nadine Bell

Cartoons: Rich Tennant, www.the5thwave.com

Composition

Project Coordinator: Emily Wichlinski

Layout and Graphics: Jonelle Burns, Lauren Goddard, Denny Hager, Joyce Haughey, Stephanie D. Jumper, Barry Offringa, Jacque Roth, Heather Ryan, Julie Trippetti, Mary Gillot Virgin

Proofreaders: Leeann Harney, Jessica Kramer

Indexer: Johnna VanHoose

Publishing and Editorial for Consumer Dummies

Diane Graves Steele, Vice President and Publisher, Consumer Dummies

Joyce Pepple, Acquisitions Director, Consumer Dummies

Kristin A. Cocks, Product Development Director, Consumer Dummies

Michael Spring, Vice President and Publisher, Travel

Kelly Regan, Editorial Director, Travel

Publishing for Technology Dummies

Andy Cummings, Vice President and Publisher, Dummies Technology/General User

Composition Services

Gerry Fahey, Vice President of Production Services

Debbie Stailey, Director of Composition Services

Contents at a Glance

Foreword...*xv*

Introduction 1

Part I: Six Sigma Basics 7
Chapter 1: Defining Six Sigma 9
Chapter 2: Examining the Principles and Language of Six Sigma............27
Chapter 3: Pinpointing the Essentials of Six Sigma 41

Part II: Understanding and Enacting the Breakthrough Strategy (DMAIC) 61
Chapter 4: Finding the Pain — Defining Projects 63
Chapter 5: Measuring the Gaps 85
Chapter 6: Measuring Capability 123
Chapter 7: Separating the Wheat from the Chaff.........................149
Chapter 8: Quantifying the Critical Few 169
Chapter 9: Achieving the Objective 195
Chapter 10: Locking in the Gains......................................217

Part III: The Six Sigma Tool and Technology Landscape 241
Chapter 11: Identifying Six Sigma Practitioner Tools 243
Chapter 12: Mastering Six Sigma Manager Tools 283

Part IV: The Part of Tens 301
Chapter 13: Ten Best Practices of Six Sigma...........................303
Chapter 14: Ten Pitfalls to Avoid 309
Chapter 15: Ten Places to Go for Help.................................313

Appendix: Glossary 319

Afterword..329

Index 329

Table of Contents

Foreword ....*xv*

Introduction 1

About This Book...1
Conventions Used in This Book 2
Foolish Assumptions 3
How This Book Is Organized..3
    Part I: Six Sigma Basics 3
    Part II: Understanding and Enacting the
        Breakthrough Strategy (DMAIC)........................4
    Part III: The Six Sigma Tool and Technology Landscape...........4
    Part IV: The Part of Tens...4
Icons Used in This Book..4
Where to Go from Here...5

Part 1: Six Sigma Basics..7

Chapter 1: Defining Six Sigma 9
The Managerial Perspective 11
    Radical corporate success 12
    Bridge between science and leadership.........................12
    Management system orientation.................................13
The Technical Perspective...16
    Product, service, and transactional quality 17
    The journey from one to many 20
    Watch out for the wiggle, bump, and jitter 22
    Why six and why sigma? (Putting the pieces together)..........23

Chapter 2: Examing the Principles and Language of Six Sigma 27
It All Begins with One Simple Equation: $Y = f(X) + \varepsilon$ 27
Determine the Cause 29
    Cause and effect 29
    There is a better way 30
    Beware superstitious delusions (that is, correlation
        doesn't imply causation) 30

Variation happens 32
    What is variation? 33
    Where does variation come from? 34
    Getting variation right is everything..................................35
Thou Shalt Measure 36
    Mind your *Y*s and *X*s 36
    The answer begins with the data 37
    The bottom line on measurement 38
The Power of Leverage...38
    The "vital few" versus the "trivial many" 39
    Finding the better way..40

Chapter 3: Pinpointing the Essentials of Six Sigma 41

The Project Strategy: DMAIC 41
Domains of Activity 43
    Thinking for breakthrough 43
    Processing for breakthrough 44
    Designing for breakthrough 44
    Managing for breakthrough..45
The People: Who You Need to Know 46
    In Six Sigma, everyone's a leader 46
    Number-crunching karate: Black Belts and their brethren............51
    Bringing the team together 54
The Lifecycle of a Six Sigma Initiative 55
    Initialize: Ready . . . Aim 55
    Deploy: Setting it all in motion 56
    Implement: Forging first successes....................................57
    Expand: Taking it everywhere..58
    Sustain: The self-healing culture 58

Part II: Understanding and Enacting the Breakthrough Strategy (DMAIC) 61

Chapter 4: Finding the Pain — Defining Projects 63

The Six Sigma Project 64
    The basics of a project 64
    The problem transformation 65
    Project responsibilities..65
Your Needs, My Needs, What Are They?....................................66
    Aligning Six Sigma with strategy 67
    Using a business case writing tool for project identification........69
    Six Sigma project definition 71
    Is it worth doing?..75

Chapter 5: Measuring the Gaps 85

The 1, 2, 3s of Statistics 85
    Why statistics? 86
    Measurement 101 87
    What does it mean? Measures of variation location 88
    How much variation is there? 91
The Long and Short of Variation 95
    Short-term variation 96
    Shift happens: Long-term variation 99
    Be all you can be: Entitlement 101
A Picture's Worth a Thousand Words 103
    Plotting and charting data 103
    Hindsight is 20/20: Behavior charts 117

Chapter 6: Measuring Capability 123

Specifications: The Voice of the Customer 123
    How close is close enough? Or why specifications? 124
    What are specifications? 124
    Do you do the RUMBA? Creating realistic specifications 125
    Don't push that big red button! What happens
        when you exceed a specification 126
Capability: Comparing the Voice of the Customer to the
  Voice of the Process 128
    Measuring yield 128
    Measuring defect rate 133
    Linking yield and defect rate 138
    Sigma (Z) score 138
    Capability indices 144
    Prescribing a capability improvement plan 147

Chapter 7: Separating the Wheat from the Chaff 149

Understanding Data Types 150
    Attribute or category data 150
    Continuous or variable data 151
Avoiding Illusion: Measurement System Capability Analysis 152
    Sources of measurement system variation 154
    Measuring measurements: Measurement
        system analysis (MSA) 156
Filling the Funnel 161
    Let the data do the talking 162
    Cast a big net 162
Mining Data for Insight 163
    Go with what you have: Observational studies ...163
    Digging in: Identifying potential sources of variation
        through graphical analysis 165

Chapter 8: Quantifying the Critical Few 169

Finding the Best Partner 169
 Viva Las Vegas: The central limit theorem....................................170
 How sure are you? Confidence intervals 171
 Confidence intervals for means...172
 Confidence intervals for standard deviations 176
 Four out of five recommend: Confidence
  intervals for proportions 178
Understanding Relationships 180
 Correlation 180
 Curve fitting 183

Chapter 9: Achieving the Objective 195

Why Experiment? The Improvement Power
 of Six Sigma Experiments 195
 What is an experiment, anyway?...195
 The purpose of Six Sigma experiments 196
 Experimenting with words 197
 The end game of Six Sigma experiments 197
Look Before You Leap: Experimental Considerations 198
 Frankenstein should have planned 198
 Simple, sequential, and systematic is best 200
2^k Factorial Experiments 202
 Plan your experiment 202
 Conduct your experiment 206
 Analyze your experiment 207
You've Only Just Begun — More Topics in Experimentation.................216

Chapter 10: Locking in the Gains 217

The Need for Control Planning..217
 The process management summary...219
 The process control plan 219
Statistical Process Control..221
Monitoring the Process: Control Chart Basics 222
 Understanding control limits 223
 Using control charts to keep processes on track..........................226
 Using control charts to detect patterns, shifts, and drifts 227
 Collecting data for control charts 229
Control Charts for Continuous Data..230
 Individuals and moving range chart ($I - MR$) 232
 Averages and ranges chart ($\overline{X} - R$ chart)................................234
 Averages and standard deviation chart ($\overline{X} - S$)........................235
Control Charts for Attribute Data 235
 The p chart for attribute data...237
 The u chart for attribute data...238
Poka-Yoke (Mistake-Proofing)..239

Part III: The Six Sigma Tool and Technology Landscape 241

Chapter 11: Identifying Six Sigma Practitioner Tools 243
The Practitioner's Toolkit 244
Process Optimization Tools...245
   The SIPOC...246
   What's critical? Look in the CT Tree...................................248
   Modeling a process 251
   Simulating a process 256
   Cause-and-effect (C&E) matrix 258
   Dem' fishbones 259
   FMEA: Failure mode effects analysis................................260
   KISS and tell: Capability-complexity analysis 262
   Funnel reports 264
   Plans 265
Statistical Analysis Tools 267
   The basics 268
   A picture's worth a thousand . . . dollars..........................268
   The time machine...270
   Analysis of variance: ANOVA 271
   If the shoe fits 271
   Design of Experiments 272
   How capable is your process? 273
   Regression 275
   Multivariate analysis..275
   Exploratory analysis 276
   Measurement systems analysis..276
   Back to the future 278
Platforms and Protocols..278
   Software products 278
   Technology architectures...280

Chapter 12: Mastering Six Sigma Manager Tools 283
The Manager's Toolkit 284
   The gallery 285
   Types of management tools 286
Through the Looking Glass..287
Project Management...288
   Eureka! 289
   Pick a winner...290
   Project definition..291
   Project planning and tracking 293
Just the Facts, Ma'am 295
Knowledge Management 298
An Apple for Your Apple 299

Part IV: The Part of Tens 301

Chapter 13: Ten Best Practices of Six Sigma 303
Set Stretch Goals 303
Target Tangible Results 304
Determine Outcomes 304
Think Before You Act 305
Put Your Faith in Data 305
Minimize Variation 306
Align Projects with Key Goals...306
Celebrate Success! 306
Involve the Owner..307
Unleash Everyone's Potential 307

Chapter 14: Ten Pitfalls to Avoid 309
Not Allowing Enough Time 309
Who's the Leader?..309
Taking Too Big a Bite 310
Focusing On Isolated Areas 310
"But We're Different"...310
Overtraining..311
Blindly Believing Your Measurement System....................311
"Remind Me Again, Is It CLs or SLs?"..................................312
Exaggerated Opportunity Counts 312
Not Leveraging Technology 312

Chapter 15: Ten Places to Go for Help 313
Colleagues...313
Six Sigma Corporations 314
Associations and Professional Societies 314
Conferences and Symposia 314
Publications 315
Web Portals 316
Periodicals 316
Technology Vendors 317
Consultants 317
Six Sigma Trainers...318

Appendix: Glossary.................................319

Afterword 329

Index.................................331

Foreword

*T*he world is on the verge of a new economic era. For the past century, the Industrial Age has been defined by tools and skills targeted at control, efficiency, specialization, delegation, scalability, and replicability. Accounting makes people an expense, a piece of equipment, an investment, and people are motivated by the great jackass theory of the carrot and stick. But although this paradigm has led to a 50-fold increase in productivity over the previous farming mindset, it has also led to a control paradigm, an entrenchment of a "leadership by position" mentality, with organizational hallmarks of lack of clarity regarding high priorities, lack of commitment or emotional connection by the workforce, lack of line-of-sight translation to specific action, disenabling systems and processes, no synergy — interpersonally and interdepartmentally — and a lack of accountability.

Studies show that the vast majority of employees possess far more talent, more intelligence, more capability, more creativity, and more ability than their jobs require or even allow. Their deep potential remains dormant, untapped, and unused. Today, the Industrial Age is ending, and the Information Age or Knowledge Worker Age is opening. This new, emerging age is defined by "leadership is a choice" with an empowerment or unleashing-potential mentality; choices guided by values in the light of unchanging principles. In the new paradigm, the greatest asset in any organization is its people — whole people — with their bodies, minds, hearts, and consciences all engaged and contributing, and all receiving benefit in the progress of the organization. A *trim tab* is a small rudder on a boat or airplane that, through its relatively small motion, allows the bigger rudder to achieve the greater effect and leverage. The leaders of the Information Age act as trim tabs within organizations. Their relatively small actions at the bottom or middle can effect a much greater change throughout an entire organization.

Six Sigma has become a key enabling skill of the new Knowledge Workers of the next generation of trim tabs. One of the great values I admire of Six Sigma is the science, the database — and the careful analytic thought processes of problem solving using that data. Six Sigma empowers and enables you to effect remarkable change, no matter your position in your organization. The maturing world has transformed the previously exclusive, academic knowledge of Six Sigma into must-have best practices for everyone wishing to advance and contribute. In a knowledge economy where 70 to 80 percent of the value added to goods and services comes from knowledge work, can you imagine the results flowing from having the entire workforce Six Sigma literate?

That's why *Six Sigma For Dummies* is a book to be read by everyone.

Stephen R. Covey

Author, *The 7 Habits of Highly Effective People* and *The 8th Habit*

Introduction

· ·

Six Sigma is the single most effective problem-solving methodology for improving business and organizational performance. There's not a business, technical, or process challenge that can't be improved with Six Sigma. The world's top corporations have used it to increase their profits collectively by more than $100 billion over the past ten years. In certain corporations, Six Sigma proficiency on your résumé is now a prerequisite to moving into a position in management.

If you're part of a *Fortune* 500 company — particularly a manufacturing company — chances are, you've heard about Six Sigma. You may even have been through a training regimen and been part of a corporate initiative or an improvement project. If so, you know the capabilities of Six Sigma; you have witnessed its achievements firsthand.

But if, like many people, you're outside of the upper echelons of big business, Six Sigma is virtually unknown. It has been too expensive and complicated for small- and medium-sized businesses, public institutions, not-for-profit organizations, educational environments, and even aspiring individuals. Its potential has remained out of reach for the vast majority of professionals and organizations world-wide.

All this is changing. As the methods and tools of Six Sigma have spread, it has become easier to understand and more straightforward to implement. The mysteries of Six Sigma have been revealed.

Simply stated, Six Sigma is about applying a structured, scientific method to improve any aspect of a business, organization, process, or person. It's about engaging in disciplined data collection and analysis to determine the best possible ways of meeting your customer's needs while satisfying yours, and minimizing wasted resources and maximizing profit in the process.

About This Book

This book makes Six Sigma accessible to you. We wrote it because Six Sigma is applicable everywhere; it's applicable not only in large and complex corporations but also in the less complex and more intimate worlds of professional performance and personal accomplishment.

We wrote this book for you, the individual. You may be a small business owner, an ambitious career person, a manager who wants to know what Six Sigma is and how to apply it, a college student or applicant who wants to have an edge on upcoming job interviews. For you, there's nowhere else but here to turn.

Six Sigma For Dummies is more than an overview or survey of Six Sigma. It is a comprehensive, actionable description of the methods and tools of Six Sigma. In this book, you find:

- ✔ A reference book that's organized into parts, chapters, and sections, so that you can flip right to what you need, when you need it
- ✔ A comprehensive text that addresses both the statistics of Six Sigma and the improvement methodology
- ✔ A guide for leading a Six Sigma initiative, selecting and managing Six Sigma projects, and executing specific Six Sigma tools and analytical procedures
- ✔ Step-by-step instructions for the Define-Measure-Analyze-Improve-Control phases of the Six Sigma process
- ✔ Instructions on where you can go for additional help, because the field of Six Sigma is much too large to fit in only 400 pages

Sure, Six Sigma is rigorous, technical, and analytical, but we've taken this difficult subject and made it understandable through examples, simple explanations, and visual aids.

Conventions Used in This Book

When a specialized word first appears in our book, we italicize it, and provide a definition. Most terms are further defined in the appendix.

For terms and phrases that industry practitioners use as acronyms, we define the term first and then use it in its abbreviated form going forward.

When we use the term *data,* we always mean it in the plural sense. While there is debate among statisticians about using *data* in both a plural and singular sense, we stick with the plural only, because our editor told us we had to. Otherwise, *datum* is the singular form.

We do use some business management and statistical concepts and language. If you want to get extra smart, check out *Managing For Dummies,* 2nd Edition, by Bob Nelson, Peter Economy, and Ken Blanchard, and *Statistics For Dummies* by Deborah Rumsey (both published by Wiley).

Foolish Assumptions

We assume you've heard about Six Sigma and are intrigued and compelled to find out more. This may be for any one or more of the following reasons:

✔ You are contemplating the application of Six Sigma in your business. and you need to understand what you may be getting yourself into.

✔ Your business is implementing Six Sigma and you need to get up to speed. Perhaps you've even been tapped to participate as a Champion, Black Belt, Green Belt, or Yellow Belt.

✔ You believe Six Sigma is a pathway to better performance in your job and can help you advance your career.

✔ You're considering a career or job change, and your opportunities require you understand Six Sigma.

✔ You're a student in industrial engineering or business school and realize that Six Sigma is part of a path to success.

We also assume that you realize Six Sigma demands a rigorous and structured approach to problem solving that calls for capturing data and applying statistical analysis to discover the true causes of the challenges you may be facing in manufacturing, service, or even transactional environments. For that reason, several chapters of this book describe and define the statistical tools of Six Sigma.

How This Book Is Organized

We break this book into four separate parts. Each is written as a standalone section, permitting you to move about the book and delve into a given topic without necessarily having to read all the proceeding material first. Anywhere we expound upon or extend other material, we reference the chapter or part of origin, so you can tie it together.

We include a Cheat Sheet at the front of this book as a handy reference of key material. And in the appendix is an extensive glossary of terms.

Part I: Six Sigma Basics

Part I is an overview of the Six Sigma methodology, the system of deployment, roles, and responsibilities. In this part, we address the key principles underlying the science of Six Sigma and its applications. Chapter 1 is a comprehensive overview of Six Sigma. Chapter 2 addresses the key principles. Chapter 3 discusses roles and phases in the implementation of a Six Sigma deployment.

Part II: Understanding and Enacting the Breakthrough Strategy (DMAIC)

Part II is the meat of the book, where we get into the depths and details of practicing Six Sigma. In seven chapters, we describe Six Sigma thoroughly, according to the DMAIC method. Chapter 4 covers the phase that defines and describes how Six Sigma projects are identified. Chapters 5, 6, and 7 cover the measurement phase. Chapter 8 is analysis; Chapter 9, improvement; and Chapter 10, control. If you fully absorb this part, you can successfully perform a Six Sigma project.

Part III: The Six Sigma Tool and Technology Landscape

In this part, we present a comprehensive listing of the tools used by Six Sigma practitioners (see Chapter 11). We also present the tools of Six Sigma management in Chapter 12.

Part IV: The Part of Tens

This summary section, in the *For Dummies* tradition, is a compilation of key reference points. Chapter 13 discusses ten practices for success. Chapter 14 addresses ten pitfalls to avoid. In Chapter 15, we tell you about ten additional places you can go for help.

Icons Used in This Book

Throughout the book, you will see small symbols called *icons* in the margins, and these highlight special types of information. We use these to help you better understand and apply the material. When you see any of the following icons, this is what they mean:

These are key points to remember that can help you implement successfully.

When you see this icon, we're cautioning you to beware of a particular risk or pitfall that could cause you trouble.

This icon flags an example from industry of real events or stories about companies that have applied Six Sigma.

This icon flags a detailed technical issue or reference. Feel free to skip right over these, if you don't want to dig deeper.

We use this icon to summarize information into short, memorable thoughts.

Where to Go from Here

The beauty of a *For Dummies* book is that you don't have to start at the beginning and slowly work your way through. Instead, each chapter is self-contained, which means you can start with whichever chapters interest you the most. You can use *Six Sigma For Dummies* as a reference book, which means you can jump in and out of certain parts, chapters, and sections as you want.

Here are some suggestions on where to start:

- If you're brand new to Six Sigma, start at the beginning, with Chapter 1.
- Want to know all about those "Belts" you're hearing about? See Chapter 3.
- If you're interested in how to begin a Six Sigma project, go to Chapter 4. To find out all about tools and technologies, check out Chapter 11.
- Want to know all the gritty statistical measurement and analysis of Six Sigma? Jump in at Chapter 5.
- If you want to understand all the lingo and terminology, see the appendix.

Part I
Six Sigma Basics

The 5th Wave — By Rich Tennant

"I'm one of the Six Sigma Black Belts in the company, but several of us still wear suspenders."

In this part . . .

Six Sigma is an applied methodology for improving business and organizational performance. But before you apply the Six Sigma methodology, you can benefit from knowing what it is, where it came from, why it works and who uses it. This part provides all this so you can understand the basics of Six Sigma.

Chapter 1

Defining Six Sigma

In This Chapter

▶ Looking at a problem-solving methodology

▶ Reviewing the precise statistical term

▶ Recognizing that Six Sigma isn't just another initiative-du-jour

▶ Identifying a formidable business force

*I*t's not often that a *For Dummies* book topic first needs a formal definition. After all, you know in general what gardening, dating, and even marathon training are. But "Six Sigma"? Even if you remember that sigma is the 18th letter of the Greek alphabet, why six of them? What happened to the first five sigma?

It's okay if you don't know what "Six Sigma" is at all, or don't understand every aspect of it. That's because Six Sigma — once a precise, narrowly-defined term — has grown over time to represent a number of concepts:

▶ *Six Sigma* is a problem-solving methodology. In fact, it's the most effective problem-solving methodology available for improving business and organizational performance.

▶ *Six Sigma performance* is the statistical term for a process that produces fewer than 3.4 defects (or errors) per million opportunities for defects.

▶ A *Six Sigma improvement* is when the key outcomes of a business or work process are improved dramatically, often by 70 percent or more.

▶ A *Six Sigma deployment* is the prescriptive rollout of the Six Sigma methodology across an organization, with assigned practices, roles, and procedures according to generally accepted standards.

▶ A *Six Sigma organization* uses Six Sigma methods and tools to improve performance: Continuously lower costs, grow revenue, improve customer satisfaction, increase capacity and capability, reduce complexity, lower cycle time, and minimize defects and errors.

No pain, no gain

The Six Sigma approach is not for the faint of heart, nor the unprepared organization. It's intense and rigorous, and it entails a thorough inspection of the way everything is done. Six Sigma sets ambitious business objectives and measures performance in a way that forces accountability. It doesn't allow a management team to become complacent, but, rather, it exposes waste that otherwise would remain largely invisible.

Six Sigma takes a business out of its comfort zone — but for a relatively short time. After the first project gains are made and the money starts flowing to the profit margin, a cultural change takes hold. The early discomfort of changing business processes gives way to success, problems become opportunities for improvement, and the organization begins to enthusiastically leverage the methods and tools of Six Sigma — more pervasively and with a keen eye on value.

Six Sigma is a methodology for minimizing mistakes and maximizing value. Every mistake an organization or person makes ultimately has a cost — a lost customer, the need to do a certain task over again, a part that has to be replaced, time or material wasted, efficiency lost, or productivity squandered. In fact, waste and mistakes cost many organizations as much as 20 to 30 percent of their revenue! That's a shocking number. Imagine throwing 20 to 30 percent of your money away in the garbage every time you cash a check. It may sound ludicrous, but that's what many organizations do.

All businesses, organizations, and individuals have room to improve. No operation is run so tightly that another ounce of inefficiency and waste can't be squeezed out. By their nature, organizations tend to become messy as they grow. Processes, technology, systems, and procedures — the ways of doing business — become cluttered with *bottlenecks,* meaning work piles up in one part of the organization while other parts sit idle with nothing to do.

Work is often performed incorrectly, or the outcome is flawed in some way. When this happens, you scrap products and services and have to do the work over again: You consume additional resources to correct a problem before it's delivered to the customer, or the customer asks later for a "redo" — a new product or a more satisfactory service.

Sometimes, flaws and defects aren't the problem, but a product or service simply takes too long to produce and deliver. Think about the problems a mortgage company would have if it processed home loans perfectly, but did so 5 times slower than the competition. That's a perfect disaster.

Six Sigma was once a quality-improvement methodology, but now it's a general-purpose approach to minimizing mistakes and maximizing value: How many products can you produce, how many services can you deliver, how many transactions can you complete to an expected level of quality in the least possible amount of time at the lowest possible cost?

Six Sigma takes effort and discipline and requires you to go through the pain of change. But soon the pain is transformed into improved performance, happier customers, lower costs, and more success.

The Managerial Perspective

While Six Sigma has its many definitions, Six Sigma action occurs on two different levels: the managerial and the technical. At the managerial level, a Six Sigma initiative includes many units, people, technologies, projects, schedules, and details to be managed and coordinated. There are also many plans to develop, actions to take, and specialized work to complete. For all of this to work in concert, and for the technical elements of Six Sigma to be effective, you have to set the proper management orientation.

From good to great the Six Sigma way

In the best-selling business book *Good to Great,* author Jim Collins studied companies that achieved a distinct break with the past by dramatically improving their performance, as reflected in market value appreciation. He set out to discover their secret — the stuff they held in the black box called "what we did to become great" and to beat the performance of the average company in their market by 3, 7, or even 18 times.

Collins' empirical research led him to several interesting conclusions. Greatness is not a function of larger-than-life leaders, exorbitant executive compensation, killer business strategies, advanced technologies, mergers and acquisitions, or big change initiatives. Over the long run, as it turns out, these are all collective crutches an organization leans on to prop itself up — but none of these enable a company to become great.

So what makes a company great? According to Collins' research, it is this: disciplined people, disciplined thought, and disciplined actions over an extended period. Having "the right people on the bus," as Collins puts it, having the "discipline to confront the most brutal facts of your current reality," in thought and in action, is the recipe for greatness.

Simply, this good-to-great result comes from the right people applying the right principles in the best possible way. Interestingly, this is what Six Sigma is all about: selecting the right people to drive and lead systematic improvement in a prescribed, disciplined, measurable, and repeatable manner.

Radical corporate success

Six Sigma performing companies realize staggering business success:

- **General Electric** profited between $7 to $10 billion from Six Sigma in about five years.

- **Dupont** added $1 billion to its bottom line within two years of initiating its Six Sigma program, and that number increased to about $2.4 billion within four years.

- **Bank of America** saved hundreds of millions of dollars within three years of launching Six Sigma, cut cycle times by more than half, and reduced the number of processing errors by an order of magnitude.

- **Honeywell** achieved record operating margins and savings of more than $2 billion in direct costs.

- **Motorola,** the place where Six Sigma began, saved $2.2 billion in a four-year time frame.

Six Sigma helps organizations achieve breakthrough improvement, not incremental improvement. In short, Six Sigma is a path to dramatic improvement in value for your customers and your company.

Bridge between science and leadership

From a management standpoint, Six Sigma culminates in the predictability and control of performance in a business or a business process, by applying the methods of science to the domain of leadership.

Early in the 20th century, Henry Ford applied the principles of science to the production of cars. By following set processes and by optimizing repeatable processes, Ford and others made goods that displayed little variation in their final states and could be mass-produced without requiring extensive education and years of finely honed skills among the assembly-line staff. We have witnessed how the achievements of machinery, technique, process, and specialization of labor collectively enable the explosion of mass-production and the consumer society. Science dictates how all the parts, materials, machines, and people on the assembly line interact to turn out many "widgets" at the highest possible speed and the lowest possible cost.

Managerially speaking, the goal of Six Sigma is to inject similar control, predictability, and consistency of results into the production of a successful organization, such that the widget comes off the production line absolutely consistently.

Countless times every day in the United States, people open a water faucet and experience the flow of clean, clear water. The reason is because reliable purification systems treat the water and pressure systems ensure the water is there. This is what Six Sigma does; it treats the processes in a business so that they deliver their intended results reliably and consistently.

The methodology of Six Sigma was first applied in a manufacturing company, but it also works in service and transactional companies (like banks and hospitals), where it has been implemented many times with great success. Six Sigma dramatically improves the way any process works — whether that process is in the chemical industry, the oil industry, the service industry, the entertainment industry, or anything else.

Management system orientation

Six Sigma is so appealing to managers because it delivers management results.

Clear value proposition and ROI

Six Sigma is characterized by an unwavering focus on business return on investment (ROI). A Six Sigma project can improve a business characteristic by 70 percent or more, stimulating increased operating margins for businesses, while at the same time increasing the value those businesses provide to their customers. Six Sigma initiatives and projects have a direct, measurable financial focus and impact.

Top commitment and accountability

A Six Sigma initiative begins at the top. The leadership and management of an organization must actively commit to the Six Sigma initiative, setting performance goals and developing tactical implementation plans. Management team members must be personally accountable for achieving the performance improvement goals they set for their respective organizations and business units.

Customer focus

Six Sigma, through its *voice of the customer (VOC)* tools, drives business processes through customer requirements. No operational, process, and business improvements can occur without a definitive understanding of who the customers are and what they need, want, and are willing to buy. Six Sigma managers become savvy about the needs and requirements of customers, in a way that also enables the business to become stronger and more profitable.

Connected business metrics

You know by now that Six Sigma is different from other performance improvement approaches in its focus on business financials and measurable operational improvements. To support this, the Six Sigma management system must include performance measures that are readily accessible and visible to everyone whose actions or decisions determine performance levels and operational quality.

Process orientation

Six Sigma improves the performance of processes — any business or work process — in how those processes effectively and efficiently transform material and other inputs into the desired outputs. This is the focal point of using Six Sigma to improve performance: the design, characterization, optimization, and validation of processes.

Project focus

The Six Sigma project is the tool by which processes and systems are characterized and optimized. Program leadership identifies opportunities for Six Sigma improvement projects and assigns Six Sigma specialists to execute them. We provide details about how to select Six Sigma projects in Chapter 4, how to implement projects in Chapters 5 through 10, and how to manage projects using tools in Chapter 12.

Enabling tools and technology

Properly managing a Six Sigma initiative that spans an entire organization or a significant part of an organization requires the ability to simultaneously manage many projects, processes, analyses, data banks, training activities, and people. Generally speaking, several classes of tools and technology are employed to accomplish this:

- ✔ Tools for designing, modeling, managing, and optimizing processes
- ✔ Tools for the broad-scale management of multiple projects across multiple organizational units
- ✔ Tools for collecting data, conducting analytical calculations, and solving performance problems
- ✔ Tools and technologies for training, educating, transferring knowledge, and managing knowledge

We provide a comprehensive view of the many Six Sigma tools and technologies in Chapters 11 and 12.

The historical perspective

The Six Sigma methodology was formalized in the mid-1980s at Motorola. New theories and ideas were combined with basic principles and statistical methods that had existed in quality engineering circles for decades. The building blocks were enhanced with business and leadership principles to form the basis of a complete management system. The result was a staggering increase in the levels of quality for several Motorola products, and the inaugural Malcolm Baldrige National Quality Award was bestowed on the company in 1988.

Everyone wanted to know how Motorola had done it. Then-president Robert Galvin chose to share Motorola's Six Sigma secret openly, and by the mid-1990s, corporations like Texas Instruments, Asea Brown Boveri, Allied Signal, and General Electric had begun to reap similar rewards. By 2000, many of the world's top corporations had a Six Sigma initiative underway, and by 2003, over $100 billion in combined savings had been tallied.

Six Sigma became the global standard of quality business practice, embraced by the American Society for Quality. Universities worldwide now offer courses. Dozens of consulting and software companies have brought products and tools to market. By the end of 2004, over 200 books on Six Sigma were in print, and entering the term "Six Sigma" into Google returned some 2,320,000 hits.

An infrastructure for change

Installing and managing a Six Sigma management system require a certain infrastructure — an underlying set of mechanisms and structures upon which to develop the Six Sigma improvement strategies and enact the tactics of project implementation and process improvement. The key elements of an effective Six Sigma infrastructure include the following:

- A fully documented Six Sigma leadership system, strategic focus, business goal configuration, deployment plans, implementation schedules, and activity tracking and reporting techniques

- A strategy, methodology, and system for training and preparing executives, managers, Champions, Black Belts, Green Belts, Yellow Belts, financial auditors, process owners, and all others involved in the Six Sigma initiative; we define and describe all the Six Sigma job roles in Chapter 3

- Competency models and compensation plans, Six Sigma participant and leader selection guidelines, position and role descriptions, reporting relationships, and career-advancement policies and plans

- Guidelines for defining project-savings criteria, aligning accounting categories with Six Sigma goals and metrics, forecasting project savings, auditing and evaluating project ROI, validating project savings, and reporting project ROI

✔ Hard criteria for selecting projects, designating project-type categories, developing project problem-definition statements, targeting intended project savings and ROI, approving selected projects, and managing projects through to completion; we give you more about project management in Chapter 4

✔ Information-technology-related structures, procedures, dashboards, tools and systems for designing and managing processes, tracking project and initiative progress, reporting results, storing information and data, and performing analytical functions; we look at these in more depth in Chapters 11 and 12

✔ A strategy for consistently communicating the Six Sigma initiative across the enterprise, and an Internet or intranet site that provides a common reference and knowledge base that contains important information, motivational content, recognition stories, educational material, contact information, and so on

✔ A management review process for assessing the effectiveness of Six Sigma from the top to the middle to the bottom of the organization:

- At the top, the focus is on the aggregate process, projects, and results for entire implementation business units.

- In the middle, the focus is on the process and results of operational units with multiple Six Sigma projects.

- At the lower levels, the focus of management review is on making sure individual projects are on track and yielding their intended process-improvement and financial results.

Complete culture change

A Six Sigma initiative often begins with outside consultants providing methods, tools, and training, but over time, the knowledge is internalized and applied organically within the organization. The ultimate goal is for everyone in the organization to have a working ability to understand customers' requirements, collect data, map processes, measure performance, identify threats and opportunities, analyze inputs and outputs, and make continuous improvements. In Chapter 3, we provide more details about culture change.

The Technical Perspective

Six Sigma performance is the statistical term for a process that produces fewer than 3.4 defects or errors per million opportunities. Behind that single statistic lies a methodology that includes a plethora of data, measurement, analysis, improvement, and control tools and supporting technologies. This section is an overview of the technical side of Six Sigma.

Quality and grade

Quality is different from *grade*. A product can be low grade but high quality, such as 87 versus 91 octane gasoline. As long as the 87 octane gas meets its required specification, it is of high quality, even though it's a lower grade. Only if a certain batch of low-grade gas doesn't meet its 87 octane requirement can you say it is of low quality, or defective.

Therefore, quality is always relative to intent. A quality $12 haircut is different from a quality $30 haircut. A quality economy car is expected to be different from a quality luxury car. A discount online stockbroker can provide a higher-quality experience than a full-service broker, relative to the expectations attached to both, respectively.

Product, service, and transactional quality

The technical objective of Six Sigma is to ensure the high quality and reliability of products, services, and transactions — the lifeblood of all businesses and organizations. Banks, government agencies, hospitals, car washes, toy makers, semiconductor plants, professional services firms — all organizations of any type — provide products, services, and transactions, or some combination of the three.

For example, most auto manufactures do much more than build cars. They also provides services, such as routine maintenance and warranty repairs, through their dealerships. Through their financing arms, they approve and process car payments, a transactional business activity.

The technical goal of Six Sigma is for products, services, and transactions all to be performed with the highest possible quality as efficiently and effectively as possible. This requires performance targets for all components in a system, and for each important characteristic of every component. For example, a car axle (component) has to have the proper form, fit, and function to perform as intended, and if it is to fit together with other components of the car.

Aiming for the target

In Six Sigma, important characteristics are referred to as CTXs, where the *C* stands for "critical," the *T* stands for "to," and the *X* represents what the characteristic is linked to: quality, cost, time, satisfaction, and so on. For example, a critical-to-quality characteristic would be called a CTQ. Graphically, you can depict the target values of any CTX in Figure 1-1.

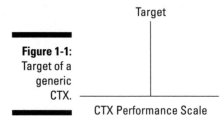

Figure 1-1:
Target of a
generic
CTX.

A performance scale in some kind of units, such as time, length, size, and so on, indicates the measured value of your CTX. The goal of Six Sigma is to come as close to your performance target as often as possible. If you're making an axle, your goal is to make all your axles for a certain car the same length every time. This is the consistency a customer needs, and the predictability a business needs.

The reality of variation

But what really happens? In reality, you can't hit the target value perfectly all the time, no matter how good you are or how hard you try. You can get close, but you will always have some variation.

In other words, every instance of a product coming off of a production line is in some way different from every other instance. The thickness of a part is never exactly the same. The amount of time it takes to execute a certain business transaction varies from instance to instance.

In the world of making products, delivering services, and conducting transactions, there is always a distribution of performance around a target. Normally, that distribution takes on the shape you see in Figure 1-2. This famous shape is called the *normal distribution*, and is also known as the *bell curve*.

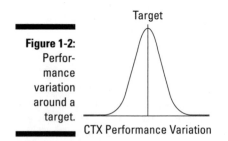

Figure 1-2:
Perfor-
mance
variation
around a
target.

Notice the shape of the normal distribution. It's symmetrical about the central line, with just as much area under the curve to the left as on the right. In Six Sigma, you encounter the normal distribution curve repeatedly, because it reveals itself again and again in the course of natural events.

Specifications have their place, and only their place

Henry Ford knew about variation nearly 100 years ago when he was mass producing his Model T cars. There is variation in everything, and all the many car parts would vary in their CTX dimensions. So what did he do? How could Henry account for this annoying phenomenon of variation?

He and the other industrialists of his day incorporated specifications and standards into their businesses. Recognizing that parts would vary at the component characteristic level, Ford designated variation limits within which to operate. By doing so, he could accept the inevitable presence of variation while not ignoring its tendency to create defects and cause business loss.

Figure 1-3 shows a performance CTX with a normal distribution and the acceptable upper and lower limits of performance. With these specifications defined, you have a way to measure quality. You have a way of bounding an acceptable extent of variation for your customers and for the business. Having performance specification limits for component characteristics gives you parameters for defining, measuring, analyzing, improving, and controlling quality.

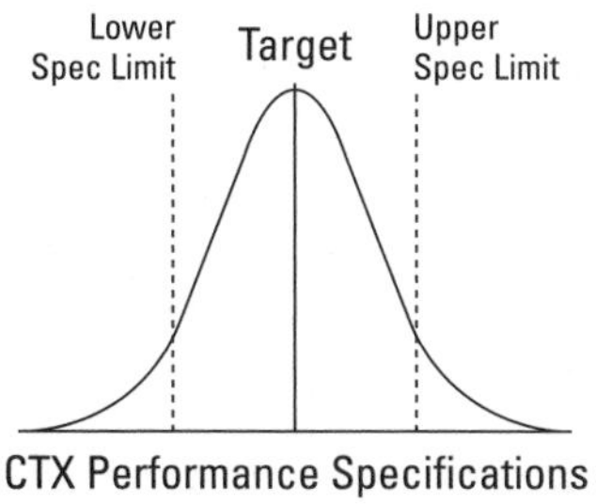

Figure 1-3:
Performance specifications around a target.

Lower Spec Limit   Target   Upper Spec Limit

CTX Performance Specifications

Consider these examples: A mortgage company has a goal of refinancing loans within two weeks of receiving a completed application. A pest-control company believes it must arrive within 30 minutes of all scheduled appointment times. An office-furniture company determines that to be competitive, it must not produce more than two defective pieces of furniture for every 100 produced.

Here are more examples:

✔ A automotive engineer designs an axle. She knows that for optimal performance within the power train, the axle needs to 3.325 inches in diameter. Realizing that there will be variation in the thousands of axles that will be produced, the engineer places an upper diameter limit on her design at 3.330 inches and a lower diameter limit of 3.320 inches. In the engineer's judgment, axles that fall within this range will be acceptably close to the target.

✔ The manager of a pizza company asks his employees to put between 7 and 9 ounces of cheese on each large pizza. His goal is 8 ounces, and he knows that having a pizza with too much or too little will lead to customer complaints.

Quality is defined by *conformance to standards or specifications.* When you operate or perform within the specification limits, you have quality. When you fall outside the limits, you have defects.

An even better definition may be this: Get as close to the target with the least amount of variation as possible. While specification limits are important and necessary, you want to focus on trying to hit your performance target and minimizing variation, because variation leads to defects and errors, which lead to poor quality, which leads to dissatisfied customers and business loss.

The journey from one to many

In the preceding section, quality is defined in terms of aiming for a performance target and achieving the least amount of variation possible — for one characteristic or one component. Now you can talk about quality in the overall assembly of a product, service, or transaction.

Consider the company which must operate at high levels of quality at the level of individual characteristics and components, because so many of them have to fit and work together to make a whole product. For example, the average car has about 10,000 individual quality characteristics, or CTXs. That's a lot of stuff that has to work together. If you work at an automotive company, how many cars do you make? How many papers have to get processed every day? How much material and supplies are ordered and purchased in every month? Millions upon millions — billions.

Suppose you have a die, and every time you roll the die and get a 1, that's considered a *defect.* With a six-sided die, then, you have one chance in six (17 percent) of rolling a defect, or a five out of six chance (83 percent) of success. But imagine now you have a pair of dice, and you roll them both together. Now the chance of success — no defects — is only 69 percent. (We show you how to calculate these probabilities in Chapter 6.) With three dice, the chance of rolling defect-free further decreases to 58 percent. Now image rolling 20 dice or 50 dice or 100 dice. With a hundred dice, you are almost certain to have a defect. (The actual probability of never getting a 1 when rolling 100 dice is less than one in 82 million!)

In Six Sigma, we call this concept of compounding defect risk *rolled throughput yield,* and we explain it mathematically in Chapter 6. In practical terms, the reality of rolled throughput yield means you have to establish an extremely high probability of success for each individual component characteristic if you ever expect your final products, services, and transactions to be highly successful and defect-free.

Exposing the hidden factory

Very few companies can actually achieve Six Sigma (fewer than 3.4 defects per million opportunities) or even five sigma performance (fewer than 233 defects per million opportunities) in their final products, because there are so many critical processes, process activities, machines, people, and materials that have to interact along a chain of causation and span of time.

Here's an example: The chemical properties of the catalyst, that is combined with the base material, that is mixed by the processing machine, that is controlled by the in-line gauges, that is operated by John, that is inspected by Sally, that is packaged by robots, that is stored in the warehouse, that is shipped to the customer via FedEx — all these have to operate in synch within certain limits of variation if the system is to reliably yield its intended outcomes. Remembering, too, that before any of this, the whole system, including the product itself, was designed by a team of engineers who are by no means infallible.

If any one of the many critical activities is compromised or doesn't function to its expectation, risk and error are propagated throughout the entire system. The system itself is also an opportunity-rich environment for hiding risk and error, because problems arising in one place and time are caused in another place and time, and the space between is extremely difficult to navigate without the proper methodologies, equipment, and people.

Among Six Sigma practitioners, this reality of fixing the results of propagated error is known as the *hidden factory* or *hidden operation.* You can almost see the wheels turning, the rework and cover ups, the hours and days of wasted time in a company of people who constantly correct mistakes. Every time a corrective action is taken or a machine is re-run, or a warranty claim is processed, you incur unnecessary rework. When you accept these events as "that's just the way it is," you've mentally hidden all of these activities from your improvement potential.

This is the hidden factory that runs in the background of all organizations. It is the factory that fixes problems, corrects mistakes, and otherwise wastes both time and money — a company's two most precious commodities. Six Sigma eliminates the hidden factory, and, as a result, returns precious time and money back to the business.

Watch out for the wiggle, bump, and jitter

Humans aren't the only ones with variable behavior. Machines vary, too. Process inputs and outputs vary, and single characteristics vary, which causes their assemblies to vary as well.

You can see variation. You can visually plot the behavior of people, processes, products, and systems and look at it like a picture. A plot like this helps you see immediately that every characteristic you can measure has a performance distribution.

Furthermore, you can plot behavior today, come back next week and plot it again, and compare the difference. What if you plotted behavior one day and it looked one way, and next week it looked different? Comparing a single snapshot to the accumulated variation over time is an example of the change in behavior from the short term to the long term. Figure 1-4 shows two probability distributions for a critical characteristic: short term (solid line) and long term (dotted line). As you can see, in the long-term the variation in the behavior of the characteristic expands.

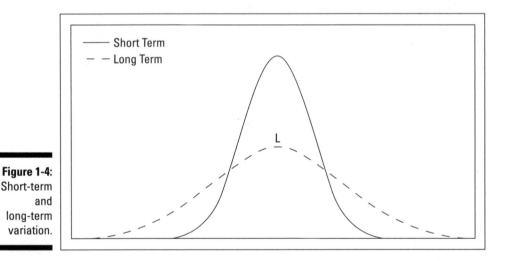

Figure 1-4:
Short-term
and
long-term
variation.

 This is a common occurrence. Here's what's happening. The probability of a defect in the short term does not account for certain changes that take place over the long term. Examples include the variation among different batches of incoming material, the impact of seasonal road traffic on delivery time, the different working styles and habits of different personnel. Joe may be a great machine operator, but he can't work 24 hours a day. Eventually, he has to be relieved by Jim, who works a little differently from Joe. Each one has their own performance variations, but combined together it enlarges the range.

Short-term variation doesn't necessarily refer to a specified period of time for every type of performance distribution. The time period involved in short-term performance variation for a restaurant meal is different from the period involved for the performance of electricity delivered to your home by a power plant. Chapter 5 provides more detail and understanding on why this is the case and what it means for the Six Sigma practitioner.

Why six and why sigma? (Putting the pieces together)

The two preceding sections describe two interesting phenomena. One is considering performance in terms of the hundreds and often thousands of separate characteristics in a product, service, transaction, process, or system. Two, whatever performance level you achieve in the short term will become eroded over the long term. The term Six Sigma comes from the statistical basis of the approach and methodology used to address these two concerns: the roll-up of characteristic behaviors and the natural increase in variation in each characteristic over the long-term.

The sigma scale is a universal measure of how well a critical characteristic performs compared to its requirements. The higher the sigma score, the more capable the characteristic. For example, if a critical characteristic is defective 31 percent of the time, you say that this characteristic operates at two sigma. But if it runs at 93.3 percent compliance, you say that it operates at three sigma. Table 1-2 shows the sigma scale.

Table 1-2	The Sigma Scale	
Sigma	*Percent Defective*	*Defects per Million*
1	69%	691,462
2	31%	308,538
3	6.7%	66,807
4	0.62%	6,210
5	0.023%	233
6	0.00034%	3.4
7	0.0000019%	0.019

If a characteristic operates at three sigma, that means that, 6.7 percent of the time, the variation in its performance exceeds acceptable levels. This could be an invoicing process that goes longer than the company's allowed time limit, or a forged bolt that is manufactured longer than customer requirements. Whatever the critical characteristic may be, if it is three sigma, it is defective 6.7 percent of the time, or 66,700 times out of a million. In Chapter 6, we explain more detail of how the sigma scale is created and why its called "sigma."

What the originators of Six Sigma discovered is that when they worked to have each critical characteristic in the system — the product, the service, the transaction — perform at a Six Sigma level, the risk of the individual characteristics being incorrect was small enough (0.00034 percent or 3.4 defects per million opportunities) that when all the parts were assembled together, the overall system still performed at an exceptional level. And even when long-term effects inevitably entered into each characteristic, the overall system performance remained high. These companies now had a method for competing at a whole new level on the global market. That's why six is the magic number.

So why six and not five sigma? Good question. For the complex products on which this method was originated, there were enough characteristics rolled together and enough long-term degradation that only six would do. Four or five sigma just didn't provide enough relief from these two constraints.

For transactional and service companies now adopting Six Sigma, their systems and environments are often less complex — they don't have as many critical characteristics coming together. So they don't necessarily need to have each critical characteristic operating at Six Sigma. In these cases, four or five may actually do.

But the magnitude of the earlier success of Six Sigma has made the name stick. And almost all companies, regardless of their size or complexity, recognize the benefits of aiming for a Six Sigma goal. Even if the milestone of Six Sigma is never reached, the act of working toward that goal drives breakthrough changes.

There are instances where great companies are able to produce Six Sigma quality in their final products, services, and transactions — especially when safety or human life is involved. For example, did you know that you are about 2,000 times more likely to reach your destination when you fly than your luggage is? That's because airline safety operates at a level higher than Six Sigma, while baggage reliability operates at about four sigma.

Table 1-3	How Good Is Good?
99% Good (3.8 Sigma)	***99.99966% Good (Six Sigma)***
20,000 lost articles of mail per hour	7 articles of lost mail per hour
Unsafe drinking water for almost 15 minutes per day	One unsafe minute of drinking water every seven months
5,000 incorrect surgical operations per week	1.7 incorrect surgical operations per week
2 short or long landings at major airports every day	1 short or long landing at major airports every five years
200,000 incorrect drug prescriptions each year	68 incorrect drug prescriptions each year
No electricity for almost 7 hours each month	One hour without electricity every 34 years
11.8 million shares incorrectly traded on the NYSE every day	4,021 shares incorrectly traded on the NYSE every day
3 warranty claims for every new automobile	1 warranty claim for every 980 new automobiles
48,000 to 96,000 deaths attributed to hospital errors each year	17 to 34 deaths attributed to hospital errors each year

Chapter 2

Examining the Principles and Language of Six Sigma

In This Chapter

▶ Understanding the fundamental principles that underlie Six Sigma

▶ Mastering the basic equation of Six Sigma: $Y = f(X) + \varepsilon$

▶ Knowing that all outcomes are determined by inputs and how they are processed

▶ Recognizing that effective control requires understanding and managing variation

▶ Seeing that you have to measure a process before you can manage it

▶ Becoming aware of the power of "leverage"

*B*eneath all the statistical analyses, the equations of probability, the charts and the experiments; below all the projects and plans, the tools and technologies; and beyond the colored belts, the catchy phrases, and dizzying arrays of terms lie several fundamental principles that beget the whole Six Sigma methodology.

Like all grand constructions, Six Sigma sits upon a solid foundation. In this chapter, you discover five basic principles. And in doing so, you will begin to think the Six Sigma way.

It All Begins with One Simple Equation: $Y = f(X) + \varepsilon$

All of Six Sigma begins with one general-purpose equation that shouldn't intimidate even the least mathematically inclined, because of its elegant simplicity. This equation is $Y = f(X) + \varepsilon$, where

- ✔ *Y* is the outcome, the result you desire or need.

- ✔ *X* represents the inputs, factors, or pieces that are needed to create the outcome. You can have several *X*s.

- ✔ *f* is the *function,* the way or process by which the inputs are transformed into the outcome.

- ✔ ε is the presence of error, the uncertainty in depending upon the *X*s and the transformation function to actually create the desired outcome.

This expression is called the *breakthrough equation*. See Figure 2-1.

The Principle of Determinism

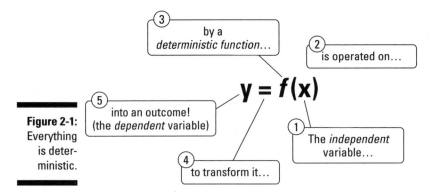

Figure 2-1: Everything is deterministic.

In other words, a certain set of inputs is transformed by some function (or process) into an output. The *Y* results from, or is a function of, the *X*s. To determine a desired outcome, you apply a transformation process or function *f* on the inputs.

You make a loaf of bread by taking flour, yeast, salt, and the other ingredients and transforming them through mixing and baking into a desired outcome. The ingredients are the *X*s, the mixing and the baking are the transformation process function *f,* and the resulting yummy loaf of bread is the *Y*.

Sound simple enough? Almost. In the real world, no matter how hard you try, there is also a degree of uncertainty or variation in the outcome. There is always some degree of uncertainty as to how well your actions produce the desired result.

Consider the loaf of bread. What if you used too little yeast, or if the oven wasn't quite hot enough? Suppose you were baking ten loaves; would they all come out exactly the same? Most likely, there would be some variation from loaf to loaf. In Six Sigma, the little error that creeps in and produces this variation is represented by the Greek letter Epsilon, or ε. Sometimes the error is your fault (you measured incorrectly), and sometimes it's just truly random error, but either way, you have variation.

Everything is deterministic. All outcomes are a result of some process or function acting on the inputs. And no matter how hard you try, there's always a little error.

Determine the Cause

We're a results-oriented society: "How'd it turn out?" "What finally happened?" "What was the final score?" "How long did it take?" "What's the bottom line?" We're always looking at the results. We're practically obsessed on them. After all, that's the whole point of all the toil and trouble in the first place, right?

But *how* did the results happen? *Why* did they happen? What *specifically* caused them to happen? You want to know the answers to these questions, because if good things happen, you want to know how to make them happen again. And if bad things happen, you just as surely want to know how to prevent them next time.

Cause and effect

All outcomes are the result of the inputs and the process that acts on them, plus the error that creates variation. A process simply operates on the inputs to create the outcomes; that is, it's the fundamental action in changing from one condition to another, in making any improvement, in adding value for yourself, your customers, and your company.

Inputs are transformed — by way of a process — into their outputs. This is how change happens. Therefore, when you understand the process, you can leverage the way the inputs are combined to produce the outcome.

Look behind every result (output) and examine the inputs, the process, and the error that combined to produce it. Seek to understand what caused the outcome. When you know the cause, you can begin to put yourself in a position to control the outcome next time — and again and again in the future. Understanding root cause is the first step to controlling outcomes.

Here's a simple example: The guy gets the girl. That's the outcome. How did that outcome happen? Well, as all razor companies would have you know, it is because he has a smooth, sexy face. What caused that? It's the result of his shaving process and choice of ingredients. What caused that? Combining hot water, shaving cream, a mirror, a particular razor, and a steady hand to get a close shave. If anything's wrong with the outcome — if the girl doesn't like the guy's scruffy face — you examine the ingredients and shaving process to determine the root cause of the problem.

Regardless of complexity, literally every result has one or more causes. The more you can single out these causes and understand them, the better your opportunity to change it for the better. In Six Sigma speak, you'd say that knowing the *Xs*, the function *f*, and the uncertainty ε means you know what caused the outcome *Y.* Cause and effect.

There is a better way

Many companies and organizations want to improve their performance. They recognize intuitively that their performance results are the outcome of all their business and work processes. These processes are quite literally "the way" business is done. So, to improve the outcomes, the company has to change the way it does business. They want to change the processes — the function *f* — and combine the business inputs in a way that produces a better outcome. It's not a wishful notion and not a trick for getting everyone to work harder. The call to change the way you do business is a legitimate search for a better way, because there is a better way. There's always a better way.

Determinism is the principle that you can create a desired outcome by configuring and controlling the inputs in a specific manner. In Six Sigma, you analyze the inputs, the process, and the variation, and then implement the best possible combination to achieve your objective. By doing so, you're exercising direct control over your environment, rather than allowing your environment to control you. You are deterministic, not reactionary, in your thinking.

Beware superstitious delusions (that is, correlation doesn't imply causation)

The more you understand the cause-and-effect relationship between inputs and outcomes, the better you can predict, determine, and control the results. Conversely, the less you understand the relationships between inputs and actions, the more difficult it is to determine and control the results.

Don't confuse coincidence, or *correlation,* with cause and effect. Just because two events happen together does not mean that one has caused the other. The Latin term for such an error is called *non causa pro causa,* which means, "non-cause for the cause." People often assume that events which are closely connected — either spatially or temporally — are somehow also connected causally.

Determinism is proactive

Determinism is about taking control. It's the opposite of believing that events unfold by chance, apart from one's influence. Surely, you don't control all the variables and processes that affect our lives. But just as surely, success is not just random luck.

If you think there really isn't much you can do to impact the world, or even your local surroundings, you're wrong. You can influence most everything around you in some way. But determinism is proactive. You must try to initiate change and believe the forces within your control are much greater than the ones outside your control.

Let go of excuses about why you can't do something — justifying a tendency to be mediocre — and realize that you can do much more than you may think! Proactivity — the willingness to do something — will fuel your determinism.

Consider this exchange between Homer and Lisa Simpson:

> **Homer:** Not a bear in sight. The "Bear Patrol" must be working like a charm!
>
> **Lisa:** That's specious reasoning, Dad.
>
> **Homer:** Thank you, dear.
>
> **Lisa:** By your logic, I could claim that this rock keeps tigers away.
>
> **Homer:** Oh, how does it work?
>
> **Lisa:** It doesn't work.
>
> **Homer:** Uh-huh.
>
> **Lisa:** It's just a stupid rock. But I don't see any tigers around, do you?
>
> **Homer:** Lisa, I want to buy your rock.

These confusions of cause versus correlation are also known as *superstitious delusions*. This is the football coach who always wears red socks, because he once won a very important game when he was wearing them. Did the socks cause his team to win? Did clothing determine the outcome of the game, or was it some other input or set of inputs?

Businesses are known to confuse correlation with causation. What about the company that ramps up capacity after a great month or quarter of sales, because they think this indicates an economic expansion? Only later do they discover that no expansion was forthcoming and that, instead, increased sales were correlated to a different factor.

Even if two variables are legitimately correlated, there is not necessarily any particular causal relationship between them. One may fluctuate in relation to the other due solely to chance (this is called *coincidence*) or, as is often the case, each is strongly affected by one or more other outside (or *confounding*) variables that you hadn't thought of.

A causal connection probably does exist if you can establish all three of the following:

✔ There is a reasonable explanation for cause and effect

✔ The connection happens under different environmental conditions

✔ You've ruled out potential outside confounding variables

One way to determine these conditions is through a designed experiment where groups strongly similar to one another in terms of the most important variables are exposed to different conditions and then analyzed to see whether the variable of interest performs differently. One or more groups is also held constant and not subjected to treatment(s) as a "control" group(s). You can find out more about this in Chapters 7 and 8.

Variation Happens

You're playing a great round of golf. Everything's dropping. All you have to do is win the last hole, and you're going to beat all your buddies for the first time ever. You step up on the 18th tee, cast an eye down the fairway, draw your club back, uncork your winning swing, and . . . splat! Right in the drink! You lose. What happened?

Variation happened. Error happened. Whatever you did seventeen times in a row, you didn't do it the last time. Dang! Consistency is a bugger. How do the pros do it?

Professional results, in anything, demand consistency. That means you get the variation in your inputs — the Xs — and the uncertainty in the transfer function — that little ε — under control.

In general, variation is undesirable, because it creates uncertainty in our ability to produce a desired outcome. In the world of business and organizational life, the goal is to produce a work product or deliver a service in a predictable manner. Variation in your results — whether in time, specification, quality, cost, or something else — is going to happen; it's inevitable.

Some variation — within limits — might be okay. A little too much variation here or there, and you might have some repairs or rework on your hands. And too much altogether, and you're either out of a job or out of business.

The characterization, measurement, analysis, and control of variation is a central theme of Six Sigma. Reduction of unwanted variation is the key to achieving Six Sigma improvements. To jump right into the statistics of variation, go to Chapter 5.

What is variation?

Very simply, *variation* is deviation from expectation. If you toss a coin, what's your the chance of it landing on heads? Fifty percent. Therefore, if you toss a coin ten times, you expect to get five heads and five tails. This is your *expectation*. Take out a coin and toss it ten times. What happened? Did you meet your expectation?

Try it again. What happened the second time? Try performing successive sets of ten coin tosses. Every time you repeat your ten coin tosses, the output — the number of heads and tails — varies. The extent to which your experience deviates from expectation is the extent to which variation has occurred.

When you closely measure any output *Y*, you find that it varies — always. Every output varies. This is important to understand: Again, every output varies. Each time you park your car, it doesn't fit exactly in the same place between the parking lines. Every single product a company makes varies from every other single instance of the same product on every dimension, such as weight, size, durability, and so on. Every time you call a company for help as a customer, you get a different level of service and you leave the call with a varying degree of satisfaction. Here's one you can probably relate to: Each and every person arrives to work at varying times each day.

Get (the) mean

If you measure the occurrence of something many times, it's going to vary around some average — or *mean* — value. The mean is the central tendency of your process. Flip that coin enough times, and you'll see that the mean will tend toward 50 percent heads, and 50 percent tails.

Variation obsession

Anytime you measure the value of a given occurrence or event, it's going to vary from the mean. A player's batting average may be .302 for the season, but Friday night he went 2-for-5 and batted .400, nearly 100 points above his average. And then Saturday he went 0-for-4. Why? The school bus usually arrives at the stop at 7:17, but today it came at 7:22; that's five minutes later than normal. Yesterday it came early at 7:15, and the kids almost missed it. Why?

These are examples of variation — the variation of occurrence versus the mean. The size, trends, nature, causes, effects, and control of this variation are the undying obsession of Six Sigma. Nothing is more examined, or more addressed in Six Sigma than this.

Variation is a serious thing

Many parts have to fit together to make a product, like a cellphone. When engineers design the parts, they account for the fact that all parts will display some amount of variation as they are produced. Variation is the degree to which a part, product, service, or transaction differs from all others in the same class or category.

In the case of a phone, each class of parts, like the plastic casing, vary in size, weight, and even color. Just as the phone cases vary, so does the clear plastic display that covers the liquid crystal display. Then you have the many hinges, buttons, antenna, internal components, and so on. All these parts have to snap and fit together well if the phone is to perform its function to your satisfaction. In other words, you can only tolerate a certain amount of variation. A little too much variation and the phone won't work properly. A little more variation and it won't work at all.

And we all know who's going to end up with the bad phone, right?

Where does variation come from?

Why does *every* output vary? Because all the input Xs vary, and because the transformation function f also varies. So how do they vary? And what makes them vary?

All variation is caused by something. Remember cause and effect: If you're going to control the outcome, you have to control the cause. Therefore, if you're going to control variation, you'd better understand what's causing it.

Causes of variation: Common versus special

Some variation is just natural; you can't eliminate it. The natural forces of nature work to mix things up. It's simply part of the normal course of events. Recall the coin-toss example; the variation in the number of heads from set to set is perfectly normal. Or consider the variation in the time between waves at the beach. Or the variation in the height of trees in a forest. These are all examples of naturally-occurring variation.

Now consider a few examples in human systems. Think about the time each day when the mailman comes. Or how long it takes to process a credit card application. Or the actual number of tiny time pills in one of those cold capsules. They all vary. And the variation is a natural part of their system.

This type of variation is called *common-cause variation*. You can act to reduce common cause variation, but you can't eliminate it. It's natural, and it's part of *every* system. It's in there and it's not going away!

The other type of variation is known as *special-cause variation*. Special cause variation is completely different — it's directly caused by something special. If the mailman usually comes at about 11:30 each day, but he gets a flat tire and doesn't come until noon, that's a special cause of variation. If it normally takes 15 minutes to process a credit card application, but the network connection went down, that's a special cause. And if there are supposed to be 600 tiny time pills in your cold capsule, but the white acetaminophen filler tube jammed and you have 550, that's special. These special causes are specific things you can identify and do something about.

With Six Sigma, you spend particular effort to identify the difference between common-cause and special-cause variation, because they're so different, and because you go to special effort to understand which type is causing the variation and how it's affecting the outcome.

We're adrift: Short-term and long-term variation

Another important characteristic of variation is the way in which it changes over time. There are short-term variations and long-term variations. The difference is important.

Here's an example: "That mailman used to come at 11:30, give or take a few minutes, but lately he's been coming later and later, and now it seems he's here closer to 12:15, which is really annoying because we're at lunch and he has to leave the packages out in the rain." In this example, the short-term variation of a few minutes was inconsequential and well within our tolerance level, but when the mean time of arrival experienced a long-term variation (perhaps caused by a seasonal shift in weather or the holidays), drifting out by 45 minutes, there was a problem.

Getting variation right is everything

In general, it's best to work on reducing special-cause variation before trying to reduce common-cause variation. The reason is because when you have special-cause variation, the process is not stable or predictable, and you can't be sure of what is happening. But after you've taken the special-cause variation out of a system or process, you can then improve its common cause variability.

For example, if a coffee house first eliminates the special employee-to-employee differences in making a cup of coffee, it can then effectively work on improving the inherent, common-cause quality of the coffee itself. If, however, the coffee house tries to fix the inherent quality of the coffee first, the special employee-to-employee differences will cloud the situation, blocking all efforts to decipher the what's really going on.

The goal is to control variation, understand it, and minimize its impact, while accepting that it is part of everyday life and a part of every organization. Just like you can understand and characterize the relationship between Xs and Y, you can characterize variation and error in the ability to produce desired outcomes consistently over time. This provides the foundation and framework for implementing real changes in the way you do what you do — changes that have the greatest probability of yielding positive results.

Thou Shalt Measure

In 1891, a British scientist named William Thompson, also called Lord Kelvin, said, "When you can measure what you are speaking about, and express it in numbers, you know something about it. But when you cannot express it in numbers, your knowledge is of a meager and unsatisfactory kind." Some wisdom is timeless, and the principle of measurement is one of the fundamental tenets of Six Sigma.

Lord Kelvin continued by saying that your opinions and ideas may be the beginning of knowledge, but they have "scarcely, in your thoughts, advanced to the state of science." Until you include measurement and numbers in your knowledge, you're bound to the world of gut-feel, guessing, and marginal improvement.

You may work very hard, and even bring significant resources to a performance problem or improvement goal, but without measuring your Ys and Xs, your ability to improve will only be, "meager and unsatisfactory."

At first, it may seem impossible to measure many of your inputs and outputs. While it may be easy at first to rationalize yourself into believing some things just aren't measurable, it's going to be much more difficult in the long term to try and achieve your goals without the data that can help you.

Mind your Ys and Xs

Measurement is the practice of collecting the data that relates to the inputs (Xs) and the given outcome (Y) that results from your process function f. Measurement is what enables you to gain a quantitative grasp on the characteristics of your various inputs and how they relate to your desired outcome.

Measuring the inputs is what gives you the profile of the way your process is playing out relative to a goal or objective. Measurement begins with the Ys, and then extends to the Xs to understand the causes.

For example, you'd probably love to have $1,000 in your wallet (the output Y). To measure how they're doing on this objective, a person could open his wallet each day and count how much money is there. He'd probably discover that his performance towards this objective is well below what he wanted. The person could then analyze the situation and discover that the amount of money in his wallet is a function of how much money he earns, how much is taken out in taxes, and how much he spends on necessities. These are the Xs.

The person can't affect the amount of money in his wallet directly. He has to do something to the identified Xs to make Y change. To affect a change in the output Y, the person would start to measure and control the performance of the causal Xs (perhaps earn more and spend less).

Many people never get past the Y. They watch it, like the money in the wallet, hoping that it will change simply by measuring it. It's easy to be guilty of such Y-dominated thinking and measurement. Consider the company that continues to work harder and force productivity in an attempt to improve results (the Y), without quantitatively investigating the contributing factors to success (the Xs of scrap, excess inventory, poor quality, and so on). This approach has a tendency to self destruct in its blind push toward a goal.

The answer begins with the data

It's easy to understand how to measure certain input and output variables because they are, by their very nature, accommodating of such measurement. Examples of this include number of calories, your weight, and the time it takes to complete a run or walk, or in business, the time it takes to complete a certain job, the number of days that transpire between a customer order, the delivery of the product, and so on. These are all numerically quantifiable measures.

Such measurement-friendly events, processes, variables, and transactions are well supported by certain measurement tools, like a bathroom scale, software, a spreadsheet, a clock, and so on. Using various quantitative scales like width, length, time, rigidity, and density, it's possible to quantify the behavior of many Ys and Xs, and their relationships.

Other Ys and Xs, however, are not so easy to measure, because they're not as easily quantified, or because the time, cost, and effort involved in doing so is extreme. How, for example, do you measure customer satisfaction — or a customer's opinions?

In these cases, measurement instruments have to be specifically designed, like a survey question that ranks responses. When such instruments are developed and employed, you can make otherwise qualitative data much more quantitative in nature.

The bottom line on measurement

Taking measurements is a matter of using information and data to quantify the relationship between inputs, outputs, and error in a given system, process, or operating model.

Even when numbers or direct measurements aren't available, there are ways to create them indirectly. In this sense, you take a deterministic approach to measurement: You don't give in to the lack of data, but you find the data you need or create estimates in accordance with sound practice.

About 100 years ago, H.G. Wells said that, "statistical thinking will one day be as necessary for efficient citizenship as the ability to read and write." We are now well into that day. Politicians don't make a statement anymore without first assessing people's opinions through polls. Businesses don't make decisions without first slicing and dicing the data. Facts and numbers are everything.

Measuring your Ys and Xs is your first step toward greater efficiency and effectiveness. It's your first step toward citizenship in the Six Sigma world of data-oriented thinking.

The Power of Leverage

If you've ever tried to move a huge rock or boulder, or even your washing machine, you can appreciate the meaning of *leverage*. While you might lift and pull on it with all your strength, the boulder won't budge. But if you use a long metal pole and an object for a fulcrum, you maximize the force of your limited strength. You use leverage to move the rock and accomplish your goal.

Life is like that: you have to expend a little effort to find the leverage. When you do, it catapults you over your problems and through the obstacles that stand between you and your goal. In Six Sigma terms, leverage is the ability to apply the critical few Xs that have the greatest impact on your desired Y.

The vast majority of leverage, or impact power, in creating any desired outcome, comes from a surprisingly small number of contributors. This is true for the simplest of goals as well as for the most complex systems. Typically, only a few select variables determine the quality of a given outcome! It all comes down to finding those critical few that give you the leverage. These vital few will enable you to move the "boulders" in your life, your process, or your organization.

The "vital few" versus the "trivial many"

The law of the "vital few versus the trivial many" comes from the work of early 20th century Italian sociologist and economist Vilfredo Pareto. You may also know this law as the *80-20 rule,* where 20 percent of the inputs in any system account for 80 percent of the influence on that system.

In his dedication to exploring the nature of individual and social action, Pareto determined mathematically that, while a great number of factors are connected to a given outcome, only a few carry the weight to change that outcome in a significant way.

In a process, a few key variables are the cause of most performance problems or defects. This principle holds true even when you analyze the impact of dozens upon dozens of variables involved in complicated assemblies and sub-assemblies with hundreds of separate parts. When you look for leverage in business, you search for the minority of variables that provide the majority of power in solving problems in manufacturing, assembly, distribution, procurement, accounting, finance, customer service, and so on.

While businesses often employ sophisticated statistical tools to find leverage, you may or may not need such tools for finding leverage as individuals. The key is to know with certainty that, whatever your goal or situation, leverage does exists; some factors in a given situation are more powerful than others.

Leverage may not exist where you think it does; the obvious is not always the answer. Look closely, apply tests, and challenge your assumptions to find the sources of leverage.

Note also that the factors that represent leverage in one situation may not represent leverage in another similar situation. Each process or problem has its own unique dynamics and interactions.

The high road

There are more factors, contingencies, and dynamics to manage than possible when trying to break through to new levels of performance and success. The natural tendency is to try and manage and control every detail, but this is a slippery slope. The trivial many will bury you in a pile of unnecessary cost, trouble, worries, wasted energy, and valueless action.

No one, and no company, has the luxury or reason to manage all the details. Instead, the right path is to manage only those that are critical to producing the outcomes you desire. Focus on the inputs that really matter. All the rest, leave alone unless they become significant.

After you determine that a factor is insignificant, don't waste time and energy putting attention on it. This spreads your energy too thin and minimizes your ability to create positive change. The key is to engage in a filtering process by which you weed out the many trivial variables that compete for your time but offer no real advantage. By doing so, you disable the force of confusion and achieve clarity of focus around your efforts to resolve an issue, solve a problem, or reach a goal.

Finding the better way

The way you find the critical few is to follow a structured process for defining, measuring, and analyzing all the cause-and-effect relationships. In Six Sigma, structured and powerful tools help you brainstorm the possible causes (Xs) of performance problems and operational issues. Collect performance data that reflects the behavior of the many Xs, as well as the behavior of your Y of concern. Analytical tools enlighten you as to which Xs are the critical ones, and which are the trivial.

The results of these operations tell you — and show you clearly — which Xs you need to focus on to impact your Y. They also show you which Xs are *out of control,* or behaving too erratically. Such variation is the primary cause of problems when it comes to performance predictability.

Having your baseline of measurements and understanding numerically how your Xs interact and impact your Y, you can then implement countermeasures — different X-related actions that ultimately improve your Y.

Using your same data framework, you can take new measurements to test the impact of your countermeasures. You have established a data-oriented baseline against which to prove that the new way of doing business is truly a better way.

You have validated that the critical few Xs are truly the critical few. This is the essence of the Six Sigma principle of finding the leverage.

Chapter 3

Pinpointing the Essentials of Six Sigma

In This Chapter

▶ Summarizing the Define-Measure-Analyze-Improve-Control (DMAIC) project methodology

▶ Understanding the many areas of Six Sigma application

▶ Reviewing roles and responsibilities in a Six Sigma deployment

▶ Following the deployment and implementation process

Six Sigma affects the lives of individuals and the conduct of organizations. Unlike most other business improvement initiatives, Six Sigma isn't like vitamins; it's not "feel good" stuff. It's an aggressive, targeted regimen. Six Sigma is a pervasive, challenging, systematic eradication of waste and inefficiency and of defects and problems that develop and hide in organizations.

This chapter discusses the five phases of the Six Sigma DMAIC project methodology. You also find out how that methodology is applied in specific areas of the organization by individuals who take on roles and responsibilities as disciplined practitioners. Finally, you see that the deployment and implementation processes follow a prescriptive roadmap.

The Project Strategy: DMAIC

At the business level, Six Sigma projects are the players in the overall game plan of a breakthrough performance improvement initiative. The business perspective is that a Six Sigma project is the agent of action that executes the business strategy and returns the results.

Every Six Sigma project follows a standardized and systematic method known as *DMAIC (Define-Measure-Analyze-Improve-Control),* a formalized problem-solving process. The DMAIC process can improve any type of process in any organization to improve its efficiency and effectiveness.

✔ **Define:** Set the context and objectives for the project.

✔ **Measure:** Get the baseline performance and capability of the process or system being improved.

✔ **Analyze:** Use data and tools to understand the cause-and-effect relationships in the process or system.

✔ **Improve:** Develop the modifications that lead to a validated improvement in the process or system.

✔ **Control:** Establish plans and procedures to ensure the improvements are sustained.

DMAIC is applied by highly trained practitioners who complete improvement projects that are managed to financial targets. In DMAIC, business processes are improved by following a structured method with set steps, or *tollgates*. Only as you start and complete one step are you ready to move on to the next. After moving through all the steps, and only when you can show that the DMAIC project has generated breakthrough benefit, can you then say you've completed a Six Sigma project.

Part II of this book covers the details of executing each of these phases in detail, including the methods and tools you need to complete a DMAIC project.

No matter how hard you try to accomplish anything, it's always easier when you follow a proven methodology. DMAIC (shown graphically in Figure 3-1) is a proven solution for process problems and improving business performance.

DMAIC Improvement Methodology

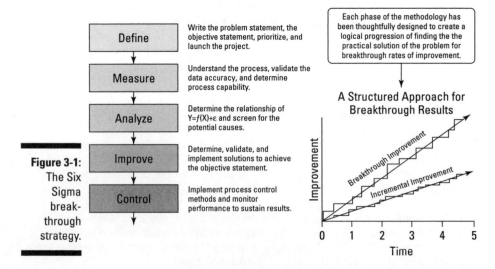

Figure 3-1: The Six Sigma breakthrough strategy.

Some companies and Six Sigma practitioners place an R for "recognize" before the D for define, indicating that you must first recognize and choose the right problem to solve or need to improve *before* you can define what the problem or need is.

Domains of Activity

There are four areas or domains of activity to which Six Sigma can be applied (each is discussed in the following sections):

- ✓ **Thinking:** The domain of thinking focuses on improving the reasoning and efficiency of *every* employee.
- ✓ **Processing:** The domain of processing focuses on improving existing processes, and a large number of employees are involved in this.
- ✓ **Designing:** Fewer people are directly involved in designing, which focuses on improving the designs of new processes.
- ✓ **Managing:** A small number of business and quality leaders are responsible for managing the overall Six Sigma initiative.

Thinking for breakthrough

Thinking for breakthrough is the realm of activity focused on the underlying principles of Six Sigma, because the performance of a business isn't guided only by directives and procedures. Improvement projects and initiatives aren't just about methods and tools. And wholesale change isn't driven by a minority but by large masses of people who together constitute real and lasting culture change.

Sweeping culture change and improvement is a function of getting everyone in an organization aligned to the same direction, values, and way of thinking. Thinking for breakthrough is a set of guiding principles that fuel culture change and get many people speaking the same language of performance improvement.

The traditional path of Six Sigma has been to first lead, and then do: First stimulate change, and then execute according to a stepwise methodology. Only after years of experience do Six Sigma change agents internalize the guiding principles of Six Sigma and apply those principles as second nature in everything they do.

Thinking for breakthrough emerged only after Six Sigma was proven and became pervasive, and only after its underlying principles were well understood by so many practitioners. Whereas processing for breakthrough and designing for breakthrough are methodology- and tool-driven, thinking for breakthrough is mind-driven.

Processing for breakthrough

Processing for breakthrough is the realm of activity that focuses on optimizing the performance of existing business and operational processes. Any process is theoretically capable of operating at its *entitlement* level, which is defined as the performance level the process has demonstrated it can operate at, even if it doesn't perform to that level all the time. See Chapter 4 for more on entitlement.

If a budgeting process was capable of operating at a 95 percent acceptance level for several weeks out of the year, you can say that 95 percent is the entitlement level for that process. Generally speaking, *entitlement* is the very best a process, product, service, or transaction can do without redesigning it.

When you are processing for Six Sigma, you take actions and implement improvements that enable your process to perform to its utmost potential all the time, not just part of the time, within the limitations of its current design. You do this by applying the DMAIC methodology through Six Sigma improvement projects — all of which are focused on improving processes that are focused on business priorities set by management.

The people who are directly responsible for processing for breakthrough are called project Champions, Master Black Belts, Black Belts, Green Belts, Yellow Belts, process owners, and sometimes White Belts. You can get a full description of who these people are and what they do in the "The People: Who You Need to Know" section in this chapter.

Designing for breakthrough

Designing for breakthrough is the realm of activity focused on optimizing the design process prior to manufacturing products, delivering services, or conducting transactions for customers. Design for Six Sigma (DFSS) is an approach for planning, configuring, qualifying, and launching products, services, transactions, processes, systems, and events that move quality upstream in an organization.

By *upstream,* we mean that DFSS methods and tools enable you to anticipate the source of development, manufacturing, or performance problems before they occur so that you can design and plan in a way that allows you to avoid them. Designing quality into products, services, transactions, processes, systems, and events from the beginning is what prevents the "hidden factory" from arising (see Chapter 1), eroding value, and, ultimately, eating away at profits.

First, DFSS reduces the risk in the performance and attributes of a design (customer satisfaction issues). Second, it reduces the risks associated with the business and operational viability of a design (provider satisfaction issues).

DFSS maximizes the confidence that a product, service, transaction, process, system, or event design will perform to its entitlement level in the presence of uncertainties that cannot be feasibly managed.

DFSS is not just an area of focus for design engineers in a company, but is applicable to the design process within any domain. DFSS enables the building of quality into processes and outcomes such that the opportunity for damaging variation and defects never occurs.

Managing for breakthrough

Managing for breakthrough entails all the plans, systems, and processes for leading a Six Sigma deployment and implementing it in an organization. This is the mechanism by which an organization drives and supports the activities in the domains of thinking, processing, and designing for breakthrough.

Because Six Sigma is an intervention that sets an organization on a new performance path, managing for breakthrough is a matter of *leadership.* Positive leadership moves people and organizations in a new direction, disrupting the status quo.

Managing for breakthrough involves selecting and training the right people; installing an improvement infrastructure; assimilating certain software tools; and establishing a management system, methods, and practices that are robust enough to set an organization on a new performance path. More information on the management aspects of selecting Six Sigma projects is in Chapter 4, and a complete run down on all the important tools for managing Six Sigma is in Chapter 12.

The executives, champions, and deployment leaders are directly responsible for managing the Six Sigma initiative. Sometimes a Six Sigma role called a Master Black Belt is also involved in managing for breakthrough. You can get a full description of who these people are and what they do in "The People: Who You Need to Know" section in this chapter.

The People: Who You Need to Know

The full deployment and implementation of a Six Sigma initiative in an organization requires the collective participation of numerous people, each of whom is responsible for fulfilling specific roles and obligations at both the managerial and technical levels. Most often, these people are drawn from within the ranks of the company and are specially trained to the requisite skills.

The rigorous nature of a Six Sigma deployment compels an organization to call on its very best people to participate. When you're involved in a Six Sigma initiative, you're working with the best and brightest, and you're part of a structured assembly of talent that works together in lockstep to achieve the breakthrough goals of Six Sigma improvement.

In Six Sigma, everyone's a leader

Six Sigma requires energized thinking, an open mind, and an unquenchable thirst for truth and betterment. The Six Sigma mindset is one that initiates change, sees problems as opportunities, and formally questions fundamental assumptions until the root causes are characterized, optimized, and controlled. These are principles and practices of leadership, and they are a fundamental part of the character of everyone who carries the Six Sigma flag.

For every participant, Six Sigma is a breakthrough leadership initiative. Just like the breakthrough performance returns realized by the organization, everyone involved in Six Sigma realizes a nearly unbounded sense of potential. Barriers and limitations melt away. Anything is possible. After you drink the Six Sigma elixir, there's no turning back — you're transformed. Energized thinking and thirst for truth become part of your being. You feel naturally compelled to question assumptions, search for root causes, and to characterize and optimize things. You become a leader.

One of the single greatest characteristics of Six Sigma is that it develops leaders. Regardless of your role or function, you develop leadership characteristics you didn't have before. Your personal and professional life will have new potential and new meaning.

From the top

A Six Sigma initiative begins with a team of executives and business-unit leaders who approve the Six Sigma deployment program, endorse projects, and are accountable for achieving the results. They inject the initial dose of vision and ambition into the organization and apply the business savvy and people skills to stimulate the drive for change.

Six Sigma is a top-down initiative. While the methods and tools of Six Sigma are applicable at all levels, breakthrough organizational performance requires a full coordinated commitment — and that can only come from the top.

You may be tempted to try to introduce a Six Sigma initiative from the bottom-up, perhaps because you see the potential of and have control over your area of business, or maybe because your senior management "just doesn't get it." And you may be successful in applying the Six Sigma methodology in your local business area to achieve a significant level of process improvement, but for the rest of the organization to embrace Six Sigma, it will have to come from the top. Prepare yourself to take your success to senior management and take it from the top going forward.

The Six Sigma deployment leader

The Six Sigma deployment leader is the single most important individual in the deployment process. The deployment leader is often a senior manager or executive who reports directly to the corporate-level person responsible for launching and sustaining Six Sigma.

The deployment leader ensures the effective alignment of corporate strategic goals with business unit deployment plans. They monitor progress and sustain performance at target levels, as Six Sigma is executed throughout the organization. In this role, the deployment leader develops the Six Sigma roll-out plan; helps select Champions, Black Belts, Green Belts, and Yellow Belts; and ensures proper training. The deployment leader also works closely with the Six Sigma Champion, and serves as a conduit between Champions and executive management, as higher-level goals and objectives are communicated downward, and as goals and plans are aligned with implementation actions.

Specific responsibilities of the deployment leader also include

- Holding accountability for the results of Six Sigma
- Driving the vision and mission for Six Sigma into the organization
- Removing barriers to successful implementations
- Internally publicizing Six Sigma goals, plans, progress, results, and best practices
- Creating and maintaining passion and commitment to Six Sigma goals
- Updating executive leadership on the progress of the business units

In large corporations made up of many business units, there may be a need for business unit level deployment leaders. Reporting directly to a business unit executive leader, the business unit deployment leader is responsible for the initialization and implementation of Six Sigma within their particular organization. In smaller organizations, the roles of the deployment leader and the Six Sigma champion may be combined and filled by a single individual.

Naturally, the Six Sigma deployment leader has a great deal of rapport among his or her peers and has typically functioned as a manager or team leader. He or she is responsible for developing and communicating the corporate vision for Six Sigma and ensuring that appropriate resources and support structures are in place.

The Six Sigma Champion

Six Sigma Champions are responsible for the dissemination and successful application of Six Sigma technical know-how. They develop a plan for transforming their organizations to "Six Sigma as the way we think and work." They are also responsible for ensuring the success of Black Belts and Green Belts, through day-to-day coaching, mentoring, resource provisioning, and removal of barriers. Champions have long-standing rapport with key managerial and staff people, and a demonstrated ability to pull people and resources together on short notice to achieve key objectives. The Six Sigma Champion:

- Identifies, selects, scopes, prioritizes, and assigns projects, and aligns projects to business strategies

- Selects Black Belts, Green Belts, and Yellow Belts, and ensures that they are appropriately trained, tasked, and deployed

- Supports Black, Green, and Yellow Belts through the removal of organizational barriers, securing necessary resources, coaching, and reviewing project implementation status

- Establishes an adequate backlog of projects and ensures that all Belts and Master Black Belts are fully dedicated to Six Sigma activities

- Reports progress against target metrics to Champions

- Promotes best-practices sharing and leverages solutions and improvements across organizational boundaries

In large corporations made up of many business units, there may be a Senior Champion, as well as business-unit-level Champions. In smaller organizations, the roles of the deployment leader and the Six Sigma Champion may be combined and filled by a single individual.

The core team

We can't overemphasize the critical importance of a cross-functional core leadership team in ensuring the efficient and effective rollout of a Six Sigma initiative. The core team is a unified body whose members perform an organizational assessment, benchmark products and services, conduct detailed gap analyses, create the operational vision, and develop implementation plans. The core team ensures completeness of deployment throughout the organization, by:

- Making the initiative highly visible through active and personalized leadership, commitment, and passion for change

- Installing the measurement system that will track the progress, install accountability into the initiative, and provide a visible dashboard of progress and efforts

- Benchmarking of products, services, and processes so that the organization can truly understand its relative position in the marketplace

- Setting stretch goals that focus on changing the process by which work gets done rather than tweaking existing processes, leading to leap-frog rates of improvement

- Providing knowledge and education to all levels of people, because certain methods and tools are necessary to initiate and sustain breakthrough improvement

- Evangelizing success stories that demonstrate how Six Sigma methods, technologies, and tools have been applied to achieve dramatic operational and financial improvements

- Developing and implementing a supporting infrastructure that enables Six Sigma to naturally occur and flourish in a company

Core team members include the following people and departments:

- Six Sigma deployment leader
- Business unit Six Sigma leaders
- Key executive representatives
- Functional representatives
- Human Resources
- Finance
- Information Technology
- Training
- Communications

Functional representatives are senior corporate staff members who run their respective departments or have large responsibility in those departments. They are well respected leaders who can drive short-cycle change initiatives because they know the people and have the knowledge they need to set new initiatives in place.

✔ **Finance representative:**

- Determines how project costs and savings will be defined, valued, and reported

- Develops a project savings audit process and leads finance participation in the project selection and review processes

- Is the single point of contact for Six Sigma finance issues and coordinates all project auditing and validation activities

- Defines accounting and budgeting requirements for Six Sigma-related expenses

✔ **Training representative:**

- Is the single point of contact for Six Sigma training issues and coordinates Six Sigma training activities for the entire corporation

- Configures all training curricula and courseware for the Six Sigma initiative, including executive, Champion, Master Black Belt, Black Belt, Green Belt, Yellow Belt, Design for Six Sigma, awareness training, and thinking for Six Sigma

- Schedules and coordinates all Six Sigma training courses, logistics, materials, and supplies and also develops training sign-up, tracking, and reporting processes

✔ **Information Technology representative:**

- Is the single point of contact for Six Sigma IT issues and coordinates Six Sigma IT activities in all organizations

- Arranges for purchase and distribution of Six Sigma software, along with the hardware necessary to support it, for training and knowledge transfer, analytical work, project management, and process improvement

- Prepares and executes plans for providing end-user support for Six Sigma software

✔ **Human Resources representative:**

- Is the single point of contact for Six Sigma human resources and coordinates all Six Sigma-related HR activities

- Writes job descriptions for all Six Sigma positions and prepares an organizational chart that identifies the roles

- Develops compensation packages for all Six Sigma positions and works with business leadership to configure reward, recognition, and career development plans

✔ **Communications representative:**

- Is the single point of contact for all Six Sigma communication activities and leads the development and implementation of communication plans

- Organizes a process for communicating internal successes and coordinates communication with stock analysts, suppliers, customers, partners, and investors

- Arranges for the distribution of reference, informational, educational, and background material throughout the company

Number-crunching karate: Black Belts and their brethren

Solving problems the Six Sigma way requires varying degrees of skill in applied statistics:

✔ Solving complex problems requires considerable statistical expertise.

✔ Solving problems of moderate complexity, or assisting in the solution of complex problems, requires a medium level of skill.

✔ Regular application of simple statistics to everyday routine work requires even less.

In Six Sigma, the highest level of skill is called *Black Belt*, the medium skill level is *Green Belt,* and the everyday level is *Yellow Belt.*

In the early 1990s, Motorola was assisting Unisys in solving complex problems associated with the production of large-scale multilayer printed circuit boards for military applications. Applying the advanced statistical analysis tools of Six Sigma solved the problem. The managers wanted to promote the value of the expertise developed in the team. One evening, unwinding after a long day's work at the Unisys facility in Salt Lake City, they hit on the idea of calling these engineers Black Belts — a term that captured the mystique of their discipline and skill. "Now that's a name I can sell!" proclaimed the Unisys manager.

And it did. As the Six Sigma methodology flourished, so too did the title of *Six Sigma Black Belt* as the master of statistical problem-solving. Later, as the need for lesser degrees of skill was identified, the terms Green Belt and Yellow Belt were added. Across the global Six Sigma landscape, you'll also find additional variants, including Blue Belt, Brown Belt, and even White Belt. You'll even hear jokes about Chartreuse Belts (part Green, part Yellow), Polka Dotted Belts, and more.

Here's one part of the martial arts metaphor that fits perfectly: A Black Belt is so expertly skilled and so experienced that they understand the true nature of their opponent, and they know how to apply the right skills and tools with grace and minimal effort to channel its energy and fully achieve their goals.

The "Belt" terminology is not universally accepted. While universally under-stood and applied as a broad standard in many companies and industries, it's downright unfashionable in some circles. But whatever your scale of measure-ment, Six Sigma practitioners have varying degrees of skill.

Master Black Belts are the trainers. They are accomplished Black Belts with teaching skills, who work with and mentor other practitioners. Black Belts are extensively trained and typically work full-time leading Six Sigma projects. Green Belts receive less training and work part-time on Six Sigma projects, either in support of Black Belt projects or leading less-complex projects of their own. Yellow Belts receive less training still, and while they may support a Green Belt or Black Belt project, they usually apply their Six Sigma knowl-edge in the course of their everyday work. The hierarchy of practitioners is shown in Figure 3-2.

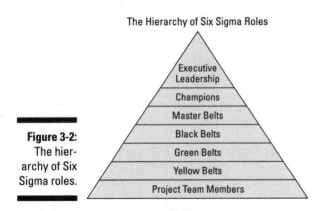

The Hierarchy of Six Sigma Roles

Figure 3-2:
The hier-archy of Six Sigma roles.

The leadership and technical roles of Six Sigma flow down through an organization in hierarchical fashion, with a very small number of leaders and champions at the top, a small number of Master Black Belts, Black Belts, and Green Belts in the middle, and a large number of Yellow Belts and team members at the bottom.

In the following sections, the roles and skills of the Six Sigma practitioners are described in further detail.

Master Black Belts

Master Black Belts (MBB) are hands-on experts who teach and mentor Black, Green, and Yellow Belts, and who often own the Six Sigma training curricula and Six Sigma knowledge content for their organizations. As mentors, MBBs consult other Belts on fundamental business issues as well as specific project application issues, challenges, and problems.

Black Belts

Black Belts are the most highly trained experts in the complete set of Six Sigma methods and tools. They are highly respected for possessing the knowledge and skill required to facilitate breakthrough-level improvements in the most complex of processes. Black Belts typically number 1 to 2 percent of the orga-nization and operate in a full-time capacity. The Black Belt

✔ Implements Six Sigma projects that historically are advertised to return a bottom-line value of $150,000 or more to the organization. A Six Sigma Black Belt may implement as many as four such projects a year.

✔ Mentors and coaches others in applying Six Sigma methods and tools

✔ Leads complex departmental, business unit, or cross-functional process improvement projects that require significant data and analytical skill.

✔ Disseminates new strategies and tools via training, workshops, case studies, local symposia, and more

✔ Discovers internal and external (suppliers and customers) opportunities for new Six Sigma projects

Green Belts

The Six Sigma Green Belt is trained and skilled to solve the majority of process problems in both transactional and manufacturing environments. Green Belts are process leaders, process owners, professional staff, operational specialists, managers, and executives who have a significant degree of business, leadership, statistical, and problem-solving skills. Green Belts typically number 5 to 10 percent of the organization. The Green Belt

✔ Implements about two projects per year that historically are advertised to return an average bottom-line value of $35,000

✔ Teaches local personnel to apply Six Sigma strategies and tools and coaches local personnel through one-on-one support

✔ Leads departmental, business unit, or cross-functional process improvement projects in environments that don't require complex data or heavy statistical analyses

✔ Disseminates new strategies and tools via training, workshops, case studies, local symposia, and more

✔ Discovers internal and external (that is, suppliers and customers) opportunities for Six Sigma projects

Yellow Belts

Everyone in the organization can apply elements of the Six Sigma methodology and improve their work environments. Everyone can assist Green Belts and Black Belts in completing projects. But not everyone needs to be immersed in the details or challenges to the extent that requires the level of training or skill of the Green Belt or Black Belt.

The Six Sigma Yellow Belt is "everyone else." Yellow Belts are staff members, administrators, operations personnel, project team members, or anyone else — technical or non-technical. Nearly anyone can identify measurement scales, define critical process factors, collect some data, characterize a process, make easy improvements, and cultivate opportunities.

The goal of the Yellow Belt is to think in a data-driven, cause-and-effect process manner, and apply this thinking to their area of work. Yellow Belts support Black Belt and Green Belt projects, and can even take on small projects of their own.

Be careful not to make generalizations about the average value of a Black Belt, Green Belt, or Yellow Belt project. Projects have a broad distribution of returns. Small projects can escalate, while high-value projects may never reach their potential. The averages we've indicated in the preceding lists are based on long-term experience across multiple companies and industries.

Bringing the team together

Each Six Sigma role-player works with other members of the team, as shown in Figure 3-3, keeping the project as the central focus.

Role Relationship Map

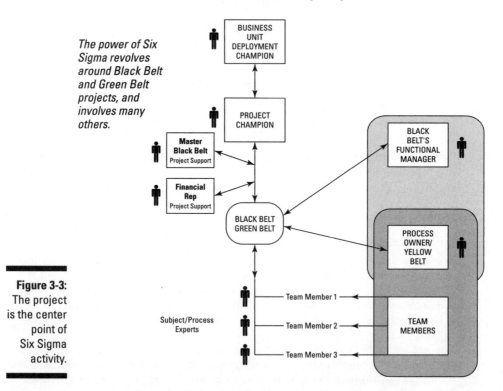

The power of Six Sigma revolves around Black Belt and Green Belt projects, and involves many others.

Figure 3-3: The project is the center point of Six Sigma activity.

The Lifecycle of a Six Sigma Initiative

A Six Sigma initiative occurs in five major stages (see Figure 3-4).

1. First, you *initialize* Six Sigma by establishing goals and installing infrastructure.

2. Second, you *deploy* the initiative by assigning, training, and equipping the staff.

3. Third, you *implement* projects and improve performance, yielding financial results.

4. Fourth, you *expand* the scope of the initiative to include additional organizational units.

5. Fifth, you *sustain* the initiative, through re-alignment, re-training, and evolution.

Each is discussed in the following sections.

Figure 3-4:
Six Sigma progresses in distinct stages.

The Lifecycle of Six Sigma

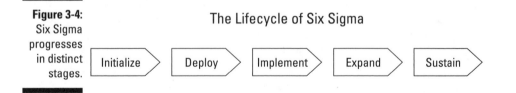

Initialize: Ready . . . Aim . . .

Six Sigma initiatives are programs. They require programmatic-type preparation and planning, beginning with a proscriptive set of readiness tasks. The initialization stage includes selecting the core team, preparing the supporting infrastructure, and enabling the processes, which must be in place to facilitate the deployment activities of the next stage (see Table 3-1).

As part of initialization, executive training prepares the executive staff and senior leaders by providing a comprehensive overview of the Six Sigma deployment process and what to expect. The executives also agree on macro items including scope, timeframes, goals, and objectives, and they issue a formal commitment statement to all employees and constituents.

The scope of the first deployments should be kept in check. The most successful Six Sigma initiatives begin with the deployment scope limited to a selected line of business or division of activity.

Table 3-1	Elements of Six Sigma Initialization
Deliverable	*Details*
Launch planning	A fully documented Six Sigma leadership system, implementation plans, schedules, and activity tracking/ reporting techniques.
Human resource guidelines	Competency models and participant selection, position and role descriptions, compensation, reporting relationships, career planning.
Communications plan	Overall strategy (who, what, and when), message content as a function of time, methods, and mediums.
Financial guidelines	Savings definitions, project forecasting, methods of evaluation, realization tracking. Integration of initiative metrics with project tracking and management software.
Project selection guidelines	Definition criteria, project type categorizations, problem statement, targeted savings values, approval process, completion requirements.
Project tracking and reporting	Organization structure definition, user manuals and training, report generation.
Management dashboard	Create an ongoing sense of urgency, and for staving off natural initiative entropy.
Information technology support	Software installations, computer needs, Intranet development, databases for final reports.

Deploy: Setting it all in motion

With a supporting infrastructure, corporate goals, and metrics established, the deploy stage begins with the selection of the Champions and the first candidate Black Belts, Green Belts, and Yellow Belts.

Champions are trained in the Six Sigma methodology, the principles of implementing Six Sigma, and in project selection, practices and tools, and begin the critical work of selecting the first Six Sigma projects.

Also, the infrastructure is deployed by the core team. This includes finance practices, including guidelines for auditing project financials; software tools for statistical analyses, project management, and process optimization; training materials, curricula, and schedules for all Belt training; and motivational communications from management. A project tracking and performance dashboard system is deployed.

According to the deployment plan, the first waves of Black Belts, Green Belts, and Yellow Belts are trained and assigned to projects.

Six Sigma deployments include the practice of conducting projects as part of the Belt training. All types of Belt training include the definition, characterization, and improvement of a work process as part of the training regimen. Although this extends the training period, trainees deliver results to the bottom line as they complete their initial training. The training has immediate-term ROI.

Implement: Forging first successes

Upon completion of the first waves of Belt training, the early successes create momentum and the Six Sigma initiative begins to gather traction. As successes continue, the initiative can become infectious and turn around even the skeptics.

In this stage, the practitioners are defining and mapping processes, identifying critical-to-quality indicators, collecting performance data, and characterizing process performance. They are conducting statistical analyses, discovering the root causes of problems and improving performance levels. Your company has begun to root out waste, increase productivity, lower costs, and decrease cycle time. Six Sigma is working!

It's important to watch the process closely. Black Belts must be assigned full time to their projects and given leverage to perform. Green Belts and even Yellow Belts must be supported in their projects. Technical issues must be addressed head-on with appropriate skill to ensure success.

Not all first projects go well — for a variety of reasons. If early high-profile projects sputter, it can threaten the success of the initiative. For this reason, be sure to choose early projects that have a manageable scope, moderate risk, and the promise of reasonable returns. Leave the big risk/high reward projects for a little later.

Expand: Taking it everywhere

Following the first successful waves of implementation, the organization expands Six Sigma into new geographies, functional areas, and lines of business.

The introduction of Six Sigma into each new line of business is an initiative unto itself and includes the stages of initialization, deployment, and implementation. The lessons learned from the first deployment are included in revisions to the implementation plans going forward.

Some form of tailoring or customization of Six Sigma is required to deploy into each new business or functional area. Examples include

- ✔ Six Sigma in engineering and design areas would employ methods and tools of a sub-field known as Design for Six Sigma (DFSS — see the "Designing for breakthrough" section), and tools like Axiomatic Design.
- ✔ Six Sigma in manufacturing includes lean practices.
- ✔ Highly computerized environments may incorporate automated process execution management tools.
- ✔ Deployment into foreign countries requires internationalization and localization of materials and tools.

Also, as the portfolio of projects grows and diversifies, it's important to apply enterprise-class tracking and management tools. Read more about these in Chapter 12.

The first few waves of projects in any given function or business area harvest what is known as the low-hanging fruit — the obvious opportunities with big returns. As the Six Sigma initiative matures, two phenomena occur:

- ✔ The biggest projects have all been completed.
- ✔ The Yellow-Belt culture is curing little problems before they become big problems.

At this point, the project-oriented Six Sigma culture begins to give way to the sustaining culture.

Sustain: The self-healing culture

Six Sigma is a problem-solving methodology. A Six Sigma deployment applies the Six Sigma suite of problem-solving tools to business challenges in a series of projects, each of which addresses technical, performance, quality, and other problems in core and enabling processes of the organization.

Through expansion, typically over a period of several years, the initiative reaches the four corners of the enterprise. Soon thereafter, all the biggest problems have been solved, and the associated big returns have come in. The first full cycle is complete. What's next?

At this point, the Six Sigma initiative changes character. The deployment leader and Champion shift the sustaining direction away from a project orientation into a process-management approach, where the tools of Six Sigma move to a supporting role — as part of how business and work processes execute most efficiently and effectively. The Six Sigma tools take their place in the organization's methodological toolbox, along with other selected tools of business performance operations.

In the sustain phase, the culture is self-healing. The Six Sigma project is used as a hot-shot tool for addressing flare-up issues that emerge from new initiatives and outside forces. Six Sigma training supports these project needs and is also integrated with other methods to support process needs. Training is used as a refresher for existing staff and to enable new hires, contractors, and acquisitions.

Part II
Understanding and Enacting the Breakthrough Strategy (DMAIC)

The 5th Wave   By Rich Tennant

"Ted and I spent over 120 man-hours together analyzing the survey data, and here's what we discovered: Ted borrows pens and never returns them, he intentionally squeaks his chair to annoy me, and, evidently, I talk in my sleep."

In this part . . .

The Six Sigma methodology is known by all as the DMAIC breakthrough strategy. That's Define, Measure, Analyze, Improve, and Control. That's all you have to do to create breakthrough performance — follow a very structured improvement process and the rest will come! We promise.

Chapter 4

Finding the Pain — Defining Projects

In This Chapter

▶ Seeing the big picture first

▶ Aligning Six Sigma with your needs

▶ Defining projects

▶ Realizing the benefits

*T*he essence of Six Sigma is to solve problems that are impacting business or personal performance. But before you can solve a problem or improve performance, you have to properly define your goal or objective — that is, you have to define the focus of your Six Sigma project. In fact, defining a project is 50 percent of the improvement game, and finding the right problems is critical to the success of your organization.

The Define stage of the breakthrough strategy (DMAIC) assumes you've identified a certain number of problems to be solved, and these problems are then converted into Six Sigma projects. A key challenge for all Six Sigma practitioners and management alike is to find these problems in a strategic way that assures maximum benefit from the application of the Six Sigma methodology.

Defining projects is about recognizing problematic areas of the business and subsequently creating a clear direction for resolving these problematic areas. It's akin to the question, "How do you eat an elephant?" The answer? One bite at a time. Problematic areas of the business (like warranty returns, accounts receivable, product yield, and customer satisfaction issues) are the elephant-sized issues of the business. More likely than not, each of these problematic areas requires that you engage in more than one Six Sigma project, thereby eating the elephant one bite at a time.

The Six Sigma Project

Six Sigma progress is obtained the old fashioned way — one project at a time. And progress is not necessarily serial, but often in parallel, as many Black Belts, Green Belts, and Yellow Belts apply the breakthrough strategy throughout an organization (see Chapter 3 for more on Belts). In essence, projects are the unit of measurement, the physical entity, by which most Six Sigma progress is accomplished. Projects represent — and in fact are — the level of granularity needed to manage a single process improvement or a large-scale business improvement effort.

The basics of a project

A Six Sigma project starts out as a practical problem that is adversely impacting the business, and ultimately ends up as a practical solution that improves business performance. Projects state performance problems in quantifiable terms that define expectations related to desired levels of performance and timing, as described in Figure 4-1.

A project:

- Has a financial impact to EBIT (Earnings Before Income Tax) or NPBIT (Net Profit Before Income Tax) or a significant strategic value
- Produces results that significantly exceed the amount of effort required to obtain the improvement
- Solves a problem that is not easily or quickly solvable using traditional methods
- Improves performance by greater than 70 percent over existing performance levels

The focus of a project is to solve a business problem that is hurting key business performance elements, such as:

- The success of the organization
- Costs
- Employee or customer satisfaction
- Process capability
- Output capacity
- Cycle time
- Revenue potential

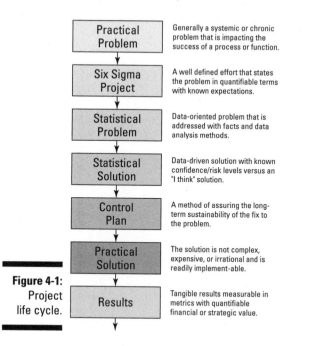

Practical Problem	Generally a systemic or chronic problem that is impacting the success of a process or function.
Six Sigma Project	A well defined effort that states the problem in quantifiable terms with known expectations.
Statistical Problem	Data-oriented problem that is addressed with facts and data analysis methods.
Statistical Solution	Data-driven solution with known confidence/risk levels versus an "I think" solution.
Control Plan	A method of assuring the long-term sustainability of the fix to the problem.
Practical Solution	The solution is not complex, expensive, or irrational and is readily implement-able.
Results	Tangible results measurable in metrics with quantifiable financial or strategic value.

Figure 4-1: Project life cycle.

The problem transformation

When a particular problem is selected to become a potential Six Sigma project, it goes through a critical metamorphosis — first from a practical business problem into a statistical problem, then into a statistical solution, and, finally, into a practical solution. When you state your problem in statistical language, you ensure that you will use data, and only data, to solve it. This forces you to abandon gut feelings, intuition, and best guesses as ways to address your problems.

Almost any problem is solvable if you throw enough time and money at it. But this does not qualify as a practical solution, and it's not the goal of a Six Sigma project. A practical solution is one that is not complex, not difficult to implement, and does not require extensive resources to affect the improvement.

Project responsibilities

There is a management framework and set of responsibilities inherent in the Six Sigma methodology that entails finding problems, defining projects, determining solutions, and implementing improvements. A Six Sigma project goes through an ownership transfer as demonstrated in Figure 4-2.

Project Responsiblities

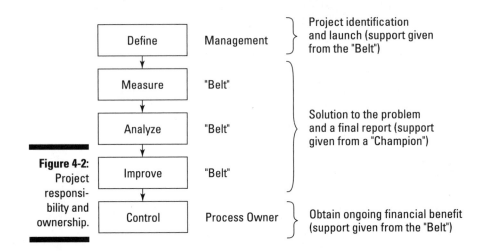

Figure 4-2: Project responsibility and ownership.

The responsibilities, accountabilities, and deliverables of a project are divided between management and the various Belts who perform problem-solving activities. Management, including the process owner, is responsible for determining priorities and focus, while non-management personnel are responsible for implementing the solution and realizing the benefits. These project lifecycle relationships prevent Six Sigma deliverables from falling into the cracks.

Six Sigma is a team effort. Even in the Define phase, where management is responsible for project identification and launch, the Belts assist. Generally speaking, Belts have 20 percent responsibility for defining and managing improvement, while management has 80 percent. When it comes to implementation — the MAIC portion of the breakthrough strategy — these percentages are reversed.

Your Needs, My Needs — What Are They?

The remarkable thing about Six Sigma is its ability to increase satisfaction for a number of different stakeholders in the business, including customers, employees, management, and owners. The common denominator holding all these groups together — and meeting their different needs — is a focus on improving business processes.

Therefore, the answer to the question "Your needs, my needs — what are they?" is ultimately the improvement of some business process, which then results in meeting the needs of one or more stakeholders. This is the bread-and-butter of Six Sigma.

Inevitably, the question arises, "Should Six Sigma projects focus on achieving benefits directly for the business or on achieving benefits directly for the customer?" While the answer depends on circumstances, any improvement to a business process usually benefits both the business *and* its customers.

For example, if you produce a product that has defects, customers will ultimately be unsatisfied, no matter how many times you inspect the products before shipment. This is because inspections are not perfect, and some percentage of the defective product will find its way to the customer.

If you do a Six Sigma project to improve product yield, it will have a positive impact — by reducing inspection, rework, scrap, inventory, and other associated costs. It will also have a positive customer impact as the probability of shipping defects is reduced, cycle time is reduced, cost is reduced, and the predictability of delivery is increased.

Isn't it now obvious that it's always good from the customer perspective to improve any process of the business? The real question is this: Where is the urgency, where is the pain, and which problem should be solved first? It's not a question of whether a project benefits the business or benefits the customer; it's simply identifying the most pressing operational problems, and fixing them — once and for all.

Aligning Six Sigma with strategy

Six Sigma is an enterprise-wide strategy that recognizes problem areas, defines improvement efforts and projects, and determines and implements data-driven breakthrough level solutions, all in a predictable and repeatable way to improve business results. To obtain the maximum benefit from Six Sigma, you must link Six Sigma with the strategic needs of the business. This approach is illustrated in Figure 4-3.

Businesses define sets of key goals and objectives for accomplishing the vision and operating plan. In turn, to achieve these key goals and objectives, critical problems are identified and solved. Keep these goals and objectives in mind when you select Six Sigma projects.

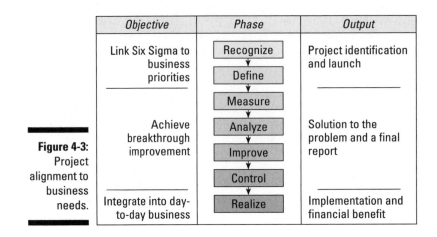

Objective	Phase	Output
Link Six Sigma to business priorities	Recognize Define	Project identification and launch
Achieve breakthrough improvement	Measure Analyze Improve Control	Solution to the problem and a final report
Integrate into day-to-day business	Realize	Implementation and financial benefit

Figure 4-3: Project alignment to business needs.

Figure 4-3 is an expanded view of the breakthrough strategy that includes a Recognize step in the beginning and a Realize step at the end. The overall strategy is to find areas of the business that are in need of improvement to meet business goals (Recognize). This leads you to determine the problems you need to solve to improve the problem areas (Define projects). Next, you determine a solution to your problem, implement the solution, and obtain the subsequent benefits.

Start by assessing the higher level needs of your organization using any knowledge obtained from the voice of the customer (VOC) and the voice of the business (VOB). The *VOC* is all the needs and expectations your customers have for your products and services. The *VOB* represents all the needs and expectations of the business. The basic idea is to assess both the VOC and VOB to identify gaps — areas where the expectations of the business and expectations of the customer are misaligned. See Chapter 6 for further details on VOC and VOB.

Problem themes start to become visible, including:

✔ Product returns or warranty costs

✔ Customer complaints

✔ Accounts receivable and invoicing issues

✔ Cycle time or responsiveness

✔ Ineffective of defective services

✔ Yield and subsequent rework or scrap

✔ Capacity constraints

✔ Excessive inventory levels

Using a business case writing tool for project identification

The use of a Six Sigma business case writing tool helps you identify the problem areas of the business, provide a summary description or characterization of the situation, and estimate the potential value of improvement projects. At this level of analysis, the intent is not to define a Six Sigma project but to identify areas where Six Sigma projects are needed.

The description of a high-level business problem doesn't have to be very detailed. The details come when defining the project itself, just prior to beginning the Measure phase of the DMAIC methodology. Examples of high-level business problems are

- Excessive warranty returns

- High accounts receivable levels

- Non-competitive product yields and cost

- Lack of customer sales order responsiveness

The potential financial benefit from improvements is the current best estimate based on the data or knowledge you have at the time. In the beginning, all you have to do is get the number in the ballpark.

The following is the structure of the business case. Use it as a template for your own organization:

> As a company, our _____ performance for the _____ area is not meeting _____. Overall, this is causing _____ problems, which are costing us as much as $_____ per _____.

Here are some examples:

- As a company, our <u>accounts receivable</u> performance for the <u>finance invoicing</u> area is not meeting <u>the goal of 47 days sales outstanding</u>. Overall this is causing <u>cash flow and budget</u> problems that are costing us as much as <u>$4 million</u> per <u>year</u>.

- As a company our <u>final process yield</u> performance for the <u>paint and polish</u> area is not meeting <u>the targeted 97 percent yield</u>. Overall this is causing <u>floor space, shipment, and resource</u> problems that are costing us as much as <u>$900,000</u> per <u>year</u>.

- As a company our <u>on-time delivery</u> performance for <u>our healthcare products</u> area is not meeting <u>the scheduling and delivery cost requirements</u>. Overall this is causing <u>delivery issues and customer dissatisfaction</u> problems that are costing us as much as <u>$3 million in lost revenues and $1.5 million in expenses</u> per <u>year</u>.

Performing the business-case writing exercise

Completing a business-case writing exercise can be an eye-opening and exhilarating experience. The process is performed as a team, where each member uses 15 to 20 sticky-back notes that contain the business-case writing template shown in the preceding section.

Each member brainstorms in silence, thinking of as many business cases as he or she can. Each written business case is a stand-alone idea that identifies problem areas of the business. When a team member has exhausted all ideas, he or she stick those notes on the wall. Each member of the team performs a similar action until all members have posted their ideas.

The business-case writing tool can also be used at the divisional, departmental, or local process levels, or even at a personal level. This tool is an adaptation of a Six Sigma tool, called an *affinity diagram,* which can have many uses — from planning a family vacation to solving a complex business problem.

An affinity diagram is the outcome of an exercise whereby members of the team write their brainstorming ideas onto small, separate pieces of paper or sticky-back notes. Then the team silently groups the individual idea notes into natural categories. The resulting collection of grouped ideas creates what is called an affinity diagram. This modified brainstorming technique has the advantage of gathering all team members' input without the inhibition of criticism, and it encourages the natural emergence of important groupings or categories of ideas.

The sorting process is an iterative process. Each member of the team reads all business case ideas and moves the ideas into common affinity clusters. Ideas move from cluster to cluster, and in 10 to 15 minutes, this step is completed.

Usually, five to ten problem areas emerge. The team leader for the exercise then writes a title for each of the clusters: warranty returns, accounts receivable, and so on. Generally there will be some duplicate ideas, and duplication indicates the strength of an idea.

Completing the business case writing exercise

The hard part is now finished, and the fun begins. With five to ten different problem areas, it's now necessary to add a little more data and do some additional categorization to take the ideas to the actionable level. The next step is to determine who is the most likely person responsible for the identified area. Because this is a group decision and is usually obvious, this step goes fast, and the responsible person's name is written on the note. Finally, the most likely owner of the whole cluster is identified.

Because everyone has been actively involved in this process, there is a sense of belief and ownership for all the issues. Another important benefit comes from each person having to read and move the notes from one cluster to another; brains are processing information and becoming knowledgeable about the broader issues facing the organization. This is a great way to create a common platform of knowledge and cooperation, which leads to involvement in improvement actions.

You now have a valuable set of data and a knowledgeable team to develop an improvement plan using Six Sigma. You know the most critical improvements needed, have an insight into the type of improvements, know who has responsibility, and have an estimate of the potential savings. You now can define specific projects to solve elephant-sized problems. You are now ready to enter the Define phase of DMAIC.

Six Sigma project definition

When defining a project, you get into the nuts and bolts of Six Sigma. It's well worth your time to do this step right, because 50 percent of your project's success depends on how well it is defined!

The following people typically identify potential projects (see Chapter 3 for the lowdown on these roles):

- Champions
- Belts
- Process leaders
- Functional managers or Process Owners

Any employee can suggest a project, but it should be considered and sponsored by one of these people.

The most common mistakes in defining a potential project are as follows:

- The scope is too broad (solving world hunger or boiling the ocean). Symptoms include considering too many Ys (outputs) for improvement (see Chapter 2 for more on what Y means), multiple goals, numerous process owners, and multiple departments. The solution: Divide the oversized problem into several projects. You know the strategy: Divide and conquer.
- The problem is too easy.
- The problem solution is known.
- It is a "just do it" solution; no problem analysis is required.
- The problem is a management issue, not a good Belt project.

Steps of the project definition process

It's best to go through a specified sequence of events or a process to ensure that a project is well defined. Generally, you can expect to perform eight specific steps in this process:

1. **Determine the *Y*: what specifically needs to be improved.**

2. **Identify the associated processes and their physical locations.**

3. **Determine the baseline performance for each *Y* chosen.**

4. **Identify the cost and impact of the problem.**

5. **Write the problem statement.**

6. **Write the objective statement.**

7. **Identify and recruit candidates for the project team.**

8. **Obtain approvals and launch.**

These steps are a combination of gathering data and organizing it into a well articulated project. It's best to have a worksheet similar to Figure 4-4 to guide you through this process.

Determining what you want to improve

You want to improve the performance of some process, but which characteristics or outputs of the process need to be improved? The next step is to identify which process output variables (*Y*s) need improvement to solve the business problem (see Figure 4-5). The *Y*s in need of improvement must be easily identifiable and quantifiable.

If there are more than two *Y*s, there's a good chance that your project is too large in scope. You may have to break the project into two or more projects to be successful.

You probably now have to get a better sense of the process steps that are involved in the performance of your *Y*. Now you can better understand who will be involved in the project, and its scope and complexity.

At this point, you need a macro process map, which is concerned with the high-level flow that generates the output of interest. (The good news is that there are several software tools used by Six Sigma practitioners, such as SigmaFlow, Visio, and iGrafx to ease the drawing of these maps.) Such a map shows the full scope of the process and includes all major areas being affected.

Figure 4-4:
Project definition worksheet.

Step	Action	Information Elements for Defining a Project	Definition/Explanation	Enter Actual Project Information Here (Examples Indicated)
1. Identify the specific problem that needs to be solved per the business case or other source.	1A	What is the actual problem?	A business condition or impediment to success, stated as the high-level effect that the problem is having on the business. This is usually in terms of cost, revenue, quality, and delivery.	High inventory levels are consuming space, asset management time, and creating cash flow issues.
	1B	Where is the problem occurring?	Define where the problem is occurring. This should include a geographic name, such as city, facility, and the high-level name for the business area (accounts receivable, purchasing, manufacturing, human relations).	Materials control organization
	1C	Over what timeframe has this problem existed?	Define when the problem first began, or the period over which it has existed. For example: The problem began in February 2004; it has existed for the last 15 months; it has always existed.	Since January 2005
	1D	Who is the customer(s) most affected by this problem?	Identify the customer who is most affected by this business problem. This could be an external or internal customer.	Product resellers
2. Determine the outputs (Ys or CTQs), what specifically needs to be improved, and the baseline performance levels.	2A	Determine the characteristics or process outputs (Ys) that will be improved if this problem is solved.	This is the name for the outcome (Y) that you intend to improve by solving the problem. This should be described by a specific name, such as product test yield, customer complaints, invoice errors, inventory levels, response time.	Raw material inventory levels
	2B	Identify the primary metric for each Y. The metric describes the problem and is used to measure and track the improvement.	The primary metric is a combination of the name for the outcome (Y) and the unit of measure associated with it. For example, motor torque percent defective, daily number of customer complaints, defects per invoice, call-back response time in minutes.	Days of inventory on hand
	2C	Estimate the magnitude of the problem using the primary metric (baseline performance).	Data is gathered to determine the performance or behavior of the primary metric, assure the data is long term and not short term. An Excel macro may be used to plot the data as a function of time, and then used to monitor the improvement as a function of time. These data establish the base from which to calculate the potential financial benefits of the project, as a function of the improvements.	Inventory levels average 31.2 days, with a high of 37.1 and a low of 28.0 days
	2D	Identify a consequential metric(s).	This is any other characteristic or process output you want to monitor to assure there is no negative impact on another area from solving the problem.	Percent of order requests not billed due to inadequate inventory on hand
3. Identify the associated process and generate a macro process map.	3A	Indicate the major high level processes(es) by names that are associated with the problem.	High-level process steps generally contain sub-processes. At this point, you are interested in identifying the process steps in order to demonstrate the overall scope of the project and to later identify process owners. Think of where the problem starts and ends as a guide, and then name the major steps	Purchasing, order replenishment, inventory reconciliation, production control, and planning
	3B	Develop a high level business process map to indicate the scope of the project.	Using the data from the above steps, draw the high level process, including as much other pertinent information as possible, such as the flow of the work, process performance data, names.	See example in Fig. 4-6
4. Identify the cost and impact of the problem.	4A	Identify the most likely cost centers that will experience a cost benefit from this project.	Who is currently experiencing additional cost because of this problem? These same cost centers will experience improved operating costs as a result of the improvement. Generally, this means some action will be taken in these areas.	Inventory control department 5422
	4B	Estimate the annual financial impact of the project. Usually, this forecast is at an 80 percent confidence level.	With the support of the financial representative, develop a reasonable estimate or targeted savings for this project. You may need to refer to your Objective Statement to identify the targeted improvement; for example, costs may be expressed as cost of labor, inventory, productivity, or material.	We could save $250,000 per year if we met industry best-in-class levels of 13.5 inventory turns.

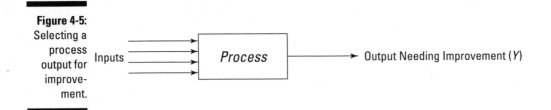

Figure 4-5:
Selecting a process output for improvement.

Figure 4-6 is an example of a pizza restaurant that is experiencing excess time to make pizzas. The macro process map illustrates the major steps in making the pizza.

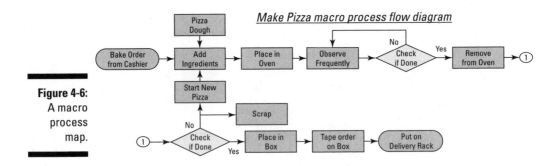

Figure 4-6:
A macro process map.

How bad is bad?

You may already have a sense of the magnitude of the problem you want to solve. Under the Six Sigma methodology, you must have more than just a sense of the magnitude; you must be able to express the magnitude of the problem (defect level) in some unit of measure (for example, hours, inches, percent late, and so on).

At this phase of your improvement effort, you may not have abundant and accurate data. While it would be handy to have data of high integrity to quantify the severity of your problem, don't be discouraged if your data is not perfect at this time. Because you will significantly improve the amount and integrity of your data when you are in the Measure phase, plan to update the quality of your data at that time.

Improvement of your data is essential, because you have to demonstrate your current performance (called the *baseline*), your desired performance (called the *objective*), and the actual data as a result of your project.

The comparison of these data is demonstrated in Figure 4-7, *a time-series chart,* a graphical method employed by Six Sigma practitioners to track the progress of improvement. In this case, the figure tracks the number of pizzas that exceeded the make time established by the restaurant in order to meet customer demands.

Verify that your data is long-term, not short-term, when estimating the baseline performance. Short-term data is a snapshot of what's happening and could mislead you; it also doesn't represent all the potential sources of variation that are contributing to your problem over the long-term, such as seasonal effects.

Improvement "Y": Percent Excessive Make Time

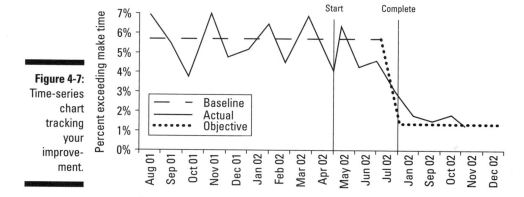

Figure 4-7:
Time-series chart tracking your improvement.

You've done well if you've gotten to this point. You've identified what needs to be improved, you know which processes are involved in creating your problem, and you've determined your current level of performance. You also may have a good estimate of how much this problem is costing you. After you set the targeted level of improvement, you can then determine the financial benefit of doing the project. Any manager worth his or her salt will be interested in this information.

Knowing the baseline level of performance allows you to calculate the potential financial benefits when you target a level of improvement.

Is it worth doing?

The Six Sigma effort is primarily aimed at cost reductions by eliminating waste (scrap, inefficiencies, excess materials, rework, and so on) that increase costs but add no value. As a general rule, Six Sigma projects should produce a financial benefit, either directly or indirectly, through cost reductions, revenue growth, balance sheet improvements, or accomplishing strategic goals.

There are three types of savings categories possible for every Six Sigma project: hard, soft, and potential.

- ✔ Hard savings reduce expenses and result in a financial improvement.

- ✔ Soft savings are financial benefits that may occur as a result of a Six Sigma project but are not accountable as a direct result of the project. Soft savings are calculated using a rational assessment of the expected benefits and a probability analysis of their likelihood.

  For example, because of a Six Sigma project, your customers may become more satisfied and place more orders. Because there are many factors affecting order rates, you can't necessarily calculate a change caused by the project. But you just know the project helped. Because these are not traceable directly to the project, they are considered soft savings.

- ✔ Potential savings are a form of hard savings, but require some action or decision to become realized. An example is a project that optimizes the design of a new product. Until the re-design is implemented, the savings are only potential.

Generally speaking, cost improvements come from reductions in labor, inventory, material, cost of money, scrap, excess equipment, space, and so on.

Cost avoidance is not an appropriate metric for determining Six Sigma savings. If a process has been improved, you can't make a projection into the future about what may have happened if the project had not been done. The vast majority of Six Sigma projects are straightforward reductions of costs, resulting in hard savings. A good way to estimate the potential value of a project is to imagine how much you could save if the problem was completely eliminated.

Describing the problem with a problem statement

The problem statement serves several purposes. First, it significantly clarifies the current situation by specifically identifying what needs to improve, the level of the problem, where it is occurring, and the financial impact of the problem. It also serves as a great communications tool, helping to get buy-in and support from others. When problem statements are well written, people readily grasp and understand what it is that you're trying to accomplish.

A problem statement should be concise and include the following:

- ✔ A description of the problem and the metric used to describe the problem
- ✔ Where the problem is occurring by process name and location
- ✔ The timeframe over which the problem has been occurring
- ✔ The size or magnitude of the problem

You must be careful to avoid underwriting a problem statement. A natural tendency is to write a problem statement too simplistically, because you're already familiar with the problem. You must remember that if you are to recruit support and resources to solve your problem, others will have to understand the context and the significance in order to support you.

Following are examples highlighting the depth and quantification of a Six Sigma project definition. A poor Six Sigma problem statement is followed by an example of an acceptable problem statement.

Example 1: Inventory levels are too high and must be reduced. How many times have you heard a problem statement like this before? Yes, it is a problem having high inventory levels, but your ability to take specific action, enlist support, and obtain improvement is significantly reduced by a problem statement containing so little information.

The problem statement cannot include any speculation about the cause of the problem or what actions will be taken to solve the problem. It's important that you don't attempt to solve the problem or bias the solution at this stage. The data and Six Sigma method will find the true causes and solutions to the problem. This is one of the ways Six Sigma prevents organizations and individuals from using gut feelings and intuition when trying to solve problems.

Here is an improved version of this problem statement:

> Inventory levels at the West Metro inventory storage process in Scottsdale are consuming space, taking up asset management time, and creating cash flow issues. Inventory levels are averaging 31.2 days, with a high of 45 days. These levels have exceeded the target of 25 days 95 percent of the time since January 2004. We could save $250,000 per year if we were at the targeted level.

Problem statements like these are effective at enlisting peoples' attention, energy, and support.

Look at the amount of information that is available in this example. You know where the problem is occurring, you know how long it has occurred, you know the magnitude of the problem, and you know how much it is costing.

Example 2: Human Resources is taking too long to fill personnel requests. Again, this is a very common problem statement. However, there is insufficient information for action to be taken. An acceptable Six Sigma rewrite may look like this:

> Recruiting time for Software Engineers for the flight systems design department in San Jose is missing the goal of 70 days 91 percent of the time. The average time to fill a request is 155 days in the human resources employee recruitment process over the past 15 months. This is adding costs of $145,000 per month in overtime, contractor labor, and rework costs.

Example 3: Our hospital has a problem with the amount of insurance claim forms submitted with errors to the insurance company. Nobody would insist that having claim forms with errors is good. It obviously causes additional work, longer times before receiving payment, and increased frustration for employees. Is this problem worthy of being worked on as stated? Maybe; maybe not. There may be other problems that are giving you worse headaches than this one.

At a minimum, some quantification of the magnitude of the problem would help you make a better decision. Is it the whole hospital or some group that is having the problem? Writing the problem statement to the standards of Six Sigma provides the level of information needed to make an informed decision:

> Insurance claim forms originating at the Fremont North Memorial emergency department are causing a loss of revenue, excessive rework costs, and delayed payment to the hospital. Forty-five percent of the claim forms have errors, with an average of 2.3 defects per form. This problem has existed since claims processing was moved to Kansas City in June 2004. Billings could increase by $3.5 million per month, rework cost could be reduced by 50 percent, and an additional 1.3 percent of revenue could be recovered if errors were occurring less than 5 percent of the time. Achieving this level of performance would increase profits by $395,000 per year.

Write the problem statement with the audience in mind. Keep in mind that you probably have to convince management to provide resources to solve the problem, you have to enlist team members to assist you, and you do not want to spend your precious time explaining over and over what you are trying to accomplish.

Perhaps you have now convinced yourself that you have a viable project, a problem worthy of being worked, and you can convince others to help. You know specifically what must be improved to make life better for everyone. Now the questions are: How much improvement do we need, and how much improvement can we make? You are ready to create the objective statement for the project.

How much improvement is enough?

You want to target the amount of improvement for the project by looking simultaneously at how much improvement you need to satisfy business requirements and how much improvement you could make given the opportunity and the power of Six Sigma. Sound confusing? Actually there are some simple guidelines to assist you here.

Setting the objective for the project's level of improvement is a triage activity. One key input is your own opinion of what success is. Another input comes from a concept called entitlement (see the following bullet list). Benchmarking is another input. Finding the hidden operation and striving for breakthrough levels of improvement are two more. Finally, listen to the needs of your customer.

Some people like to go right to the cash. They establish some threshold of savings and try to configure the amount of improvement required to achieve the savings. While this is okay in some cases, the best strategy is to strive for an aggressive but rational level of improvement, and to let the dollars flow later. There is plenty of experiential evidence to justify the return on investment for Six Sigma and typical project savings.

Instead, ask yourself the following questions:

- **How much am I entitled to?** Entitlement is an extremely powerful Six Sigma concept, used to determine the potential level of improvement. It is also an eye-opening concept, which, when understood, can change the way you think about everything. *Entitlement* is the best performance a process, as currently designed, has demonstrated in actual operation.

  Suppose that you have a business process that, over a long-term period, has a 90 percent average yield. In other words, 90 percent of the time, it delivers to requirements. Now imagine that you observe the same process delivering at a 98 percent level for a few weeks or some other short period. When this happens, you may have considered it to be incidental or just plain lucky. You may have even made an off-the-cuff remark to the effect that: The sun, moon, and stars all lined up during that period of above-average performance.

  In Six Sigma speak, however, you would say: The conditions or inputs to this process (the Xs) all combined in such a way that they delivered the observed improved performance (the Y). (If you need help with the equation $Y = f(X)$, flip to Chapter 2.) Therefore, if you can determine the right alignment or settings or values for the inputs leading to this improved performance, you're entitled to operate at this performance level all the time! This is the entitlement level of performance for the process.

  There is a saying, "You can't unscramble scrambled eggs, but you can unscramble entitlement!" When determining the amount of improvement, always take entitlement into consideration.

- **Other hidden opportunities exist.** The hidden factory (see Chapter 1) is another Six Sigma concept that can change the way you think about the work in your company. The *hidden factory* is work that is done above and beyond what is required to produce a product or a service. The hidden factory is also the work that gets ingrained into the organization when you forget to ask yourself, "Why are we doing this, since this is not adding any value?"

  There are many reasons for this, and you may have experienced something like this: "Over a year ago, we did this quick fix on a problem, followed by an additional inspection to make sure the problem was contained." Is it possible that the quick fix became part of normal procedures? Have you ever heard the saying, "That's the way we have always done it." If you have heard this, you probably have a hidden operation opportunity to find.

Figure 4-8 shows a view of the hidden operation. At some point in almost every process that exists, you will find a sequence of steps that are very similar to these. Work is done on the product or service during one of the process steps called "Op i," which is a form of shorthand for naming this process step. You also see the next work step in the process is operation "$i + 1$," which in shorthand means the next work step in the process.

Between these two work steps in the process is an inspection or verification step. When there is a verification step in a process, you have a high potential for a hidden operation to exist. Refer to the area below the dashed line in Figure 4-7 — it's the extra analysis, repair, scrap, and so on that occur when a product or service has been deemed to not meet requirements.

All these steps add cost because the product or service was not correct the first time. Most organizations just accept these types of additional steps as, "That's the way we do things here, and that's the way we have always done it." When this occurs, you have mentally hidden this operation.

Finding the hidden operation and quantifying its effect helps you further understand your potential level of improvement when writing your objective statement.

✓ **Going for breakthrough improvement.** Another important approach is to anticipate a breakthrough level of improvement from your project to determine the amount of improvement you should attempt. This approach may be less obvious until you have experienced or felt the power of Six Sigma in solving problems. You probably have a sense of how much improvement you can achieve using methods with which you are currently familiar, commonly called traditional methods.

Figure 4-9 shows the difference between breakthrough improvement and the more traditional incremental rates of improvement that you're probably used to.

Always consider a 70 percent improvement over baseline performance as one possible way to determine the target improvement in your objective statement. Such rates of improvement are defined as "breakthrough" rates. For example, if you have a process step with a 10 percent problem for a particular characteristic, a Six Sigma project should be able to lower the defect rate to less than a 3 percent problem. Although this rate of improvement does not necessarily hold true for all projects, it is an average, and most actual projects will be somewhat higher or lower.

Objective statement basics

The objective statement directly addresses the information in the problem statement. Just like the problem statement, the objective statement must contain certain information in order for it to be effective. A good objective statement contains all of the following elements: Improve some *metric* from some *baseline* to some *goal* in some amount of *time* with some *impact* against some corporate *goal* or *objective*. This timeline should be aggressive but realistic.

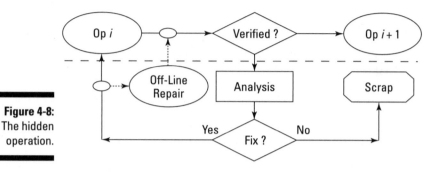

Figure 4-8:
The hidden
operation.

Simply stated, you need to indicate what level of improvement is expected
from this project. This is a specific, quantifiable amount of improvement
planned above the baseline performance that was indicated in the problem
statement. You need to determine how long it will take to complete this
project and to achieve your goal.

Start with the baseline performance you established in the problem statement.
After you have set your improvement goal, you can estimate the financial
benefit of achieving this goal. This should be an aggressive, but reasonable
estimate, and you shouldn't worry about being accurate to the nearest penny.

You then estimate the financial benefit by assessing what will be different at
the new operating level versus what it is today. Your task, with the assistance
of the financial organization, is to identify the differences and to estimate the
annual benefit.

It's always good to link Six Sigma projects to the key goals and objectives of
the organization. Aside from the common sense of doing this, it is a good way
to roll up all projects and the accumulated benefits related to the company's
goals and objectives. In some businesses, Six Sigma has created, for the first
time, the ability to quantitatively link improvement effort to strategy.

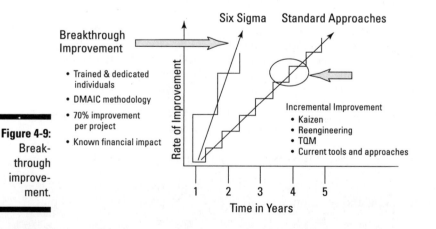

Figure 4-9:
Break-
through
improve-
ment.

Writing an objective statement

Objective statements tell you where you're going or where you need to go. The following are several Six Sigma–style objective statements that you can adapt for your projects.

If you wrote a poor objective statement about high inventories, it may look like this:

> Reduce inventory levels as soon as possible.

Could you succeed at this? Can you get excited about working on this project? Well, it may depend more on the mood of your boss than anything else! Consider your attitude and the enthusiasm of your boss if the statement looked something like this:

> Reduce raw material inventory levels from 31.2 days average to 23 days average with a maximum of 27 days by August 1, 2004. This project will save $235,000 per year for interest, space, and personnel in support of our corporate goal to improve asset management and ROI.

Are you now chomping at the bit to get started? Do you know where the goal line is now? Do you know how long you have? Do you know how much benefit you will create? Will your team know their effort will be for a good cause? Do you think you can do it ? Now you see how high the mountain is that you have to climb.

If you were the manager needing software engineers to complete a design, would you sign up for an aggressive schedule and put your career on the line based on this objective statement?

> Improve how long it takes for human resources to fill personnel requests.

Unless you have nothing better to do, you probably should look the other way when volunteers are being recruited to take on this project. But your adrenalin might get flowing if it were worded like this:

> Reduce the software engineer recruiting time from an average of 155 days to 51 days, with an upper limit of 65 days. This will meet the current maximum goal of 70 days greater than 99 percent of the time. The new goal will be achieved by June 1, 2004. It will support our Employer of Choice goal and achieve an annualized savings of $145,000 per month.

Finally, one more example. In addition to being another poor objective statement, this example has an additional no-no. Here it is:

> Re-train employees to eliminate inaccurate claims forms.

The no-no here is the inclusion of the solution, "re-train employees." If you already know the solution, why bother with the project in the first place?

Keep in mind the objective statement template: Improve some *metric* from some *baseline* level to some *goal* by some *time* to achieve some *benefit* and improve upon some corporate *goal* or *objective*.

This example includes all the necessary information:

Reduce the defects per form from 2.3 DPU to less than 0.1 DPU by September 15, 2004. This will increase revenue collection by $3.2 million per month resulting in an additional $25,000 profit per month at an 8 percent profit margin. This project supports the corporate goal to increase revenue by 15 percent per year.

These examples demonstrate the style and types of problem and objective statements generated by Six Sigma improvement efforts. Such statements are part of the reason Six Sigma projects are effective and can generate breakthrough levels of improvement. You are almost ready to start your own improvement projects. Just hold on for a couple more details, and your project will be ready for the Measure phase discussed in Chapter 5.

Launching a project

Your next step is to identify who has to approve the project. Although this seems like an easy step that requires little effort, don't take it lightly — it's vitally important! You have probably been involved in task force teams in the past when things were pushed through and there just wasn't enough thought given to who should be involved, provide support, or provide resources. Are any of these efforts really successful?

Six Sigma treats this process differently. Because you know so much about the problem, where it's occurring, how long it has existed, its impact, and the benefits of eliminating it, you're the best person to know who should approve your effort and, more importantly, why they should approve your project. You are always better off getting buy-in at the front of the effort than waiting until the last minute.

Imagine if someone came to you and said, "We did this project thing and have determined that you need to change your headcount, modify a piece of equipment, and provide a set of ongoing controls." Your good work will probably go to waste, and you'd probably also create a lot of stress for yourself and the organization.

Refer to the macro process map in Figure 4-6. Referencing this map may help you identify the process owners and others you may need to approve your project.

The key individual to identify is the process owner. This is the person who has the primary responsibility for the results of the process associated with the problem you are going to solve. If additional approvals are required, it will become obvious when the process owners are known.

Don't forget to also ask for approval from the person who will be leading the project.

You must now decide what skill levels, in the form of Six Sigma Belts, are required to solve this problem. Figure 4-10 assists you in making this decision. From experience, we know that a large number of smaller problems exist, followed by fewer process optimization problems, and then finally a few issues that aren't really process problems, but more likely management problems.

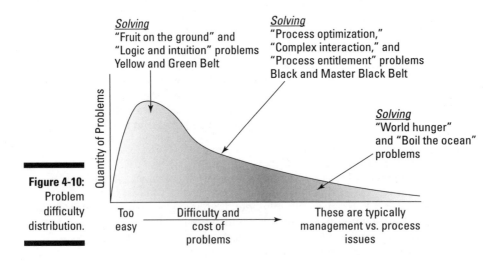

Figure 4-10: Problem difficulty distribution.

Finally, you have to identify which project team will be associated with the improvement, unless you believe you can accomplish the improvement goal by yourself. Be wary of going it alone: Very few people have all the skills necessary to take on process improvement projects. Usually, three to six team members, all of whom have expertise from the areas associated with the project, are sufficient. If you have enlisted the process owners into your project, identifying these individuals will be easy.

The project is now assigned, launched, and ready to enter the Measure phase of the breakthrough strategy (see Chapter 5). You are already on the road to breakthrough improvement!

Chapter 5

Measuring the Gaps

. . . .

In This Chapter

▶ Understanding the basics of statistics and measurement

▶ Seeing the difference between short-term and long-term variation

▶ Plotting and graphing data to gain insight

. . . .

Developing a problem statement and forming an objective statement is only your first step to better performance. The second step of the Six Sigma methodology is to measure performance — and by doing so, to determine the vital few factors that influence the behavior of your process.

Measure is generally the most difficult and time-consuming phase in the DMAIC methodology. But if you do it well — and do it right the first time — you save yourself a lot of trouble later and maximize your chance of improvement. The only way to do this is to measure and observe your critical-to-*X* (CTX) characteristics (see Chapter 1 for an explanation of CTXs).

When you enter the world of measurement and statistics, you discover the ultimate source of problem-solving power: data. While the idea of data may not be exciting to some, it should be very exciting to a Six Sigma practitioner who is tasked with improving a process, an operational unit, or an entire organization.

The 1, 2, 3s of Statistics

Statistics is the distilling of numbers, data, and measurements into knowledge and insight. If you understand a little bit about statistics, you can create a data-leveraging environment in which you gain the utmost value from the information you have.

Why statistics?

Variation is everywhere, and it diminishes your ability to consistently produce quality results, meet schedules, and stay under budget. This is why organizations have performance problems, and it's why you define those problems with a problem and an objective statement for improvement.

So what is the next step? How do you begin to approach the nagging problem of variation and achieve your improvement objective? In 1891, the famous scientist Lord Kelvin provided insight that is valuable today. He said:

> When you can measure what you are speaking about, and express it in numbers, you know something about it; but when you cannot express it in numbers, your knowledge is of a meager and unsatisfactory kind. It may be the beginning of knowledge, but you have scarcely, in your thoughts, advanced to the state of science.

In other words, until you include science, measurement, and numbers in your improvement efforts, you're bound to remain in the world of gut feel, educated guessing, and marginal improvement power. You may work hard and you may marshal significant resources, but your gains will be meager and unsatisfactory.

This is where statistics comes into play. Statistics is the branch of the mathematical sciences used to describe performance with measurements and numbers (believe it or not, many people have spent their life's energy furthering statistical theory, methods, and applications). Statistics is what takes you out of the realm of intuition and guessing and into the realm of objective truth.

When you hear statistics mentioned, do you retreat in terror? If so, you wouldn't be the first, or the last. Aside from pure fear, statistics are often disdained because of their historical misapplication, summarized succinctly by A.E. Houseman: "Statistics in the hand of an engineer are like a lamppost to a drunk — they're used more for support than illumination." And British Prime Minister, Benjamin Disraeli: "There are three kinds of lies: lies, damn lies, and statistics."

Others, however, have seen past the terror and misapplication, discerning the true power of statistics. One was H.G. Wells, who predicted that statistical thinking would someday be as essential for citizenship as the ability to read and write. And that is why you are reading this book. Because you, too, recognize (at least enough to pick up this book) that statistics — and their embodiment in Six Sigma — are like vegetables: They're not always what you want to eat, but you know they're good for you.

In fact, the effectiveness of Six Sigma is dependent upon taking accurate and appropriate performance measurements, so you can, as Lord Kelvin suggests, advance your improvement efforts to a state of scientific certainty.

Measurement 101

To begin your journey into the world of Six Sigma measurement and statistics, suppose you need to find out how long it takes to fill out a certain purchase order form. Each time the form is filled out you record the elapsed time to the nearest second and plot the result as a dot along a horizontal time scale. The first three measurements — of 41, 50, and 47 seconds — are shown in Figure 5-1.

Figure 5-1:
First three measure-ments for filling out a purchase order form.

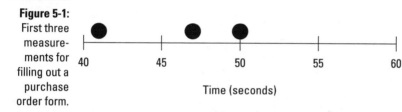

Time (seconds)

Notice that the recorded results reveal that variation is inherent in the process. Continuing the study, you take a total of 100 purchase order time measure-ments. Whenever you encounter a measurement that already has a recording (like 47 seconds), you simply stack another dot on top of the previous dot. The completed chart with all 100 measurements, is shown in Figure 5-2.

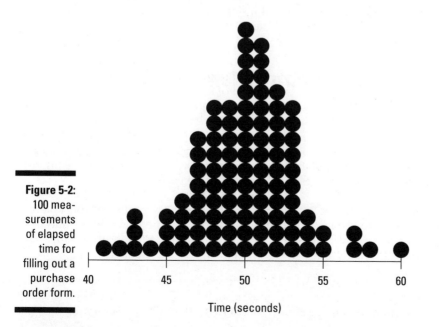

Figure 5-2:
100 mea-surements of elapsed time for filling out a purchase order form.

Time (seconds)

Notice in Figure 5-2 that the output values that occur often pile up with multiple dots. For example, 50 seconds is the purchase order completion time observed more than any other. Consequently, it has the highest peak in the chart (15 occurrences). Output values that were observed less often have lower heights, and output values that were never observed have no dot at all.

Figure 5-2 graphically describes how the measured output is *distributed* along the time scale. Looking at the chart, you can predict that if you were to measure another cycle of the purchase order process, the elapsed time would most likely be around 50 seconds. The chart also shows that times longer or shorter than about 50 seconds would be less likely to occur than those around 50 seconds. A completion time of 30 seconds, for example, is just not going to happen. Nor will one of 80 seconds.

Distribution is the statistical term used to describe the relative likelihood of observing values for a variable factor. Synonymous terms include *probability distribution* and *probability density function*.

Distributions are critically important in creating problem and objective statements for your Six Sigma project. (See Chapter 4 for details of how to create effective problem and objective statements). The reason is because you need to know how your process is performing in terms of its output if you are to properly define what needs to be improved.

Understanding distributions is also critical for understanding the behavior of the critical *X*s (CTXs) in your process — the few factors or variables that determine the quality and consistency of your expected output. If your output metric is "purchase order completion time," then will have certain input factors to Measure, Analyze, Improve, and Control.

What does it mean? Measures of variation location

Suppose you know that the purchase order completion time is a variable with distributed output values. But, following Lord Kelvin's admonition, you may ask, "How can I describe this distribution numerically?" Where is the distribution located (central tendency) along the scale of measure?

A distribution can have infinitely many points, and it's important to fix a location for the distribution so you can then understand the variation around that location. To do this, statisticians have developed three different measures of a distribution's location: the mode, the mean, and the median.

Mode

The *mode* is the value observed most frequently and is associated with the highest peak of a distribution. If 10 students take an exam, and three score 60, three score 70, and four score 80, 80 is the mode because it occurs more frequently than any other value.

Although it is simple and intuitive, using the mode as the measure of variation location has a drawback: Many distributions don't have a single clear peak and some have more than one peak of roughly the same height. In these cases, the presentation of a single mode metric by itself does little to deepen your knowledge of the variation.

Mean

The most common measure of central tendency is the *mean* — widely called the *average*. Examples of averages are everywhere — the Dow Jones industrial average, grade point average, the average temperature in your hometown and the list goes on.

It's important to understand that the mean is theoretical rather than real; while the mean may not have actually occurred within your measurements, it is the value most likely to occur *next* in a sequence or population of data. The mean, therefore, is a mental model by which the Six Sigma practitioner can make comparisons, make predictions, interpret data, and anchor much of the analytical work that is done in order to save money in operations, make customers more satisfied, and improve products and services.

So how is the mean calculated? It's really very simple. Imagine having ten paper cups, each holding a different amount of water. What is the average amount of water in a paper cup? How do you determine the answer? Consider combining the contents of each of the ten cups into a large bowl. You'd simply measure the collected amount and divide it by the number of paper cups. This tells you how much water would be in each paper cup if the amounts were forced to be equal — or *average*.

Mathematically, this process for calculating the mean is written as

$$\overline{x} = \frac{\sum x_i}{n}$$

where

- $\overline{x}$ (pronounced ex bar) is the symbol representing the calculated mean.
- Σ is the Greek capital letter sigma. In the shorthand of math, it tells you to sum up (add) all the individual measurements.

  ✔ x_i represents each of the individual measurement values.

  ✔ n is the number of individual measurements in your data set.

So, for the purchasing order example discussed in the preceding section, the mean ($\bar{x}$) is found by adding up each of the $n = 100$ time measurements and dividing the result by $n = 100$. The result is an $\bar{x}$ of 49.9 seconds. Computing the mean for any distribution is never any harder than that.

Median

The *median* is the point along the scale of measure where half the data are below and half are above. The median is the preferred measure of variation location when your collected data contains outliers, or extreme data points well outside the range of other data. An *outlier* is a recorded observation that is well outside the range of variation of the rest of the data.

For example, the median is often used when communicating home prices because it is usually more reflective of the central tendency of the distribution of all prices. Suppose you have a set of homes with prices of $158,000, $200,000, $178,000, $125,000, and $535,000. The average price is $239,200. The median, however, is $178,000. Figure 5-3 shows the raw data of home prices with the mean and median specified. Note that the median represents the location of the distributed home prices better than the mean. That's because the calculated value of the mean is pulled up away from the more accurate location value by the presence of the outlier — the $535,000 home.

The median is the preferred communicator of variation location when the data you are describing contains outliers.

Figure 5-3:
Graphical
comparison
of the mean
and median.

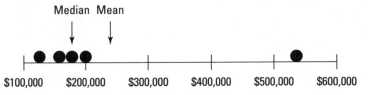

Median Mean

$100,000 $200,000 $300,000 $400,000 $500,000 $600,000

Beware when someone communicates only the average to you when describing a distributed variable. Without your knowing, he or she could have included an outlier (accidentally or on purpose) that has biased the calculated mean value.

Putting all three together

Table 5-1 describes the mode, mean, and median of variation location. But although measures of variation location are indispensable, they don't tell the whole story. The mode, mean, and median all fail to communicate the critical information of how spread out or how widely or narrowly dispersed the data is around its central location point. The following section gives you some additional options.

Table 5-1   Summary of Statistical Measures of Variation Location

Measure of Variation Location	Definition	Comment
Mode	Peak of distribution	Problematic, seldom used
Mean (average)	$\bar{x} = \dfrac{\sum x_i}{n}$	Most common and familiar
Median	Point where half of data are below and half are above	Used when data contains outliers

How much variation is there?

Two sets of measurements having identical means may contain raw data values that are distributed very differently. A second measure is needed in addition to the measure of location. You need to be able to quantify how widely or narrowly dispersed the data are around their central location.

The simplest measure of the spread of your data is its range. The *range* of a distribution is defined as the difference between the largest and the smallest observed data values. Mathematically, this is written as

$$R = x_{MAX} - x_{MIN}$$

where

- R is the calculated range
- x_{MAX} is the largest observed measurement
- x_{MIN} is the smallest observed measurement

In the preceding purchase order example, the range is simply the longest recorded time to fill out the form (60 seconds) minus the shortest time (41 seconds), or $R = 19$ seconds.

Calculating the range works just as well when you only have two recorded measurements as it does when you have 1,000. But obviously, outliers directly affect its calculated value. (By their very nature, outliers end up being the x_{MAX} or x_{MIN} used to calculate the range.)

Is there another way to quantify a distribution's degree of dispersion that avoids the problem of outliers? Look at any single recorded measurement. How far is it from the central location of the data set? Mathematically this problem is written as

$$x_i - \overline{x}$$

✔ x_i represents any single recorded measurement from your set of data

✔ $\overline{x}$ is the calculated mean of your collected observations

$x_i - \overline{x}$ then acts as a numerical "score" for each data point. Like in golf, the lower the magnitude of the score, the better (the less it varies from the central location).

You've probably played around with numbers enough, however, to recognize a problem with this scoring system. When x_i is less than the mean ($\overline{x}$), the score ($x_i - \overline{x}$) ends up being less than zero. That won't work! A point being above or below the central location doesn't matter; it's how far away it is that counts. And negative scores make things too complicated. There needs to be a way to score each data point that looks only at its distance from the central location regardless of which direction.

For example

$$\left(x_i - \overline{x}\right)^2$$

The parentheses and the raised "2" tell you to take the quantity $x_i - \overline{x}$ and multiply it together twice. For example, $(2)^2 = 2 \times 2$ and $(-3)^2 = -3 \times -3$. Notice that no matter whether the quantity you are multiplying by itself is positive or negative, the resulting answer is always positive: $2 \times 2 = 4$ and $-3 \times -3 = 9$.

The area of a square is the length of any one of its sides (called l for length) multiplied by itself, that is l^2. This is why mathematicians call this operation *squaring* and the numerical result a *square*. In Six Sigma you hear the term "squares" often. Every time you do, remember the mathematicians and know that some quantity is being multiplied by itself.

A side benefit of squaring each individual score is that it penalizes points that are farther away from the central location disproportionately more than those that are close. Figure 5-4 shows a plot of $(x_i - \overline{x})^2$ output values versus input values for $x_i - \overline{x}$.

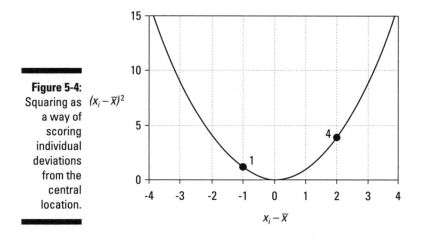

Figure 5-4:
Squaring as a way of scoring individual deviations from the central location.

Referring to Figure 5-4, if an individual data point is one unit away from the central location (either above or below), $x_i - \overline{x} = 1$ and $(x_i - \overline{x})^2 = 1$. If a different point is twice as far away, however, with $x_i - \overline{x} = 2$, then $(x_i - \overline{x})^2 = 4$, resulting in a score that is not twice as bad, but *four times* worse.

To create an overall, combined score for the entire data set, simply add all the individual squared scores together. Mathematicians write this as

$$\sum(x_i - \overline{x})^2$$

Σ is the Greek capital letter sigma, which tells you to add up all the individual squared scores.

Statisticians call this result the *summed squared error,* or SSE for short.

In the field of statistics, *error* doesn't mean something is wrong. The term simply means a calculated deviation from a comparison value. In this case, error is the difference between the mean and the individual observations.

Having totaled up all the individual squared scores, what is the typical (average) squared score? To find out, you divide the summed squared error by the number of *independent* data points in our collection, like this:

$$\sigma^2 = \frac{\sum (x_i - \overline{x})^2}{n-1}$$

where n is the total number of data points you have collected.

Statisticians call this averaged squared error score the *variance* and give it the symbol σ^2.

Right now, one of two things has happened. Either your eyes have glazed over, or you are saying, "Hold on a minute. Why did you divide by one less than the number of measurements I collected ($n-1$) instead of by the total I collected (n)? That doesn't seem right."

Assuming your eyes are not glazed over, you've asked an outstanding question. In the equation for the variance, notice that the mean ($\overline{x}$) is included. This is where you lose the *independence* of one of your collected measurements.

It's like having a full five gallon bucket and dividing the contents completely into ten new buckets. Even though the amounts you pour into the first nine buckets can vary independently from each other, when you get to the tenth bucket there is no more freedom — what you have is exactly what remains. In the same way, using the mean ($\overline{x}$) reduces the number of independent measurements available to compute the variance.

A final problem lingers with the development of a measure of how widely or narrowly your collected data is distributed. What are the units associated with the computed variance? In the preceding purchase order example, your measurements have been in seconds. That means the variance comes out as seconds^2. In the real world, what are seconds^2? No one knows (and anyone who thinks they do ought to be avoided!)

The person who originally solved this last issue must have known the answer from the beginning. Notice that the symbol for the variance is σ^2. And as you've likely guessed, the solution is simply to reverse the squaring done previously to your measurements. Mathematicians call this reverse-squaring operation the *square root* and give it a special operator symbol ($\sqrt{}$).

Applying it vigorously to the variance introduces the greatly anticipated measure sought after, namely, the standard deviation:

$$\sigma = \sqrt{\frac{\sum(x_i - \overline{x})^2}{n-1}}$$

The standard deviation is by far the most commonly used measure of dispersion. Represented by the Greek lower case letter sigma, it occurs throughout statistics and Six Sigma — to which the quality initiative owes its name.

What is the real-world meaning of the standard deviation metric? Its units are exactly the same as your original measurements. So for the purchase order example, its units are seconds. The standard deviation represents the typical (average) distance from the central location you expect to observe. See Table 5-2.

Table 5-2   Summary of Statistical Measures of Variation Spread

Measure of variation spread	Definition	Comments
Range	$R = x_{MAX} - x_{MIN}$	Simple. Preferred metric for sets of data with few (2 to 5) members. Drawback: Greatly influenced by outliers.
Variance	$\sigma^2 = \dfrac{\sum(x_i - \overline{x})^2}{n-1}$	Theoretically useful, but lacks direct tie to reality.
Standard deviation	$\sigma = \sqrt{\dfrac{\sum(x_i - \overline{x})^2}{n-1}}$	Most commonly used.

Armed with two quantities — a measure of location and a measure of spread — you can now describe any type of distribution in scientific terms. Lord Kelvin would be proud.

The Long and Short of Variation

Peeling the layers of the onion back, there is another aspect of variation you need to know about: the difference between long- and short-term variation.

Short-term variation

Suppose you monitor certain characteristics of a process — such as the volume of inbound calls per hour at a customer call center — over an extended period. After each hour, you measure and record the number of calls received. To review what you've observed, you graph your collected measurements as a sequence of connected points along an axis representing time, as shown in Figure 5-5.

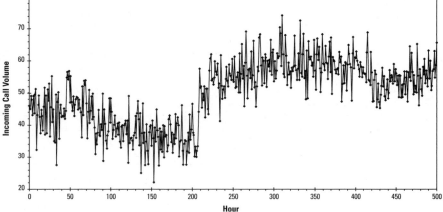

Figure 5-5: The observed output behavior of a process over an extended period of inbound calls at a customer call center.

Although the points graphed in Figure 5-5 represent the number of incoming calls per hour, you should recognize that it could also represent any process characteristic in any type of company. All process characteristics vary from cycle to cycle: the exact length of newly manufactured pencils, the time required to fill out an invoice, the number of calls per hour, and so on.

If you zoom in on a narrow portion of the graph, as shown in Figure 5-6, you can see from the scattered points that the output certainly does vary for each measurement cycle. But you can also notice that the variation is not limitless. It lies within upper and lower boundary limits — represented by the dashed, horizontal lines.

In fact, for any selected *short period of time*, the process essentially varies within the same rough limits. (Try it for yourself. Pick any short time segment of Figure 5-5 and eyeball the vertical variation limits with your thumb and index finger. Now, keeping the distance between your fingers fixed, move to a differ-ent time section of the graph. Do your eyeballed limits capture the output variation for other short-time segments?)

This natural level of variation is called the *short-term* variation of a process. Often, it is designated with a simple *ST* notation.

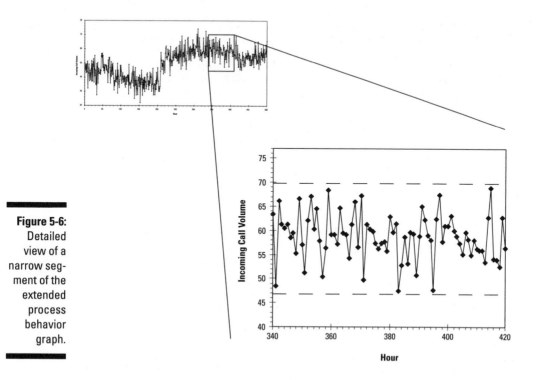

Figure 5-6:
Detailed
view of a
narrow seg-
ment of the
extended
process
behavior
graph.

Short-term variation is purely *random*. This means that, like rolling a pair of dice, you cannot predict what the next output value will be. If you could, Las Vegas would be bankrupt in a week!

Short-term variation is caused by the combined effect of all the little things that are too hard to include in your understanding of the process. Even Einstein would find it too difficult to determine exactly how the microscopic textures of the dice contribute to their spin as they contact the felt surface of the table. Or how the drag of the swirling air on the corner of the airborne dice alters their tumble. Yet these factors — and many more — are real and do add up to affect the outcome of the roll.

This is the reality of short-term variation in any and all processes, from rolling dice to preparing a meal to writing a memo to launching a rocket: The complete chain of causation is unknown and unknowable. Like rolling dice, your ability to understand the full depth of causation for any process is ultimately limited.

Because these small forces are present to some degree in all processes, they are referred to as *common*. Consequently, the short-term variation they cause is sometimes called *common cause variation*.

Now that you know what short-term variation is, you need to know how to quantify it. The formula for calculating the standard deviation given back in Table 5-2 does not account for any short- or long-term effects. It just looks at the overall variation in all the measurements. But never fear, hard-working statisticians have developed a way to extract the level of the short-term variation out from the overall variation.

The quickest way to get to the short-term variation is to analyze the separation or differences between sequential measurements of a critical characteristic. The difference between any two sequential measurements can be thought of as a kind of range. For a sequence of measurements

$$x_1, x_2, \ldots x_{n-1}, x_n$$

the difference or range between the first and second measurements can be written as

$$R_1 = |x_1 - x_2|$$

In general, the difference between any two sequential measurements is

$$R_i = |x_i - x_{i+1}|$$

And the average range or difference between sequential points is

$$\overline{R} = \frac{1}{n-1} \sum_{i=1}^{n-1} R_i$$

The way to calculate the short-term standard deviation from these sequential, between-point ranges is to take their average and multiply it by a special correction factor based on the range between two sequential measurements:

$$\sigma_{ST} = \frac{\overline{R}}{1.128}$$

WARNING!

Never try to calculate a characteristic's short-term standard deviation on anything other than a sequential set of measurements. That is, only perform this calculation on a set of measurements that are in the order that the measurements were taken. This is because the calculation of the short-term standard deviation is based upon the natural ranges that occur between the characteristic's measurements; if the order of the measurements is altered at all, it directly effects the calculated value of the short-term standard deviation.

Shift happens: Long-term variation

Take another look at the extended process behavior graph in Figure 5-5 in the preceding section. Something else besides pure random variation is going on here. Notice that the range of short-term variation doesn't stay locked at a single level. Instead, it "shifts and drifts" up and down over time. These bumps and currents — called *disturbances to the process* — are emphasized with overlaid lines in Figure 5-7.

Figure 5-7:
Non-random disturbances overlaid on the extended process behavior graph.

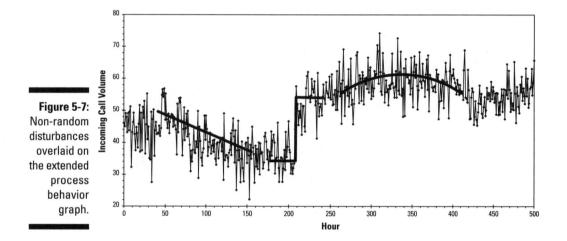

When these underlying disturbances are added to the natural short-term variation, the overall combination is called the *long-term variation of the process*. In many cases, it is written with a simple *LT* notation.

As opposed to random, short-term variation, these underlying disturbances are *non-random* over the long-term. You can approximate them with a line, a step, a curve, or a repeated pattern. When gambling in Las Vegas, you know that the long-term disturbance will result in your losing all your money. (*Note:* You can prevent this by quitting while you're ahead in the short term.)

The great thing about long-term variation is that you don't have to be Einstein to figure it out. With the proper detection techniques and tools, you can see what part(s) of your process is affected by non-random forces. If the process is to assemble a proposal, and if the critical output of that process is how long it takes to create the proposal, you want to look at the variation patterns in the output of the process.

Figure 5-7 shows just the *output variation,* or changes in the number of incoming calls at a call center per hour. If the output metric varies in a non-random way, it is safe to say that some combination of special cause factors has affected the volume of incoming calls.

When we say *special cause,* we mean that the output has varied to an extent that is inconsistent with what you would expect from purely normal, short-term, natural — or random — influences. You know that something non-random has occurred and, therefore, you know that you can find the cause and solve the problem.

A good way of depicting the difference between short-term and long-term variation in a process is with the use of two "probability distributions," as shown in Figure 5-8. Notice that, over time, the long-term variation is wider than the inherent, short-term variation.

Figure 5-8:
Long-term (LT) and short-term (ST) process variation summarized as probability distributions.

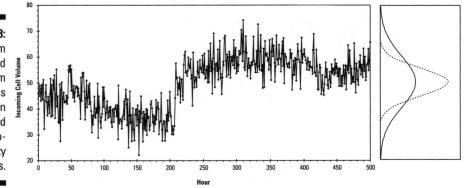

Non-random variation is caused by *special* forces whose effects on the process are readily observed and understood. Consequently, this non-random variation is also called *special cause variation* or *assignable cause variation.*

Calculating the long-term variation of a characteristic is identical to calculating its overall variation. Therefore, the overall standard deviation is the formula you use to quantify the level of long-term variation in a characteristic. See Table 5-3.

Table 5-3	**Formulas for Calculating Short-Term and Long-Term Standard Deviation**
Short-Term Standard Deviation	*Long-Term Deviation*
$\sigma_{ST} = \dfrac{\bar{R}}{1.128}$	$\sigma_{LT} = \sqrt{\dfrac{\sum(x_i - \bar{x})^2}{n-1}}$

The calculated short-term variation should always be less than or equal to the calculated long-term variation.

This is the crux of the difference between common cause and special cause variation: If you can't see microscopically enough to understand exactly why some variation occurred, you surely can't do anything to stop it from occurring again (the dice example). On the other hand, if you can see and understand why variations happen, you have a reasonable opportunity to stop the problematic variations from happening at all.

For any example of special cause variation, notice that you can immediately create solutions to solve the problems. You can conduct routine preventive maintenance on your drills. You can make the maintenance procedure so easy that anyone can understand and adhere to it. You can create redundant systems in case equipment breaks down or in the advent of losing a principal leader. And so on.

Poka-Yoke is a Japanese term that means "mistake-proof." It is a fundamental concept behind the practice of making processes so easy and simple to follow that even a child can perform them. Essentially, when you Poka-Yoke a process, you vaccinate it against error (see Chapter 10 for details on Poka-Yoke).

Be all you can be: Entitlement

For every process, there is natural, short-term variation happening concurrently with an underlying, long-term, shift-and-drift variation. The short-term component comes from the unaccounted common causes rooted within the process. The long-term component is the result of factors you can detect — special causes. Suppose that you want to reduce the overall level of variation in your process. What do you do? How will your new understanding of short-term and long-term variation guide your approach?

Imagine you identify and remove all of the non-random, special causes affecting your process. You're left, then, with process that is influenced by only random, short-term variation. It's guaranteed: You find that further shrinking the output variation is difficult — very, very difficult. That's because further shrinking requires discovering what previously was unknown about the inner workings of your process. You need to identify, understand, prioritize, and fix the myriad of embedded, common factors jiggling the process output.

This hard wall in the improvement path leads to the idea of entitlement. *Entitlement* is the level of variation that is naturally built into a process. It is the amount of variation you can expect from a process under the best conditions — even when all the special causes are identified and eliminated. (Of course, you can see that this is just another name for short-term variation.)

What's the difference between short-term and long-term variation?

Short-term variation is synonymous with common cause variation — because all the non-random influencing factors have not had time to express themselves or exert their effect on the outcome. Long-term variation is synonymous with special cause variation, because non-random influencing factors have had time to express themselves and affect the outcome. Therefore, there is no set time period where short-term variation transitions into long-term variation for every process characteristic. The transition point depends totally on the process and the time it takes to sufficiently characterize the process.

Some things can go wrong (*assignable causes*) in a manufacturing environment:

✔ **Tool wear:** The bit that drilled holes in your new assemble-it-yourself desk was too worn down at the time it was employed during the manufacturing process. You, and 500 other people who bought tables from the same production batch, now struggle to assemble your desks while muttering unkind words about the manufacturer.

✔ **Changes in machine operator:** Jack replaces Jill on the printing press but doesn't do his required maintenance. Print quality suffers,

customers are unhappy, and the finger-pointing begins.

✔ **Differences between raw materials:** Print quality also suffers non-randomly when Jill is on her shift, because the quality of the ink is sometimes compromised by the supplier, and at other times the ink is slightly off its target color value.

Some things can also go wrong (also *assignable causes*) in a service environment:

✔ **Equipment breakdown:** Your computer crashes, preventing you from providing great customer service at the call center. The jet carrying the express mail needs unscheduled maintenance at the airport, thus making the deliveries late.

✔ **External forces:** Traffic jam patterns in certain geographical areas negatively impact the productivity of a trucking company. Inventory gets backlogged, and deliveries are late.

✔ **Health of service provider:** The lead litigator in a very important case becomes ill and cannot perform his duties. His colleagues do not have the depth of knowledge and experience to maintain the momentum created.

Long-term variation is always greater than short-term, or entitlement, variation.

Short-term, or entitlement, variation is what you use to compare the capability of different processes to meet a specified goal. For example, creating a shaped plastic part using an injection mold machine may have an entitlement variation of ±0.002 inches. The process of cutting plastic with a milling machine, on the other hand, may have an entitlement variation of ±0.0005 inches. In this case, the milling machine process has the better level of entitlement. It has less inherent, short-term variation.

Clearly, a fundamental task in Six Sigma is to observe processes and understand their levels of short-term variation and long-term variation. The only way to really know the capability of a process is to engage in an effort to gather and understand sufficient data about how the process is working. By doing this, you begin to reach the heart of Six Sigma: measuring the gaps between current performance and entitlement performance and addressing those gaps.

A Picture's Worth a Thousand Words

Crunching numbers and data into statistics — like a mean or a standard deviation — provides numerical insight into the inner workings and outside influences of a process. Pictures of data, however, often serve as a more intuitive way of gaining the same insights. These pictures — called *graphs* or *plots* — are definitely better than numbers at communicating your gained insight to others.

Using visual material to communicate data is your best way of getting improvement team members to be integral parts of the Six Sigma breakthrough process. When team members can see the reality of performance for themselves, they are more motivated to contribute and participate in measurement and improvement efforts. Also, your visual pictures are an effective and essential prop for communicating your project details to management.

Plotting and charting data

The chief purpose of plotting and charting data is to graphically show the central tendency and the spread of variation in a measured item of interest. You can do this in a couple of different ways, each with its advantages and disadvantages.

Creating dot plots and histograms

Dot plots and histograms both do the same thing, they show *where* the variation occurs in a critical characteristic. Is the variation all lumped together within a narrow interval? Or is it evenly spread out over a wide range? A dot plot or a histogram reveals the answer.

After collecting measurements or data for a characteristic, create a *dot plot,* or *histogram,* for it by using the following steps:

1. **Create a horizontal line, representing the scale of measure for the characteristic.**

   This scale can be in millimeters for length, pounds for weight, minutes for time, number of defects found on an inspected part, or anything else that quantifies what it is about the characteristic you're interested in.

   2. **Divide the horizontal scale of measure into equal chunks or "buckets" along its length.**

      Select a bucket width that makes it so that there are about 10 to 20 equal divisions between the largest and the smallest observed values for the characteristic.

   3. **For each observed measurement of the characteristic, locate its value along the horizontal scale of measure and place a dot for it in its corresponding "bucket."**

      If another observed measurement falls into the same "bucket," stack the second (or third, or fourth) dot above the previous one.

      It is not a requirement to use dots. You can use whatever symbol or character is available or easy for you to draw.

   4. **Repeat Step 3 until all the observed measurements are placed onto the plot.**

To create a histogram (so that you can impress your peers with a graph that has a much more complicated-sounding name), replace each of the stacks of dots with a solid vertical bar of the same height as its corresponding stack of dots.

Interpreting dot plots and histograms

A dot plot and its fancy cousin, a histogram, offer ready access to a wealth of information about the variation of a characteristic's performance.

   ✓ **Variation shape:** Is the variation of a characteristic lumped around a single spot? Or is it spread out evenly across a range of values? A dot plot or histogram reveals the answer immediately. Figure 5-9 shows a variation shape that is *normally* distributed or bell shaped. For a normal distribution, most of the observed values of the characteristic are close to a central point with fewer and fewer appearing as you get farther away from the central tendency. Figure 5-10 shows a *uniformly* distributed variation for a characteristic.

   For a uniformly distributed characteristic, the variation is evenly spread out across a bounded range. That is, you're just as likely to observe a value for a characteristic at one end of the interval as you are at the other, or anywhere in between. Figure 5-11 shows a *skewed* distribution shape. A skewed distribution is a variation shape that is not symmetrical. Either one side or the other of the distribution extends out farther than the other side.

✔ **Variation mode:** The mode of a distribution is its most likely value, or in other words, its peak. Usually, the variation in a characteristic has a single peak, as seen in Figure 5-12.

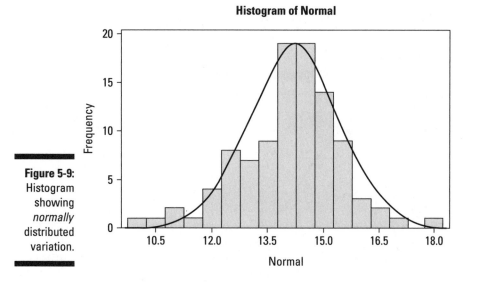

Histogram of Normal

Figure 5-9: Histogram showing *normally* distributed variation.

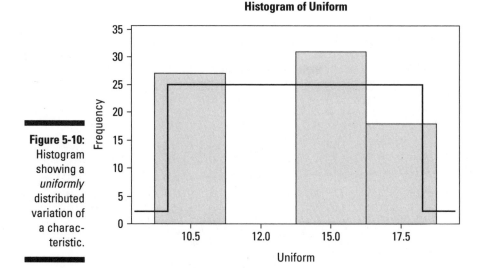

Histogram of Uniform

Figure 5-10: Histogram showing a *uniformly* distributed variation of a characteristic.

A histogram showing two or more distinct peaks is *multi-modal*. This means that two or more values dominate the variation. Multiple major peaks is not usual. It typically means that there is a factor affecting the characteristic's performance that causes the entire system to behave schizophrenically.

But sometimes, a characteristic displays two or more modes, like shown in Figure 5-13.

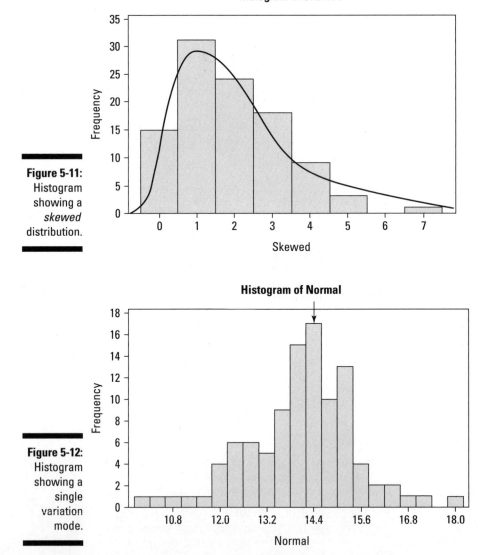

Histogram of Skewed

Figure 5-11: Histogram showing a *skewed* distribution.

Histogram of Normal

Figure 5-12: Histogram showing a single variation mode.

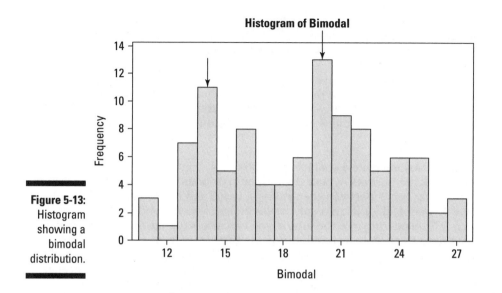

Figure 5-13:
Histogram
showing a
bimodal
distribution.

When you encounter a multi-modal distribution, always dig deeper to discover what factor or factors is causing the characteristic's schizophrenic behavior.

✔ **Variation average:** Without having to crunch any numbers, you can visually estimate a characteristic's mean or average value from a dot plot or histogram.

Hold your index finger up against the horizontal axis of the dot plot or histogram. Move your extended finger back and forth across the horizontal axis until you find the point where the middle knuckle of your finger balances your distribution equally on each side. Voila! The point along the horizontal axis where you've located your finger is the approximate average value of the variation.

✔ **Variation range:** The extent or width of variation present in a characteristic is immediately recognized in a dot plot or histogram. The difference between the greatest observed value x_{MAX} and the smallest observed value x_{MIN} creates what is called the *range* of the distribution. The symbol R always represents the range. The range is calculated by

$$R = x_{MAX} - x_{MIN}$$

✔ **Outliers:** Outliers are measured observations that don't seem to fit the grouping of the rest of the observations. They're either too far to the right or too far to the left of the rest of the data to be concluded as coming from the same set of circumstances that created all the other points.

And that is exactly their value. When you see an outlier or outliers on a dot plot or histogram, you immediately know that something is probably different about the conditions that created those points, whether in the set-up or execution of the process, or in the way the process was measured.

Investigate all outliers. Find out what caused their value to be so different from all the other observed values. Isolating the cause almost always leads to the discovery of what factors are degrading the performance of the characteristic.

If you want to get more quantitative with your dot plots and histograms, you can use them to calculate the proportion of observations you've measured within an interval of interest. Or you can use them to predict the likelihood of observing certain values in the future. (Seeing into the future is definitely powerful stuff!)

Suppose you measure a characteristic 50 times. Counting and adding up what's in each of the buckets of your dot plot or histogram, you observe 17 measurements that occur between the values of, say, 5 and 6. You can conclude, then, that 17 out of 50, or 34 percent, of your measurements ended up between 5 and 6. Now peering into the future, you can also say that if the characteristic continues to operate as it did during the time of your measurements, that 34 percent of future observations (that you haven't even made yet) will end up being between 5 and 6! The casinos of Las Vegas thrive in business because they use Six Sigma in this way to know what will happen in the future, say, when you sit down for a game of craps.

Creating box and whisker plots

The problem with dot plots and histograms is that they only allow you to effectively look at one characteristic's performance at a time. When you need to compare distributions, few things are quicker to do or more easy to interpret than a box and whiskers plot. Like putting two people back-to-back to see who is taller, box and whisker plots allow you to directly compare two or more variation distributions.

Box and whisker plots are sometimes simply called *box plots.* A box and whisker plot is made up of a *box* representing the central mass of the variation and thin lines, called *whiskers,* extending out on either side representing the thinning tails of the distribution. An example of a box plot is shown in Figure 5-14.

To create a box and whisker plot:

1. **Rank the captured set of data measurements for the characteristic.**

   Reorder the captured data from the least to the greatest values.

2. **Determine the median of the data.**

   Find the observation value in the rank ordered data where half of the data lies above and half lies below.

Box Plot of Characteristic

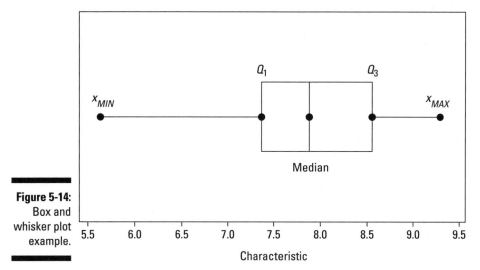

Box Plot of Characteristic

Figure 5-14:
Box and
whisker plot
example.

When the number of observed points in your data set n is odd, the median is the

$$\left[\frac{n+1}{2}\right] \text{th}$$

value in the rank ordered sequence.

When the number of observed points in your data set n is even, the median is the average of the

$$\left[\frac{n}{2}\right] \text{th}$$

and the

$$\left[\frac{n}{2}+1\right] \text{th}$$

values in the rank order sequence.

3. **Find the first quartile Q_1.**

   The first quartile is the point in your rank ordered sequence, where 25 percent of the observed data fall below this value.

4. **Find the third quartile Q_3.**

   The third quartile is the point in your rank ordered sequence, where 75 percent of the observed data fall below this value.

5. **Find the largest observed value x_{MAX}.**

6. **Find the smallest observed value x_{MIN}.**

7. **Create a horizontal line, representing the scale of measure for the characteristic.**

   This scale could be in millimeters for length, pounds for weight, minutes for time, number of defects found on an inspected part, or anything else that quantifies what it is about the characteristic you're interested in.

8. **Construct the box.**

   Draw a box spanning from the first quartile Q_1 to the third quartile Q_3 and draw a vertical line in the box corresponding to the calculated median value.

9. **Construct the whiskers.**

   Draw two horizontal lines, one extending out from the Q_1 value to the smallest observed observation x_{MIN}, and another extending out from the Q_3 value to the greatest observed value x_{MAX}.

10. **Repeat Steps 1 through 9 for each additional characteristic to be plotted and compared against the same horizontal scale.**

When you have a large set of data for a characteristic, you may find value in extending the whiskers out only to the 10th and 90th percentiles, or to the 5th and 95th percentiles, and so on. Then when outlier data points fall beyond these ends of the whiskers, you can draw them as disconnected dots or stars. This is a great way of graphically identifying and communicating the presence of outliers in your data.

Interpreting box and whisker plots

Box and whisker plots are ideal for comparing two or more variation distributions. These may be before and after views of a process or characteristic. Or they may be several alternative ways of conducting an operation. Essentially, when you want to quickly find out if two or more variation distributions are different (or the same) then you create a box plot. Figure 5-15 is an example of using box plots to compare distributions *A, B,* and *C.*

In Figure 5-15, distribution *B* clearly has the lowest level. But it still overlaps the performance of distribution *A*, indicating that it may not be that different. Distribution *C*, on the other hand, has a much higher value and no overlap with distributions *A* and *B*. It also has a much broader spread to its variation.

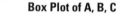

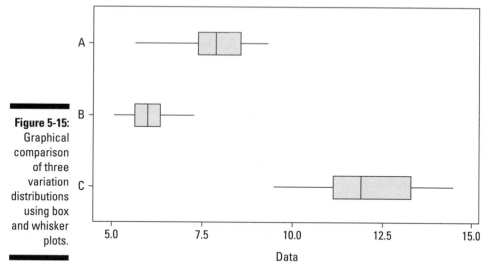

Figure 5-15:
Graphical
comparison
of three
variation
distributions
using box
and whisker
plots.

Things to look for in comparative box plots:

- ✔ Differences or similarities in location of the median
- ✔ Differences or similarities in box widths
- ✔ Differences or similarities in whisker-to-whisker spread
- ✔ Overlap or gaps between distributions
- ✔ Skewed or asymmetrical variation in distributions
- ✔ The presence of outliers

Creating scatter plots

Dot plots, histograms, and box plots chart only one distribution (characteristic) at a time. Often, you need to explore the relationship between two characteristics. To do this, you use a *scatter plot*. Scatter plots get their name from their appearance — a scattered cluster of dots on a graph.

The key to creating a scatter plot is in the capturing of the measurement data. To investigate the relationship between two characteristics, you need to capture measurements from the two characteristics simultaneously. So at each measurement time, you have to take simultaneous measurements for each of the characteristics you are interested in. If you are interested in exploring the relationship between characteristics X and Y, at each point of measurement, you have to collect and record values for X and Y.

The two characteristics being plotted can be two inputs. Or, alternatively, one can be an input and the other can be an output. As long as your measurements are made simultaneously, it doesn't matter if they are inputs or outputs.

With this simultaneous data collected, you're now ready to create a scatter plot:

1. **Form points from the collected data.**

   At each of the measurement times, pair the simultaneously measured values for the two characteristics together to form an *x-y* point that can be plotted on a two-axis graph.

2. **Create a two-axis plotting framework.**

   Create two axes, one horizontal and the other vertical, with each being assigned to one of the two characteristics under investigation.

   The scale for each axis could be in millimeters for length, pounds for weight, minutes for time, number of defects found on an inspected part, or anything else that quantifies what it is about the characteristics you're interested in.

3. **Plot each formed point on the two-axis framework.**

   Figure 5-16 shows a sample set of simultaneous measurement data and a corresponding scatter plot.

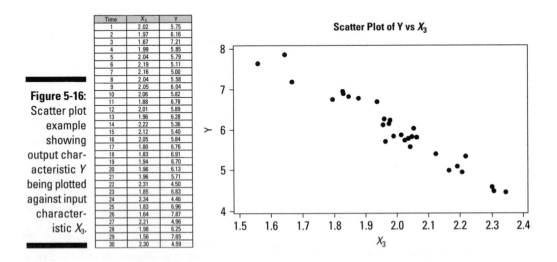

Figure 5-16: Scatter plot example showing output characteristic Y being plotted against input characteristic X_3.

Time	X_3	Y
1	2.02	5.75
2	1.97	6.16
3	1.67	7.21
4	1.99	5.85
5	2.04	5.79
6	2.19	5.11
7	2.16	5.00
8	2.04	5.58
9	2.05	6.04
10	2.06	5.82
11	1.88	6.78
12	2.01	5.89
13	1.96	6.28
14	2.22	5.36
15	2.12	5.40
16	2.05	5.84
17	1.80	6.76
18	1.83	6.91
19	1.94	6.70
20	1.96	6.13
21	1.96	5.71
22	2.31	4.50
23	1.85	6.83
24	2.34	4.46
25	1.83	6.96
26	1.64	7.87
27	2.21	4.96
28	1.98	6.25
29	1.56	7.65
30	2.30	4.59

Scatter plots can also be created when one of the characteristic data types is not measured on a continues scale, but fits into discrete categories. For example, the characteristic of sales volume (measured on the continuous dollar scale) can be plotted against marketing plans 1 and 2 (measured by two discrete categories). Figure 5-17 shows an example of this type of category data scatter plot.

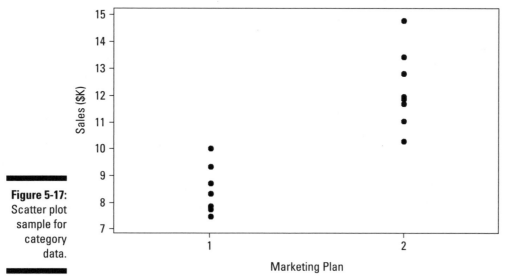

Scatter Plot of Sales ($K) vs Marketing Plan

Figure 5-17:
Scatter plot sample for category data.

Interpreting scatter plots

A scatter plot tells you graphically how two characteristics are related. They may be strongly related or not related at all. A scatter plot immediately tells you the answer. *Correlation* is the word used to quantify how closely related two characteristics are to each other.

Things to look for in a scatter plot:

✔ **Amount of correlation:** If two characteristics are not related, the scatter plot of the two should appear as a random cloud of points, like shown in Figure 5-18.

When two characteristics are unrelated, there is no pattern or trend or grouping among the plotted points. It is instead a random scattering of points.

On the other hand, when two characteristics are related, a pattern, trend, shape, or grouping in the plotted points emerges. For example, Figure 5-19 shows the earlier scatter plot of Figure 5-16 with an overlaid line to highlight the trend.

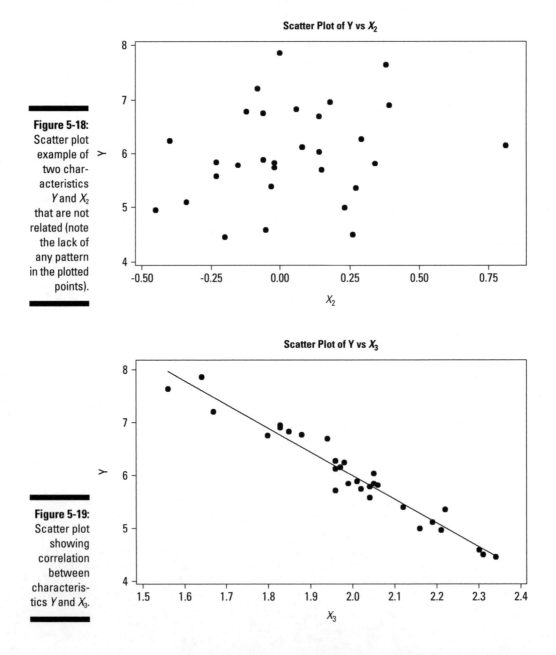

Figure 5-18: Scatter plot example of two characteristics Y and X_2 that are not related (note the lack of any pattern in the plotted points).

Figure 5-19: Scatter plot showing correlation between characteristics Y and X_3.

Whenever you can naturally fit a drawn line to a set of plotted points, as in Figure 5-19, you know that the characteristics are correlated. The *amount* of correlation is determined by how closely or tightly the plotted points fit a drawn line. If a line can only loosely fit the plotted points, there is only a slight relationship between the characteristics. If, however, the plotted points are tightly clustered around a line, there is a high correlation between the characteristics.

Of course, the reason you should be concerned with how closely certain input and output characteristics are related is because you're trying to find operational leverage. You are looking for the factors or variables that can positively influence your desired performance improvement outcome as defined by your project objective statement. See Chapter 2 for a deeper discussion of this concept.

How closely clustered do the scatter plot's points need to be before there is evidence of significant correlation? A good rule of thumb is the *fat pencil test*. Imagine laying a fat pencil on top of the drawn line fitting the plotted points. If the fat pencil body covers up the plotted points, it passes the test, and you can conclude that there is enough correlation between the two characteristics to call it significant.

✔ **Direction of correlation:** Two characteristics are *positively correlated* if the relationship indicates that an increase in one characteristic translates into an increase in the other. Figure 5-20 shows a scatter plot with a positive correlation between two characteristics.

Two characteristics are *negatively correlated* if the relationship indicates that an increase in one characteristic translates into a decrease in the other, and vice versa. The earlier Figure 5-19 shows a scatter plot with a negative correlation between two characteristics.

✔ **Strength of effect:** Scatter plots also graphically show the strength or magnitude of the effect one characteristic has on the other. Two characteristics may be strongly correlated (that is, tightly clustered around a fitted line). Yet a large change in one characteristic may still lead to only a small change in the other. Alternatively, there are situations where a small change in one characteristic is magnified as a large change in the other.

The way to visualize this strength of effect between two characteristics is to look at the slope of the line fitted to the scatter plot points. Figure 5-21 shows three scatter plots, one for each of three input characteristics' effects on an output characteristic *Y*. The steepness of the slope of the fitted lines determines how strong an effect the input has on the output. Steep slopes mean strong effect.

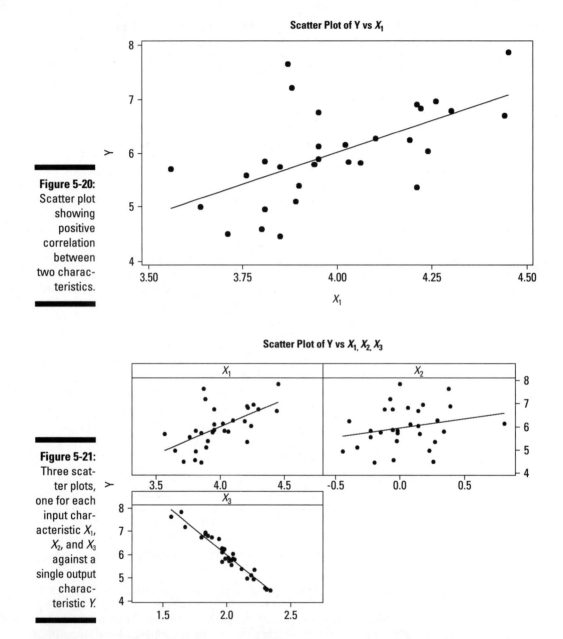

Figure 5-20:
Scatter plot showing positive correlation between two characteristics.

Figure 5-21:
Three scatter plots, one for each input characteristic X_1, X_2, and X_3 against a single output characteristic Y.

The slope of a line is how steep it is. The slope is quantified mathematically by comparing how much the line climbs up to how much it runs across between two points. This comparison is formed from a ratio of *rise* to *run*.

For example, given two points on a line (x_1, y_1) and (x_2, y_2), the slope is calculated by

$$\frac{rise}{run} = \frac{y_2 - y_1}{x_2 - x_1}$$

If the calculated slope is zero, that means the line is horizontal or flat. A negative slope means that the line slopes down from left to right. And a positive slope indicates a line that slopes up from left to right.

As the calculated slope value gets farther away from zero (either positively or negatively), the steepness of the line increases. When you get to a slope of positive infinity or negative infinity, you have yourself a vertical, straight up-and-down line.

In Figure 5-21, you can compare the slopes of the fitted lines for each input characteristic X_1, X_2, and X_3 to the output characteristic Y. The scatter plot showing a correlation with the greatest slope indicates the greatest impact or effect on the output. So in Figure 5-21, characteristic X_3 has the greatest effect on the output Y.

Another way to say this is that if you wanted to effect a one-unit change in the output Y, then input characteristic X_3 would have to be modified the least to get that change in the output. X_3 is the largest point of leverage among the input characteristics.

When you use a scatter plot to determine the strength of effect one characteristic has on another, it is often called a *main effects plot*. You can read a lot more about main effects plots in Chapter 9.

Scatter plots are a simple yet extremely powerful tool you can use to explore and quantify the relationship between two or more characteristics. It really is the start of getting to the fundamental $Y = f(X)$ relationship at the heart of Six Sigma improvement. Scatter plots start to get at the heart of how certain variables impact other variables, how certain inputs either inhibit or enhance your ability to create your desired outcomes.

Hindsight is 20/20: Behavior charts

Dot plots, histograms, box plots, and scatter plots all ignore a critical element: time. None of these graphical methods takes into account the order in which the measured data is observed. Time or order are critical factors, especially when you're trying to figure out the causes behind variation and changes in process behavior.

Creating a characteristic or process behavior chart

To investigate the behavior of a characteristic or process, plot your observed measurements one at a time along an axis representing time or order, in the exact sequence the measurements occurred in real life.

To create a characteristic or process behavior chart:

1. **Create a horizontal scale representing time or order.**

   You usually do this by creating an axis for the order in which the measurements occurred, called their *run order.*

2. **Create a vertical axis representing the scale of measure for the characteristic.**

   This scale could be in millimeters for length, pounds for weight, minutes for time, number of defects found on an inspected part, or anything else that quantifies what it is about the characteristic you're interested in.

   Set the maximum and minimum values on this vertical scale just slightly larger and slightly lower than the maximum and minimum observed data values, respectively.

3. **Plot each observation as a dot using its order and measurement.**

4. **Connect the dots.**

   Draw a line between each sequential point to emphasize the change that occurs between observations.

Figure 5-22 shows an example of a behavior chart for the completion time of an assembly process.

Interpreting characteristic or process behavior charts

Under normal conditions, a process or characteristic should behave normally. This statement is more profound than it sounds. The performance of every process or characteristic has natural variation. A behavior chart graphically shows how that variation plays out over time.

Like in Figure 5-22, a process or characteristic has variation that bounces around a central, horizontal level on the behavior chart. Most of the observed variation will be clustered close to this central level. Also, every now and then, there will be excursions that are farther away from the center. The variation will be completely random over time, without patterns or trends. This type of behavior is the definition of *normal,* and is analogous to the entitlement level of variation covered in "Be all you can be: Entitlement" section.

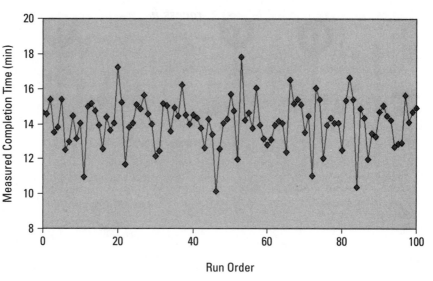

A behavior chart not only allows you to see the normal behavior of a process or characteristic, it also allows you to quickly detect *non-normal* behavior — variation above and beyond the expected normal level. The causes of non-normal behavior are the assignable or special causes spoken of earlier in this chapter that erode and degrade entitlement performance over the long term. Behavior charts form the foundation of detecting and finding the root cause of non-normal behavior.

Things to look for in process and characteristic behavior charts:

✔ **Variation beyond expected limits:** Outliers are measurement observations that occur beyond the limits of the normal short-term variation you expect out of the process or characteristic.

Outliers are non-normal because you don't expect to see them. It's like rolling five doubles in a row with a pair of dice. Five doubles in a row is possible, but when it happens, you suspect that something out of the ordinary is at play, like maybe a loaded pair of dice. ("Loaded" is just another way of saying the dice are acting non-normal.)

Figure 5-23 shows an example of a behavior chart showing evidence of variation beyond expected levels.

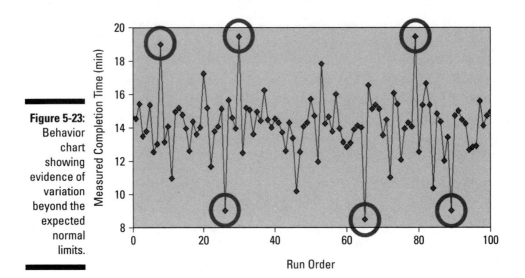

Figure 5-23:
Behavior
chart
showing
evidence of
variation
beyond the
expected
normal
limits.

When you see excessive variation like this, use the time scale or run order of the behavior chart as a starting point to discover what conditions or factors are causing the non-normal variation. Go back to that point in time identified by the chart and ask yourself. what was different at this point in time to take the characteristic or process behavior out of its normal course? The answer allows you to identify and manage the factor or factors influencing the process or characteristic performance.

Typical causes of outliers include worker inattention, measurement errors, and other one-time changes to the process's or characteristic's environment. For example, there may be a data outlier for purchase order processing due to an emergency in the office where two workers had to leave at the same time — thereby leaving a purchase order in the queue for an excessive period of time.

In Chapter 10, you find out much more about detecting evidence of this type of special-cause variation in the performance of your process or characteristic.

✔ **Trends:** Trend is a steady, gradual increase or decrease in the central tendency of the process or characteristic as it plays out over time. If all the conditions in the system stay constant, the level of performance of the process or characteristic will also stay level. The presence of a trend in a graphical behavior plot is evidence that something out of the ordinary has happened to move the location of the process or characteristic behavior. Figure 5-24 shows a sample of a trend in a process behavior chart.

Just like with any other evidence of non-normal behavior, when you see a trend in a behavior chart, you need to look closer at the system to uncover what is causing the changed performance.

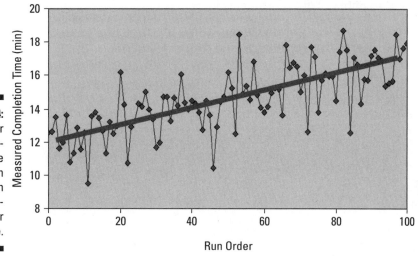

Figure 5-24:
Behavior
chart show-
ing evidence
of a trend in
the location
of the varia-
tion center
over time.

Trends in performance are almost always caused by system factors that
gradually change over time, like temperature, tool wear, machine maintenance, rising costs, and so on.

✔ **Runs:** Run is a sequence of consecutive observations that are each
increasingly larger or smaller than the previous observation. Figure 5-25
shows an example of two runs, one increasing and one decreasing, within
a behavior chart.

Runs can be caused by faulty equipment, calibration issues, and cumulative effects, among other things.

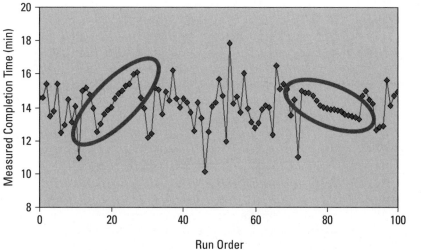

Figure 5-25:
Behavior
chart with
evidence of
a run. A
string of
consecutive
points that
increase or
decrease
are not
normal
behavior.

✔ **Shifts:** Shifts are sudden jumps, up or down, in the process's or characteristic's center of variation. Something in the system changes permanently — a piece of equipment, a new operator, a change in material, a new procedure. Clearly, shifts are non-normal behavior.

Figure 5-26 shows an example of a process or characteristic that has experienced a shift in the center level of its variation.

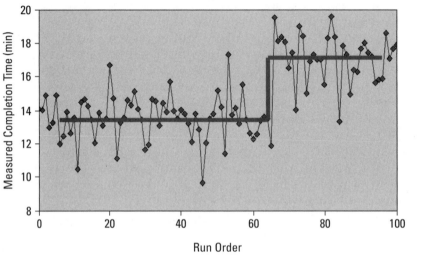

Figure 5-26: Behavior chart with evidence of a non-normal shift affecting the level of the central tendency of the variation.

Chapter 6

Measuring Capability

· ·

In This Chapter

▶ Understanding specifications and how they relate to defects and errors

▶ Knowing how to calculate and interpret measures of yield and defect rate

▶ Calculating and interpreting the sigma score (Z) of a process or characteristic

▶ Calculating and interpreting short- and long-term capability indices (C_P, C_{PK}, P_P, and P_{PK})

· ·

*W*hen you distill your measurements of a process or characteristic into statistical metrics, like a mean $\bar{x}$ and a standard deviation σ, you describe its properties. The process cycles on and on, and the characteristic is created over and over again. But each time a new instance happens, it's slightly different than the one before. This variation affects the performance of the larger system and, ultimately, impacts the customer.

This chapter is about two voices — the voice of the process and the voice of the customer — and the effect each has on the other. In Six Sigma, this relationship is called *capability*. Capability is how well the voice of your process or characteristic matches up with the voice of your customer, or how well your process performs in meeting customer expectations.

In the DMAIC strategy, you use capability calculations to quantify and communicate the performance of characteristics and processes relative to their requirements. These capability metrics allow you to know where to focus your attention and to verify that real improvement has been made.

Specifications: The Voice of the Customer

When you buy a Coca-Cola, you, as a customer, expect a certain experience. You expect it to be the same each time you open a new can. If there were too much sugar one time, or not enough secret ingredient another time, you'd notice and feel dissatisfied. The Coca-Cola company knows this about you, its customer, and so it very carefully controls the amounts and makeup of each ingredient going into its drinks.

The way Coca-Cola controls its product is through *specifications*. Each specification represents what the customer requires in order to be satisfied.

How close is close enough? Or why specifications?

Before the 1800s, all products were manufactured one at a time by craftsmen. A gunsmith, for example, would shape a single barrel of a gun, and then expertly carve a single wooden stock to match the barrel's dimensions. The pieces fit together because the craftsman adjusted each part to match the other.

A revolution was ignited when specialists were engaged to separately create each of the components of a product. Because the specialists each focused on a smaller area, they became more expert and efficient in producing that piece. The overall result was an economy that produced goods and services much more quickly and at a much lower cost than before.

It was in this environment of economic revolution that specifications were born. In order for Billy Bob's barrels to fit into Cletus's wooden stocks, there had to be some formal coordination. Specifications told the specialists what size or shape to make their parts. That way, when all the separate parts were assembled together, they would still fit.

What are specifications?

Specifications are performance values beyond which the performance of a process or characteristic is considered unacceptable. Spending more than $200 a month on movie tickets is probably considered unacceptable for your personal budget. But what about $100? Or $50? At what dollar value is movie ticket spending acceptable or unacceptable? A *specification* is that value separating acceptable from unacceptable performance. This definition holds for all process or characteristic performance measures.

There are several different types of specifications (see Figure 6-1):

- **Specification limit (SL):** Any value designating acceptable from unacceptable performance.

- **One-sided specification:** A specification limit that designates only a single transition point from acceptable to unacceptable performance. For example, if you care only that the characteristic or process performance not exceed a certain upper value, that is a one-sided specification.

- **Two-sided specification:** A pair of specification limits creating an interval of acceptable performance between the two limits.

- ✔ **Upper specification limit (USL):** A value designating an upper limit above which the process or characteristic performance is unacceptable.

- ✔ **Lower specification limit (LSL):** A value designating a lower limit below which the process or characteristic performance is unacceptable.

- ✔ **Target (T):** The single designated value you wish the process or characteristic to perform at. (A specification target is an *ideal*. Variation prevents the process or characteristic from exactly hitting the target every time.)

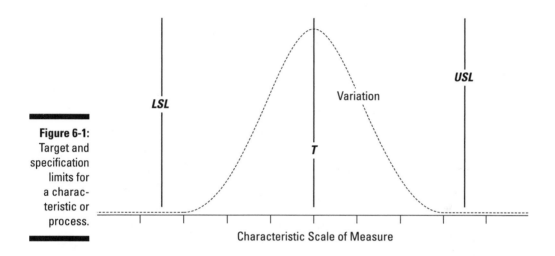

Figure 6-1:
Target and specification limits for a characteristic or process.

Characteristic Scale of Measure

If set up correctly, specifications represent the range of values a characteristic can be at and still be acceptable to the customer. Often, customers are not directly involved in your work. You never directly interact with them or see them. But a characteristic's specification is always available to you! In this way, specifications are said to represent the *voice of the customer* (or *VOC* for short).

Do you do the RUMBA? Creating realistic specifications

Specifications should never be arbitrary. Unless they actually represent the values that separate good from bad performance, they become a stumbling block to progress. If a specification is set too loosely, your customer will be dissatisfied or upset with the performance of what you provide — even though it meets its specification. If a specification is set too tightly, you spend more resources than you should to always perform within your overly narrow goalpost.

Imagine a specification requiring a delivered pizza to be between 120.4°F and 120.6°F when it arrives at the customer's door. To be within this required temperature range, the pizza company would have to take some pretty complicated and expensive actions. Maybe they'd have to use space-age ceramic pizza boxes made out of space shuttle tiles. In any case, it would take a lot of work and expense to meet that specification.

But do customers really require this extent of control over the temperature of their pizzas? Probably not. A less troublesome specification, and one just as satisfactory to the customer, might be 115°F to 125°F.

A mind-jogging acronym, RUMBA, is used in Six Sigma to help you evaluate the appropriateness of any specification:

- ✔ **Reasonable:** Is the specification based on a realistic assessment of the customer's actual needs? Does the specification relate directly to the performance of the characteristic?

- ✔ **Understandable:** Is the specification clearly stated and defined so that there can be no argument about its interpretation?

- ✔ **Measurable:** Can you measure the characteristic's performance against the specification? If not, there will be a lot of debate between you and your customer as to whether the specification has been met or not.

- ✔ **Believable:** Have you bought into the specification setting? Can you and your coworker peers strive to meet the specification?

- ✔ **Attainable or achievable:** Can the level and range of the specification be reached?

You need to review each specification to make sure that it passes the RUMBA test. If it falls short in any of the RUMBA categories, begin to develop a plan to bring the rogue specification back into control.

Very often, an improvement project is fast-tracked or solved through a simple review and adjustment of the involved specifications. The performance of the characteristic or process never has to be changed. Always review the appropriateness of specifications early in your Six Sigma project.

Don't push that big red button! What happens when you exceed a specification

So what happens when a characteristic's performance exceeds a specification? Does the system involved immediately stop working? Well, that depends. If the amount of departure from the specification limits is significant, maybe the system will indeed break. But what if the specification is exceeded only by a teeny bit?

Figure 6-2 shows four different points, each representing a different performance scenario.

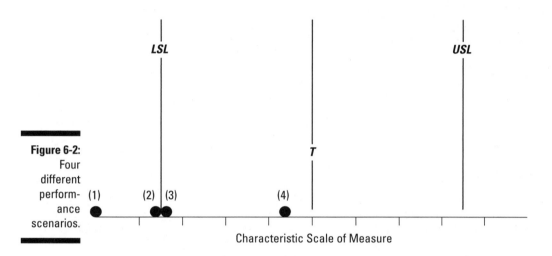

Point 4 in Figure 6-2 is clearly the best; it's closest to the ideal specified target
value for the characteristic. Point 1 is well beyond the lower specification limit.
But what about points 2 and 3? Is Point 2 much more likely than Point 3 to
create a defective condition? The answer is no. Points 2 and 3 are about equal
in their likelihood of causing a problem. Why treat real-world observations
like Point 2 differently from observations like Point 3?

A traditional view of quality has been:

> quality = compliance with specifications

This all-or-nothing perspective is flawed. Quality and the cost associated with
poor quality rarely behave this digitally. Realistically, problems and associated
costs increase more and more the farther and farther performance strays
from the specified ideal target. A better definition of quality is:

> quality = on-target performance with as little variation as possible

The target, not the limits, is the most important part of a specification. Getting
a characteristic to operate on target with as little variation as possible should
be the focus of improvement and cost reduction efforts.

Figure 6-3 graphically compares the flawed traditional and the Six Sigma per-
spectives on specifications and their relation to quality.

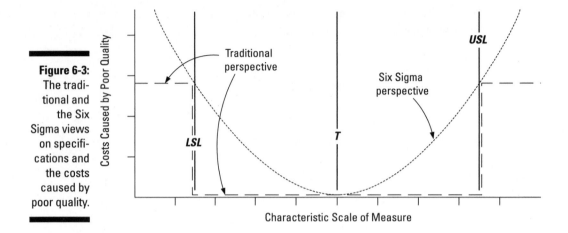

Figure 6-3:
The tradi-
tional and
the Six
Sigma views
on specifi-
cations and
the costs
caused by
poor quality.

The loss curve shown in Figure 6-3 is often called a *Taguchi loss function*, due to the pioneering work of Dr. Genichi Taguchi in the areas of optimization and robust design. As the figure shows, the traditional perspective is a hit or miss view, where unnecessary cost is incurred only when specifications are missed. The Six Sigma view is one in which additional cost is incurred as performance moves away from the target.

Capability: Comparing the Voice of the Customer to the Voice of the Process

Creating a specification is one thing. Meeting that specification through your processes and characteristics is another. A central task of Six Sigma is to understand how well your processes or characteristics meet their associated customer specifications.

Measuring yield

In the simplest terms, a process or characteristic can either meet or not meet its specification. Just as when you harvest the fruit from an apple tree, the *yield* of a characteristic or process relates to how much good stuff — performance within specifications — you get out.

Traditional yield: Output versus input

Traditionally, yield is the proportion of correct items (conforming to specifications) you get out of a process compared to the number of raw items you put into it. Figure 6-4 illustrates the idea of traditional yield.

Figure 6-4:
The tradi-
tional view
of yield and
of output
compared
to input.

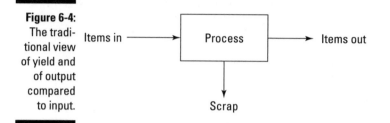

So, for the process of inflating the tires on cars in an assembly line, a study may reveal that of the 352 cars that went through the tire inflation process during a day's production, 347 were later found to have a pressure within the required specification limits. In this case, the traditional yield is

$$Y = \frac{out}{in} = \frac{347}{352} = 0.986 \text{ or } 98.6\%$$

Converting from a proportion like 0.986 to perhaps a more familiar percentage scale is done by simply multiplying the proportion by 100. To go from percentage back to proportion, divide the percentage by 100.

Always perform mathematical operations on proportions, not on percentages.

The traditional calculation of yield is often employed on the last, final inspection step of a process to measure the effectiveness of the overall process.

The Six Sigma perspective: First time yield (FTY)

The results of calculating yield the traditional way are misleading. Take a closer look at the tire-inflating example process in Figure 6-5.

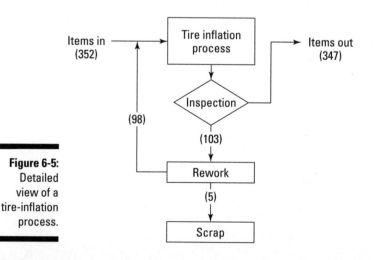

Figure 6-5:
Detailed
view of a
tire-inflation
process.

After inflation, the tire is immediately inspected to make sure it meets the required pressure specification limits. In the example, 103 tires are detected that don't comply with the pressure specification. Of course, the operators of the process reviewed each of these 103 and corrected (or *reworked*) 98 of them, leaving only five that were not able to be brought back within the correct pressure range and had to be scrapped.

With this detailed information, you now know that the proportion of tires going through the inflation process correctly the *first time* is

$$\frac{249}{352} = 0.707 \text{ or } 70.7\%$$

This calculation of yield is appropriately called *first time yield* or FTY for short. First time yield is often much different than traditional yield. That's because, unlike traditional yield, it captures the harsh reality of the effectiveness of the process, including inspection and rework.

Uncovering the hidden factory

Figure 6-6 shows the tire inflation process again, this time with the previously hidden, but now revealed, part of the process clearly identified.

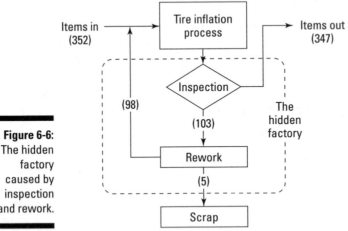

Figure 6-6: The hidden factory caused by inspection and rework.

The hidden factory is a natural outgrowth of the inability to correctly comply with required specifications the first time through the process. Here and there throughout organizations, hidden factories arise and become entrenched as tacit appendages of the standard processes. Measuring yield using the first time yield method forces you to objectively review and acknowledge the effectiveness of your processes.

In the case of the example tire inflation process, the hidden factor of in-process inspection and rework accounts for 98.6% – 70.7% = 27.9% of production. All together, value-sapping hidden factories within organizations combine to consume valuable resources and time.

Rolled throughput yield (RTY)

In reality, individual process steps are strung together to create an overall process structure for accomplishing complex tasks. One way Six Sigma quantifies the complexity of a system is to count the number of processes involved.

For example, Figure 6-7 illustrates a purchase order process that is made up of five individual process steps.

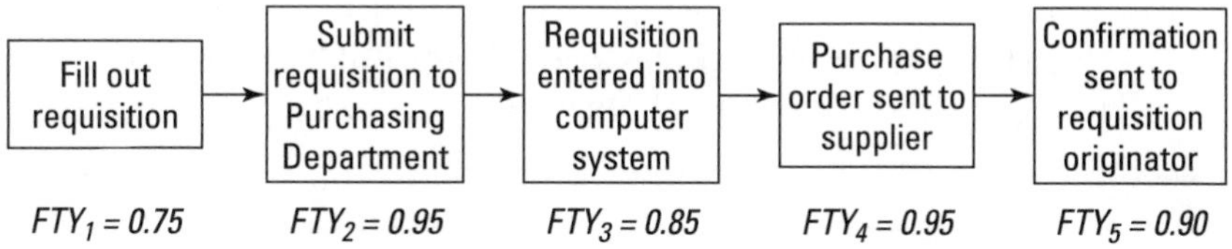

Figure 6-7:
Several smaller process steps link together to create a complex process.

Fill out requisition	Submit requisition to Purchasing Department	Requisition entered into computer system	Purchase order sent to supplier	Confirmation sent to requisition originator
$FTY_1 = 0.75$	$FTY_2 = 0.95$	$FTY_3 = 0.85$	$FTY_4 = 0.95$	$FTY_5 = 0.90$

How do you calculate the overall yield for a string of processes? The answer: You multiply the first time yields for each step together, creating what is called the *rolled throughput yield (RTY)*.

For the purchase order example given in the preceding section, the rolled throughput yield for this five-step process is

$$RTY = FTY_1 \times FTY_2 \times FTY_3 \times FTY_4 \times FTY_5$$
$$RTY = 0.75 \times 0.95 \times 0.85 \times 0.95 \times 0.90$$
$$RTY = 0.518$$

That means that the chance of a purchase order going through the process the first time with no rework or scrap is only 51.8 percent! (The last "confirmation" step in the process acts as a final test. With this last step having a 90 percent yield, there must be a lot of hidden factory stuff going on to drop the *RTY* down to 51.8 percent.)

Like a chain that is only as strong as its weakest link, rolled throughput yield can never be greater than the lowest first time yield within the system. To immediately improve the overall system performance, focus first on the individual process step with the lowest first time yield. Then move on to the step with the next lowest first time yield.

The formula for rolled throughput yield can be simplified as

$$RTY = \prod_{i=1}^{n} FTY_i$$

where the Greek letter pi ($\prod$) tells you to multiply all the first time yields of the system together. (See Table 6-1 for a summary of yield metrics.)

Even if the first time yields of the individual process steps are high, if the overall process becomes more and more complex (that is, more and more process steps), the system rolled throughput yield will continue to erode. Figure 6-8 charts how complexity degrades rolled throughput yield for different levels of individual first time yield.

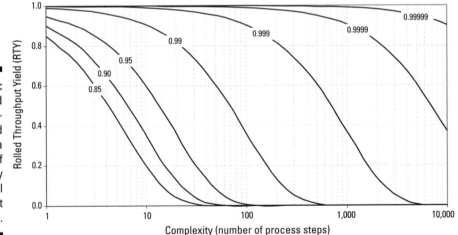

Figure 6-8: Rolled throughput yield *(RTY)* as a function of complexity for several constant *FTY* values.

For very complex systems — like automobiles, aircraft, data switching systems, enterprise-level business processes, and so on — a very high individual first time yield must be achieved in order to have any hope of an acceptable rolled throughput yield.

Table 6-1	Summary of Yield Metrics	
Metric Name	*Calculation Formula*	*Description*
Traditional yield (Y)	$Y = \dfrac{out}{in} = \dfrac{in - scrap}{in} = 1 - \dfrac{scrap}{in}$	Is a misleading perspective that obscures the impact of inspection and rework.
First time yield (FTY)	$FTY = \dfrac{in - scrap - rework}{in} = 1 - \dfrac{scrap + rework}{in}$	Shows the likelihood of an item passing through a process successfully the very first time. Includes the effects of inspection, rework and scrap.
Rolled throughput yield (RTY)	$RTY = \prod\limits_{i=1}^{n} FTY_i$	The combined overall yield of an entire process stream. Tells you the likelihood of an item passing through all process steps successfully the first time.

Measuring defect rate

The complimentary measurement of yield is defects. If your yield is 90 percent, there naturally must be 10 percent defects. Measuring defects and calculating the rate or how often they occur is like looking at the flip side of the yield coin.

Defects equal failure

When a process or characteristic doesn't perform within its specifications, it is considered defective. Or in other words, it produces a non-compliant condition, called a *defect.*

Defining a defect as a non-compliance with specifications may seem overly simplified. Just because a characteristic exceeds a specification doesn't necessarily mean that the system it is part of will break or stop functioning. It may or may not. For example, misspelling a customer's name on a billing statement (a defect or non-compliance with specifications) may or may not turn into a complaint (a failure) that costs money to correct.

But over and over again, experts have verified that product or process failures are directly related to compliance with specifications; the less you are compliant with specifications, the more likely you are to have a failure or breakdown.

So given the difficulty in directly linking compliance with specifications to product or process performance, the safe thing to do is to make sure you strive to comply with specifications. The absence or reduction of non-compliance with specifications will always reduce failures or breakdowns in your customers' experiences.

Defects per ubiquitous unit (DPU)

Six Sigma applies to all areas of business and productivity — manufacturing, design, sales, office administration, accounts receivable, healthcare, finance, and so on. Each of these areas works on and produces different things — products, services, processes, environments, solutions, among others.

To bridge these diverse disciplines, in Six Sigma you call the item you are working on a *unit*. A unit may be a discretely manufactured product. Or it may be an invoice that crosses your desk. It may be a month's worth of continually produced product. It may be a hospital patient or a new design. Whatever it is you do, in Six Sigma it is called a *unit*.

A basic assessment of characteristic or process capability is to measure the total number of defects that occur over a known number of units. This is then transformed into a calculation of how often defects occur on a single unit, like this

$$DPU = \frac{number\ of\ defects\ observed}{number\ of\ units\ inspected}$$

where DPU stands for defects per unit.

For example, if you process 23 loan applications during a month and find 11 defects — misspelled names, missing prior residence information, incorrect loan amounts — then the DPU for your loan application process is

$$DPU = \frac{11}{23} = 0.478$$

That means that for every two loans that leave your desk, you expect to see about one defect.

Leveling the field: Defects per opportunity (DPO) and per million opportunities (DPMO)

A DPU of 0.478 for an automobile is viewed very differently than the same per unit defect rate on a bicycle. That's because the automobile, with all its thousands of parts, dimensions, and integrated systems, has many more opportunities for defects than the bicycle has. A DPU of 0.478 on an automobile is evidence of a much lower defect rate than the same *DPU* on a relatively simpler bicycle. It's just not a fair comparison.

⋯ contrast the defect rates of things that have very different ⋯ he key is in transforming the defect rate into terms ⋯ whatever it is or however complex it may be.

⋯ en any different units is opportunity. For any ⋯ ransaction, or environment, an *opportunity* is a ⋯ could either turn out as a defect or as a success. ⋯ pportunity is defined as compliance to the oppor-

⋯ include:

⋯ cal dimension of diameter on an automobile axle.

⋯ ocess, the applicant's mailing address on a loan

⋯ the correct medial history records into the

⋯ tail store environment, the placement of clearance

✔ In a manufacturing process, the tightening of a bolt to the correct torque.

The number of opportunities inherent to a unit, whatever that unit may be, is a direct measure of its complexity. In fact, when you want to know how complex a unit is, you count or estimate how may opportunities there are for success or failure. Individual characteristics that are critical to the performance of the system are opportunities. Characteristics that have a specification represent opportunities.

The way to level the playing field so you can directly compare the defect rates of systems with very different complexities is to create a per-opportunity defect rate. This measurement of capability is called *defects per opportunity* (or *DPO*) and is calculated as

$$DPO = \frac{number\ of\ defects\ observed\ on\ a\ unit}{number\ of\ opportunities\ on\ a\ unit}$$

With a calculated DPO measurement, you can now fairly compare how capable an automobile is to a bicycle. For example, you may observe 158 out-of-specification characteristics on an automobile. After some study, you also determine that there are 14,550 opportunities for success or failure within that automobile. Its *DPO* is then

$$DPO = \frac{158}{14,550} = 0.011$$

days prior to the date of return) will be issued for returns within 30 days of purchase for (i) new and unread books (except textbooks and study aids, computer books, medical books, and audio books) and (ii) unopened music/DVDs/audio (opened music/DVDs/audio may not be returned but may be exchanged only for the same title and only if defective). Even with a receipt, a store credit will be issued for (i) purchases made by check less than 7 days prior to the date of return or (ii) when a gift receipt is presented. After 30 days with a receipt, store credit will be given on all returns for (i) new and unread books (except textbooks and study aids, computer books, medical books, and audio books) and (ii) unopened music or DVD's, at Barnes & Noble's lowest selling price. *A valid government issued photo ID is required for all no-receipt returns.* Study aids, computer books, medical books, and audio books may only be returned within 14 days of purchase with an original sales receipt (store credit will be given for

For a bicycle, on the other hand, you may find only two non-compliant characteristics among its 173 critical characteristics. So its *DPO* is

$$DPO = \frac{2}{173} = 0.012$$

Even though an automobile and a bicycle are two very different items with very different levels of complexity, the *DPO* calculations tell you that they both have about the same real defect rate. You only observe more defects on the automobile because there are many more opportunities for defects.

Be careful not to overly estimate the number of opportunities on a unit. You can artificially make the *DPO* of your product, process, or service look better than it really is by inflating its number of opportunities. For example, you could count the correct name on a patient record as a single opportunity for success or failure; whether the name on the form is right or wrong. Or you could say that there's one opportunity for the correct spelling, another for the correct font, another for the correct darkness of the printed text, another for the name's placement within the form box, and so on. Playing opportunity counting games only shrinks your ability to make an honest assessment and begin to make real improvement.

When the number of opportunities on a unit gets large and the number of observed defects gets small, calculated *DPO* measurements become so small they are hard to work with. For example, two commercial airline crashes (defects) observed out of 6 million flights in a year translates into

$$DPO = \frac{2}{6,000,000} = 0.000000333$$

0.000000333 is definitely an inconvenient number to work with!

You may also want to estimate out into the future, to know how many defects will pile up after running the process or observing the characteristic for a long time. After all, *DPU* and *DPO* look only at a single unit or a single opportunity.

A simple way to solve both of these problems is to count the number of defects over a larger number of opportunities. For example, how many defects occur over a set of one million opportunities? This defect rate measurement is called *defects per million opportunities* (or *DPMO*) and is used very frequently in Six Sigma.

When a process is repeated over and over again many times — like an automobile assembly process, or an Internet order process, or a hospital check-in process — *DPMO* becomes a convenient way to measure capability. Six Sigma is famous for its defect rate goal of 3.4 defects per million opportunities.

When calculating *DPMO*, you don't want to actually measure the defects over a million opportunities. That would take way too long. Instead, the way you calculate *DPMO* is using *DPO* as an estimate, like this

$$DPMO = DPO \times 1,000,000$$

This also means you can track backward, going from DPMO to DPO:

$$DPO = \frac{DPMO}{1,000,000}$$

A common alternative form of *DPMO* is *DPPM* — defective parts per million. *DPPM* is often used when assessing the defect rate of a continuous material or process where the "part" is the opportunity. Like in ongoing shipments of bolts to a supplier, the cumulative number of defective bolts found compared to the total number shipped over time can be translated into *DPPM*. (See Table 6-2 for a summary of defect rate metrics.)

Table 6-2	Summary of Defect Rate Metrics	
Metric Name	*Calculation Formula*	*Description*
Defects per unit (*DPU*)	$DPU = \dfrac{\text{number of defects observed}}{\text{number of units inspected}}$	*DPU* provides a measurement of the average number of defects on a single unit.
Defects per opportunity (*DPO*)	$DPO = \dfrac{\text{number of defects observed on a unit}}{\text{number of opportunities on a unit}}$	*DPO* measure the number of defects that occur per opportunity for success or failure. *DPO* allows you to fairly compare the defect rates of things with very different levels of complexity.
Defects per million opportunities (*DPMO*)	$DPMO = DPO \times 1,000,000$	*DPMO* is the average number of defects found over a million opportunities. It is best used when the process or characteristic is repeated many times.
Defective parts per million (*DPPM*)	$DPPM = DPO \times 1,000,000$	*DPPM* is synonymous with *DPMO*.

Linking yield and defect rate

You can calculate the yield of a process or characteristic. You can also calculate the defect rate of a process or characteristic. Are these two measures related? In fact, they are.

When you have an overall process with a relatively low defect rate, say, a process that produces units with a DPU less than 0.10 (or 10 percent), you can mathematically link the process defect rate to the overall process yield:

$$RTY = e^{-DPU}$$

where e in the equation is a mathematical constant equal to 2.718. There will be a function or key for raising e to a number on any scientific calculator or any spreadsheet computer program. (Look for the e^x key on your calculator.)

The actual value of the constant e is 2.71828182845905. . . . The decimal digits of e go on forever, never repeating. But you don't need to know the details of this curious constant called e to excel at Six Sigma. If, however, you feel yourself compelled to know more, you can proudly claim the title of "math geek." And by all means, find yourself a copy of _Calculus For Dummies_ by Mark Ryan (Wiley) to find out more about the fascinating number e!

The power of this mathematical link between yield and defects, is that if you can only measure or have only measurements of the defect rate of a process, you can still calculate its rolled throughput yield.

A little bit of algebraic contortions provides an equation to calculate _DPU_ based only upon the rolled throughput yield of a process:

$$DPU = -\ln(RTY)$$

where ln is the natural logarithm. (**_Hint:_** There's an ln button on every scientific calculator.)

Sigma (Z) score

From a quality perspective, Six Sigma is defined as 3.4 defects per million opportunities. This is called a Six Sigma level of quality. What is this famous sigma level or score? Sigma scores are thrown about so much, you definitely need to be comfortable understanding what they are and how they are calculated.

How many standard deviations can fit?

Figure 6-9 illustrates a process or characteristic performance distribution compared to its one-sided specification.

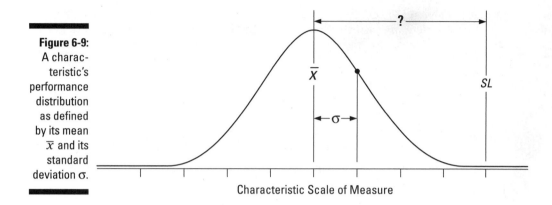

Figure 6-9:
A charac-
teristic's
performance
distribution
as defined
by its mean
$\overline{x}$ and its
standard
deviation σ.

Characteristic Scale of Measure

The central tendency of the performance distribution is defined by its mean. The amount of variation in the performance, or the width of the distribution, is defined by its standard deviation σ. The question is, how many standard deviations can you fit between the process or characteristic's mean and its specification limit *SL*?

Graphically, in Figure 6-9, you can see that four standard deviations can fit between the mean and the specification limit. The exact number can always be calculated (even without a graph!) by the formula

$$Z = \frac{|SL - \overline{x}|}{\sigma}$$

Calculating *Z* tells you exactly how many standard deviations can fit between the mean and specification limit of any process or specification. In Six Sigma, you call this value the *sigma score* of the process or characteristic.

Statisticians usually call this same value the *Z* score or *normal* score. In Six Sigma, however, you need to be careful not to confuse the sigma score (sometimes called a *sigma value,* or even simpler just *sigma*) with the standard deviation represented by the Greek letter σ. *Z* score, *Z* value, *Z,* sigma score, sigma value, and sigma are all different names for how many standard deviations can fit between the mean and the specification limit. Things get confused when practitioners call the standard deviation "sigma." In this book, we always call the standard deviation the standard deviation. To avoid the confusion yourself, whenever you are reading or speaking about a σ, don't call it "sigma." Instead, call out "standard deviation" for what the symbol always represents.

Use a sigma (*Z*) score only on a characteristic that is approximately normal. That means its distribution needs to be bell shaped. When the distribution is far from normal, the formula for calculating the sigma score (*Z*) breaks down. The quickest way to check whether the distribution is approximately normal is to create a dot plot or histogram. (See Chapter 5 to do this.)

A low sigma (Z) score means that a significant part of the tail of the distribution is extending past the specification limit. So the higher the sigma (Z) score, the fewer the defects. A process or characteristic gets a good sigma (Z) score when the variation distribution is safely away from the edge of the specification cliff.

There are three ways a sigma (Z) score can change:

- ✔ The location of the central tendency of the distribution, the mean, moves either closer or farther from the specification limit.
- ✔ The width of the distribution, as defined by the standard deviation σ, gets either wider or narrower.
- ✔ The location of the specification limit *SL* moves either closer or farther from the characteristic or process variation.

Actually, changes to $\bar{x}$ and σ usually happen at the same time, with both simultaneously contributing to a change in the computed sigma (Z) score.

Short-term versus long-term sigma score

From the mean $\bar{x}$ and the standard deviation σ, you can calculate a sigma (Z) score. A wrinkle here is that you must know what type of standard deviation you are using to calculate the sigma (Z) score: Is it a short-term standard deviation σ_{ST}, or is it a long-term standard deviation σ_{LT}? (To understand the critical differences in short- and long-term standard deviations, and the implications, see Chapter 5.)

If you are using a short-term standard deviation, the sigma (Z) score you calculate is a short-term sigma score Z_{ST}:

$$Z_{ST} = \frac{|SL - \bar{x}|}{\sigma_{ST}}$$

If, however, you have a long-term standard deviation, you can calculate the long-term sigma score Z_{LT}:

$$Z_{LT} = \frac{|SL - \bar{x}|}{\sigma_{LT}}$$

Short-term variation performance, as quantified by the short-term sigma score Z_{ST}, represents the best variation performance that you can expect out of your currently configured process. It is an *idealistic* measure of capability. It is also the easiest type of data to collect — you just go and quickly grab a relatively small sample of measurements from the process or characteristic.

But in the real world, a process or characteristic doesn't operate ideally like it does in the short-term. Its performance is degraded by shift, drift, and trend influences.

At the heart of Six Sigma is a method that combines the best of both worlds. It allows you to leverage the economy of short-term variation data while projecting realistic, long-term performance versus the process's or characteristic's specifications.

Shifty business: Linking short-term capability to long-term performance with the 1.5-sigma shift

Figure 6-10 shows the short-term variation of a process or characteristic and its expanded, long-term variation.

Figure 6-10:
A characteristic with short-term variation that complies with specifications, but with an expanded long-term variation that creates defects.

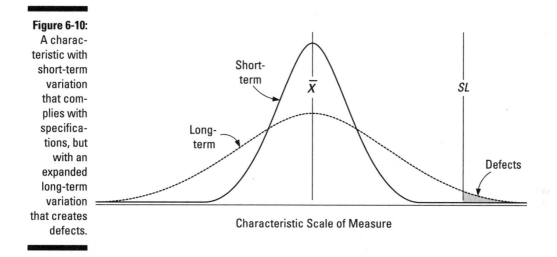

Characteristic Scale of Measure

The characteristic or process shown in Figure 6-10 stays within specifications during the short-term. It looks like there aren't problems. But over the long term, disturbances to the problem cause it to expand and sometimes create defects beyond the specification limit.

One mathematical way to simulate the effect of these degrading, long-term influences is to artificially move the short-term distribution closer to the specification limit until the amount of defects for the short-term distribution is the same as that for the long-term distribution. This approach is shown in Figure 6-11.

Early practitioners of Six Sigma proposed that mathematically shifting a characteristic's or process's short-term distribution closer to its specification limit by a distance of 1.5 times its short-term standard deviation (σ_{ST}) would approximate the amount of defects occurring in the long term. This breakthrough can be applied directly to the calculation of short-term and long-term sigma (Z) scores.

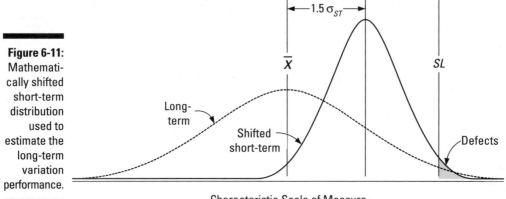

Figure 6-11:
Mathemati-
cally shifted
short-term
distribution
used to
estimate the
long-term
variation
performance.

Characteristic Scale of Measure

Because Z_{ST} represents the number of short-term standard deviations between the variation center and the specification, the sigma (Z) score of the shifted distribution is

$$Z_{\text{shifted}} = Z_{ST} - 1.5$$

But with the shifted distribution being equivalent, defect-wise, to the long-term distribution, the preceding equation can be rewritten as

$$Z_{LT} = Z_{ST} - 1.5$$

So what Six Sigma practitioners do is measure the short-term variability of a process or characteristic and calculate its short-term sigma score Z_{ST}. Then they immediately translate this to the expected long-term defect rate performance, using the 1.5 short-term standard deviation shift. This long-term sigma score, Z_{LT}, is communicated in terms of defects per million opportunities, DPMO.

Table 6-3 is a look-up table that Six Sigma practitioners carry around in their pockets and use over and over until they have it memorized (or until it is worn out, whichever happens first). They figure the Z_{ST} for any process or characteristic, and then translate that into a long-term defect rate DPMO. Or, in reverse, they first find the DPMO, and then translate that back to a short-term sigma score Z_{ST}.

Table 6-3	Sigma Score Table: $Z \leftrightarrow$ DPMO
Z	*DPMO*
0.0	933,193
0.5	841,345

Z	DPMO
1.0	691,462
1.5	500,000
2.0	308,538
2.5	158,655
3.0	66,807
3.5	22,750
4.0	6,210
4.5	1,350
5.0	233
5.5	32
6.0	3.4

Note: Paired table values are long-term for DPMO and short-term for Z (example, a long-term DPMO of 6,210 is the result of a process with a short-term sigma score of 4.0). Add 1.5 to corresponding Z values to obtain short-term equivalents (example, a short-term DPMO of 32 is the result of a process with a short-term sigma score of 4.0).

What's your sigma, baby?

As you work in Six Sigma, you may hear someone ask, "What's the sigma of the process?" And the response you'll hear back is, "2 sigma" or "3.3 sigma" or such-and-such sigmas. The question these people are really asking is, "What is the short-term sigma score Z_{ST} corresponding to the long-term defect rate of the process?"

After only a few times looking up sigma score values in Table 6-3, you begin to get a feel for this famous scale of capability. You may even be able to approximate sigma scores for defect rate values that fall between the rows of the table. Like a *DPMO* of 20,000. Its sigma score is about 3.6, a value just a little larger than the 3.5 corresponding to the *DPMO* of 22,750 in the table.

The sigma score can be applied to the performance of anything that has a specification and a defect rate: the performance of the mail system in delivering letters to the correct address, the ability of an automobile manufacturer to produce a door that fits to the body within a required dimensional tolerance, or a repeated budgeting process that must be completed within its specified schedule window.

All these sigma scores can be directly compared to see how capable the process or characteristic is. And when you communicate this capability with a sigma score, everyone else in Six Sigma knows exactly what you're talking about.

Capability indices

Yet another set of measures exists to quantify the capability of a process or characteristic to meet its specifications. This last set are indices that directly compare the voice of the process to the voice of the customer.

Short-term capability index (C_P)

The simplest capability index is called C_P. It compares the width of a two-sided specification to the effective short-term width of the process. Determining the width between the two rigid specification limits is easy. It is simply the distance between the upper specification limit *USL* and the lower specification limit *LSL*. But with variation that trails out at the tails, how do you determine the width of the *process*?

To get over this hurdle, Six Sigma practitioners have defined the effective *limits* of any process as being three standard deviations away from the average level. At this setting, these limits surround 99.7 percent, or virtually all, of the variation in the process. This is shown graphically in Figure 6-12.

Figure 6-12:
The effective width of a process or characteristic is ±3 standard deviations, containing 99.7 percent of the process variation.

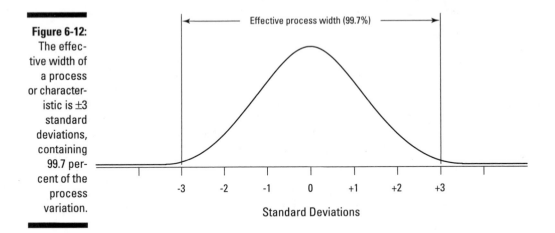

So to compare the width of the specification to the short-term width of the process, you use the formula:

$$C_P = \frac{USL - LSL}{6\sigma_{ST}}$$

where *USL – LSL* represents the voice of the customer's requirements and $6\sigma_{ST}$ represents the inherent voice of the process.

A calculated C_P value equal to 1 means that the voice of the customer is equal to the voice of the process. A C_P value less than 1 means that the process is wider than the specification, with defects spilling out over the edges. A C_P value greater than 1 means that the effective width of the process variation is less than the required specification, with fewer defects occurring.

C_P is a measure of short-term process or characteristic capability. Use only the short-term standard deviation to calculate its value. Using a long-term standard deviation in its calculation gives you incorrect results.

Adjusted short-term capability index (C_{PK})

A problem with the short-term capability index C_P is that it only compares the widths of the specification and the process. Figure 6-13 illustrates this problem.

Figure 6-13:
Two
distribu-
tions, one
centered
and one
offset
from the
specifica-
tion limits.

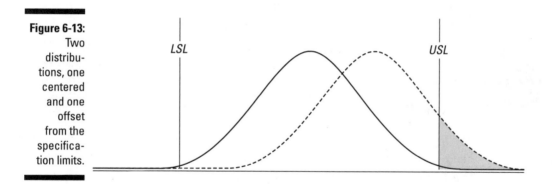

In Figure 6-13, both the distribution drawn with the solid line and the distribution drawn with the dotted line have the same calculated C_P. That's because they both have the same specification width and the same process width. But they are not equally capable. Because it is offset from the center of the specification, the dotted line distribution has many more defects than the solid distribution.

You can compensate for this by adjusting the C_P calculation for how far it is offset. To do this, you simply compare the distance from the distribution center $\bar{x}$ to each of the specification limits with the half-width of the short-term variation that should exist between the center of the distribution and the specification limit, like this

$$C_{PU} = \frac{USL - \bar{x}}{3\sigma_{ST}}, \text{ and}$$

$$C_{PL} = \frac{\bar{x} - LSL}{3\sigma_{ST}}$$

The smallest value you calculate of C_{PU} and C_{PL} is called the adjusted short-term capability index C_{PK}. So the formula for C_{PK} can be written as

$$C_{PK} = \min\left(C_{PU}, C_{PL}\right) = \min\left(\frac{USL - \bar{x}}{3\sigma_{ST}}, \frac{\bar{x} - LSL}{3\sigma_{ST}}\right)$$

where the *min* in the equation tells you to choose the smallest of the values in parentheses.

If the characteristic or process variation is centered between its specification limits, the calculated value for C_{PK} will be equal to the calculated value for C_P. But as soon as the process variation moves off the specification center, it's penalized in proportion to how far it is offset.

C_{PK} is very useful and very widely used. That's because it compares the width of the specification with the width of the process while also accounting for any error in the location of the central tendency. This is a much more realistic approach than what the C_P method offers.

Generally, a C_{PK} greater than 1.33 indicates that a process or characteristic is capable in the short-term. Values less than this tell you that the variation is either too wide compared to the specification or that the location of the variation is offset from the center of the specification. Or it may be a combination of both width and location. The only way to know for sure is to create a graph and begin to review the details.

Long-term capability indices (P_P and P_{PK})

The same capability indices that you calculate for short-term variation, C_P and C_{PK}, can also be calculated for long-term variation. To differentiate them from their short-term counterparts, these long-term capability indices are called P_P and P_{PK}. The only difference in their formulas is that you use σ_{LT} in place of σ_{ST}.

Long-term capability indices are important because no process or characteristic operates in just the short term. Every process extends out over time to create long-term performance. Table 6-4 summarizes each of the short- and long-term capability indices.

Table 6-4	Summary of Short- and Long-Term Capability Indices	
Index Name	**Formula**	**Description**
Short-term capability index	$C_P = \dfrac{USL - LSL}{6\sigma_{ST}}$	Compares the width of the specification to the short-term width of the process

Index Name	Formula	Description
Adjusted short-term capability index	$C_{PK} = \min\left(\dfrac{USL - \bar{x}}{3\sigma_{ST}}, \dfrac{\bar{x} - LSL}{3\sigma_{ST}} \right)$	Compares the width of the specification to the short-term width of the process and accounts for off-centering of the process from the specification
Long-term capability index	$P_P = \dfrac{USL - LSL}{6\sigma_{LT}}$	Compares the width of the specification to the long-term width of the process
Adjusted long-term capability index	$P_{PK} = \min\left(\dfrac{USL - \bar{x}}{3\sigma_{LT}}, \dfrac{\bar{x} - LSL}{3\sigma_{LT}} \right)$	Compares the width of the specification to the long-term width of the process and accounts for off-centering of the process from the specification

Prescribing a capability improvement plan

When you know what the short- and long-term capability indices of a process or characteristic are, what do you do? How can you use these four indices to chart out a plan for improvement?

Table 6-5 outlines the various scenarios that may occur when measuring the capability of a process or characteristic. The table also describes an improvement plan for each scenario.

Table 6-5	Prescriptive Capability Improvement Plan	
Symptom	**Diagnosis**	**Prescription**
$C_P = C_{PK}$ and $P_P = P_{PK}$	Overall, your process or characteristic is centered within its specifications.	As needed, focus on reducing the long-term variation in your process or characteristic while maintaining on-center performance.

continued

Table 6-5 *(continued)*

Symptom	Diagnosis	Prescription
$C_P = P_P$ and $C_{PK} = P_{PK}$	Your process or characteristic suffers from a consistent offset in its center location.	Focus on correcting the set point of your process or characteristic until it is centered.
$C_P = P_{PK}$	Your process is operating at its entitlement level of variation.	Continue to monitor the capability of your process. Redesign your process to improve its entitlement level of performance.

Chapter 7

Separating the Wheat from the Chaff

In This Chapter

▶ Differentiating between the different types of data — attribute and continuous

▶ Understanding measurement system capability

▶ Separating the critical few performance influencers from the trivial many

▶ Using observational studies as a funneling tool

*I*n Chapters 4, 5, and 6, many different ways are introduced to identify and discover all the possible variables — the Xs — influencing an important outcome, process, or characteristic — the Y. This chapter covers how to start to whittle this large list of potential influencers to a handful of variables on which to focus your improvement efforts.

Just like an experienced whittler selects a different knife for carving different types of wood, you need to choose among many different Six Sigma tools to narrow your field of suspect variables. What tool you choose depends a lot on what type of data you are using. So it's important for you to assess what type of data you have.

An area of potential influence that is often overlooked in Six Sigma projects is your measurement system itself. In Six Sigma, data forms the foundation of your knowledge and decisions. Imagine what would happen if all your analysis and decisions were based on faulty data. You need to immediately eliminate the chance that the measurements you are using are creating an illusion.

Reducing a large collection of potential factors down to a smaller area of focus allows you to concentrate your limited resources on the items that really will have an impact on improvement. In this whole process, you want to have your choices guided by the data, rather than opinion or guesses.

Understanding Data Types

All data are not created equal. Before you can do much else, you first need to know what type of performance data you have. Just as knowing what the fish are biting tells you which lure to use, knowing what kind of data you are dealing with tells you which tools to use.

Attribute or category data

Some data consist of measurements that describe an attribute of the characteristic or process. When these attributes are named categories, the data are called *attribute* or *category* data.

Attribute data are all around you.

- Telephone area codes are attribute data.
- S, M, L, XL, XXL clothing sizes are attribute data.
- "Pass" or "fail" judgments pronounced on just-assembled products are attribute data.
- "Good" or "bad" assessments of the output from a process are attribute data.
- When studying the performance of automobiles, manufacturer names like Ford, Chevy, and GM are attribute data.

How do you know whether you are working with attribute data? The telltale test is to ask yourself: Can I meaningfully add or subtract values of this data?

If the answer is "no," what you have is attribute data. For example, what do you get when you add a S-sized shirt to a M-sized shirt? There is no meaningful answer to this question. Or, if you subtract telephone area code 415 from area code 213 does the resulting area code of 202 mean something? Of course not! And so you know that you're dealing with attribute data.

What you can do with attribute data is count how many times each category or attribute appears. For example, you may find that a process produces 152 "good" items and 28 "bad" items over a given period of time. You use the results of these type of counting studies as the starting point for many of the analyses discussed in Chapters 8, 9, and 10.

Lord Kelvin said, "When you can measure what you are speaking about, and express it in numbers, you know something about it; but when you cannot express it in numbers, your knowledge is of a meager and unsatisfactory kind." Measuring with attribute data is a first step in getting to a satisfactory knowledge of what you are trying to improve. Even though there are limitations to what you can do with it, attribute data is a giant first step into the world of Six Sigma improvement.

A subset category of attribute data that provides a little more horsepower is called *ordinal* or *rank order* data. Ordinal data is attribute data that can be logically placed in an order from smallest to greatest or in an order of time. Like the months of the year: January, February, March, and so on. If you have "month" data on a set of last year's invoices, you can sort them into buckets of occurrence starting with January, and then move on through the year. Or you may not have actual completion times, but you may have data about which employee finished a task first, second, third, and so on. In this case, you have a powerful set of ordinal data that you can use to begin analysis and improvement.

Continuous or variable data

Keep in mind the question you asked yourself to find out whether the data you have is attribute data: Can I meaningfully add or subtract values of this data?

If the answer to this question is "yes," the data you are working with is called *continuous* or *variable* data.

Both *continuous* and *variable* are bad names for this type of data, but for historical reasons, these are the names that have stuck. The name continuous is meant to convey the idea that this data type can have any value from a continuous scale, like the reading on a mercury thermometer. Variable is meant to say the same thing — that the measured values can vary anywhere along a given scale. You can get 98.23°F or 98.25°F or 98.37°F. The problem is that no matter how continuous or variable you think your scale of measure is, as soon as you write down a measurement on paper or record it in a computer you always truncate its reading to some fixed length, making it no longer continuous. The important thing to remember is that when you have data that can be meaningfully added or subtracted, you have what is called continuous or variable data. For example, a count of the number of children in each household can only occur in integer values. (You can't physically have 2.3 children. The scale of measure of children in a household is not continuous at all.) But you can take the integer measurement from each household and perform mathematical operations to calculate a meaningful average or standard deviation. Being able to mathematically operate on continuous data is what sets it apart from attribute data. (See Table 7-1 for a summary of data types.)

Table 7-1	Summary of Data Types	
Data Type	*Description*	*Examples*
Attribute or category	Data observations fall into discrete, named value categories. No mathematical operations can be performed on the raw data. You can count the number of occurrences you see of each category.	Eye color: brown, blue, green Location: Factory 1, Factory 2, Factory 3 Inspection result: pass, fail Size: large, medium, small Fit check: go, no-go Questionnaire response: yes, no Attendance: present, absent Employee: Fred, Suzanne, Holly Processing: Treatment A, Treatment B
Continuous	Data observations can take on numerical value and are not confined to nominal categories. Data values can be meaningfully added and subtracted.	Bank account balance: dollars Length: meters Time: seconds Electrical current: amps Survey response: 1 = disagree, 2 = neutral, 3 = agree

Examples of continuous data include:

- A numbered GPA scale representing letter grades at school
- The temperature in your oven
- The amount of money you spend on groceries
- The time it takes to complete a process task
- The gas mileage of your car

Avoiding Illusion: Measurement System Capability Analysis

Measurement is critical. It is the foundation of knowledge and subsequent improvement. It is the way you verify that you have the right answer, have corrected the problem, or have improved the situation.

Measurement is unavoidable. That's because nothing is observed outside of the filter of some kind of measurement system — your eyes, your brain, your perception; a physical ruler, a stopwatch; or a laser interferometer. Everything comes to you through some kind of measurement system lens. You need to know whether your measurement system is giving you a clear picture of reality.

Measurement itself is a process you can never avoid. The act of measuring is a process all by itself. And as with any other process, it has variation within it. Think back to the last time you watched an Olympic ice skating competition. In that situation, expert judges act as the measurement system. Imagine showing a series of judges a recording of an ice skater's routine. It's likely that each judge would give the routine different marks. This is evidence of variation in the measurement system. If you came back a year later with the same recording to the same series of judges, you'd almost certainly get a different score from each judge. In fact, the variability in this Olympic example is parallel to how it is with every measurement system.

Everything you see is through an imperfect lens of measurement. Any time you place something into a category or quantify one of its attributes, you are doing so through an imperfect measurement system. Figure 7-1 illustrates this concept.

Figure 7-1: Everything you observe has the added variation of your measurement system.

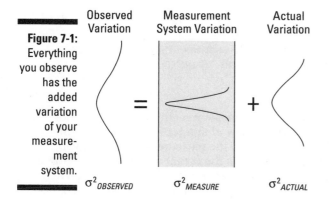

Observed Variation = Measurement System Variation + Actual Variation

$\sigma^2_{OBSERVED}$　　　$\sigma^2_{MEASURE}$　　　σ^2_{ACTUAL}

Six Sigma teaches that data and measurements are the starting point of knowledge and improvement. Before you get too far down the improvement road, however, you need to determine whether your measurement system is clouding your observations to the point of illusion — whether what you see is not what really is.

Sources of measurement system variation

There are several aspects of a measurement system that affect how much clouding variation it contributes to your observations.

Measurement resolution

Resolution is a comparison of the smallest increment your measurement system can provide to the characteristic you are trying to measure. For example, imagine measuring a grain of sand with a tape measure. You'd be kidding yourself if you treated the results of this measurement system seriously. The ⅟₁₆th-inch increments on the tape measure are not fine enough to discern the much, much smaller grain of sand. What you need instead is a system, like maybe a microscope, that can measure in increments of 1/1,000th of an inch. Then you could trust your measurements of the sand grain sizes.

A good rule of thumb is to use a measurement system with at least ten increments within the specification width you are measuring or within the process variation you are trying to observe. So, as an example, for measuring the variation of a process that should be completed between 9 and 10 minutes, you want to use a measurement system with increments of no more than 0.1 minutes.

The idea of resolution also applies when you are measuring attribute data. A customer survey that allows only responses of "satisfied" and "dissatisfied" offers less resolution than one where the customer can mark "delighted," "satisfied," "indifferent," "dissatisfied," and "disgusted."

Measurement accuracy

Accuracy describes how centered your measurement system's variation is with the actual variation of the process or characteristic. Figure 7-2 shows this visually. In (a), the dots representing the measurement system variability are centered on the target that represents the actual variation of the process or characteristic being measured. The measurement system depicted in (a) is accurate. In (b), the measurement system variation is offset, or biased, from the center of the actual process or characteristic variation. The (b) measurement system is not accurate.

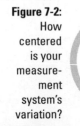

Figure 7-2:
How
centered
is your
measure-
ment
system's
variation?

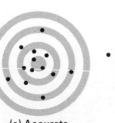

(a) Accurate   (b) Not accurate

Several conditions can cause accuracy problems in your measurement system. Sometimes a measurement system can have problems with *linearity*. Good linearity is when the centering and the magnitude of the measurement system variation is consistent across its range of operation. A measurement system has poor linearity when its centering or magnitude of variation changes across its range of variation. A *stable* measurement system is one that stays centered and free of offset changes. In an instable measurement system, the location of its variation center bounces around.

Measurement precision

Accuracy and precision are two distinct properties of a measurement system. Accuracy describes how centered your measurement system is compared to the actual variation. *Precision* describes how widely spread the variation of your measurement system is compared to the actual variation of the process or characteristic you are measuring. Figure 7-3 illustrates the idea of measurement precision. In (a), the dots representing the measurement system variability are clustered tightly together compared to the target representing the actual variation of the process or characteristic being measured. The measurement system depicted in (a) is precise even though it is not accurate in its location. In (b), the measurement system variation varies widely compared to the actual process or characteristic variation. Although the (b) measurement system is accurate in its location, it is not precise.

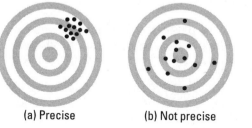

Figure 7-3:
Measurement system variation.

(a) Precise   (b) Not precise

Measurement system precision is made up of two components that you hear talked about a lot in Six Sigma: repeatability and reproducibility.

- *Repeatability* is the part of measurement variation that occurs when you repeat measurements with the same item, the same measurement setup, and the same equipment, under the identical conditions. In a way, repeatability can be thought of as the short-term part of measurement system variation.

- *Reproducibility* is the part of measurement variation that occurs when you repeat measurements with different items and different measurement setups, under different environmental conditions. Reproducibility captures all the long-term variation influences in your measurement system.

Together, the metrics of repeatability and reproducibility capture all of your measurement system's precision. In Six Sigma there's an acronym (of course!) for repeatability and reproducibility — R&R. You see this acronym used to describe how precise a measurement gauge is, as in its gauge R&R. (When you hear "R&R" don't think of "rest and relaxation" or of a railroad line. Instead, think of how good your measurement system is.)

Measuring measurements: Measurement system analysis (MSA)

So how do you measure the goodness of your measurement system? There are several ways for you to do this, depending on the type of measurement data you are collecting and the type of measurement system you are using. Typical measurement system analyses (MSA) include audits, attribute studies, and gage or continuous variable studies.

Audit measurement system studies

An *audit* is a measurement system study where you compare your measurements to a known, correct standard. For example, you may compare what your computer system says you have in inventory (your measurement system) to what is actually in your physical inventory warehouse. Any differences between the two reflect variation in your measurement system.

For example, read the following paragraph as quickly as you can. As you're reading, circle each occurrence of the sixth letter of the alphabet — either lower or upper case. Do not go back or reread parts of the paragraph.

> The necessity of training Farm Hands for first class farms in the fatherly handling of farm livestock is foremost in the minds of Farm Owners. Since the forefathers of the farm owners trained the Farm Hands for first class farms in the fatherly handling of farm livestock, the Farm Owners feel they should carry on with the family tradition of training Farm Hands of first class farms in the fatherly handling of farm livestock because they believe it is the basis of good fundamental farm management.

Now, count how many *f*s you found in the paragraph. How many did you find? Going through this paragraph slowly and carefully, you will find exactly 36 *f*s.

Reading through the paragraph quickly, circling *f*s, is a type of measurement system. (It is a lot like the inspections that are placed in a process to verify the quality of what is being produced.) How good was your measurement system? Of the 36 *f*s, what percentage did you find? This analysis of how well you did is an audit of your measurement system.

A visual inspection system

A computer disk drive manufacturer in the mid 1980s was experiencing a nagging problem with poor yields. The principle concern was that the sensitive magnetic media coating the disks was in some way defective. As a result, a collection of very demanding standards was put in place and a battery of stringent tests was implemented with the hope of detecting and removing media problems from the system.

At one point, design engineers at the company happened to notice some visual defects and spots in the magnetic coating on the disk. They concluded that this was the long sought-after cause of their persistent yield problems. Engineering immediately requested that Manufacturing implement a final visual inspection of each disk to be done at the end the already onerous test cycle. With the implementation of this new inspection, the disk reject rate jumped from 8 to 10 percent. At $30 a disk, the scrap bill neared $300,000 per month!

With no real improvement evident, Engineering proposed to further tighten the specifications on the magnetic disk media. With mounting assembly and scrap costs, Manufacturing asked that an expert from Engineering audit their test and inspection process one last time before tightening the specs again.

Upon arrival at the manufacturing facility the Engineering expert reviewed the entire test and inspection process. He then decided to run some experiments to validate the final visual inspection process on the disks. His first experiment was to send a bunch of previously rejected disks back through the final inspection process without the inspectors' knowledge. The results were so startling he reran the experiment several times: Each time the previously inspected disks were secretly sent back through the final visual inspection process, an additional 10 percent of the disks would be rejected!

Armed with this new insight, the engineer tried another test. This time he took a bunch of disks that had already passed the final inspection step and secretly reinserted them back into the inspection process. Even with these "passed" disks, the inspectors continued to find ten percent of the previously passed disks to be visually defective.

As a final confirmation, the engineer sent a collection of passed disks and a collection of failed disks into the final stages of the assembly process. At the end of the assembly process, the disk drives with the rejected media actually had a slightly higher final performance yield than those with disks passing the visual inspection.

Clearly, this company was living in a measurement system illusion. The visual inspection system they had added provided no benefit to the company but was costing over $300,000 per month in incorrectly rejected disk media.

Industrial engineers have found human screening or inspection measurement systems to be consistently about 80 percent effective. Yet most people act under an illusion that the outcome of a screening operation is 100 percent correct. Performing a simple data audit tells you how effective your measurement system is.

What can you do to improve the effectiveness of a screening or inspection measurement system?

✔ Divide a large screening task into smaller pieces and assign it among several individuals.

✔ Clarify inspection criteria with pictures, examples, and so on.

✔ Use successive inspectors to incrementally increase the effectiveness of the inspection.

✔ Incorporate technology or automation to remove human error.

Pareto diagrams are a great diagnostic tool for detecting problems with a measurement system. Vilfredo Pareto (1848–1923) was an Italian economist who proposed that 80 percent of an economy's wealth is held by 20 percent of its population. Since Pareto proposed his famous principle, other researchers have confirmed that it also applies to many other phenomena, including the distribution of measured defects. For example, it has been found that 80 percent of the observed defects on a product or in a process can be attributed to 20 percent of the possible causes. What this means is that when you create a bar chart of the observed number of each type of defect on an item, and then sort the order of the bars from most frequently observed defects to the least frequently observed, only the first few defect categories should have a significant contribution to the overall defect count. So if your measurement system divides things up into multiple defect categories and a Pareto diagram shows approximately equal contribution from each category, you should suspect that something is wrong with your measurement system. Instead, a healthy measurement system should show that only a few defect categories make up the bulk of the observed defects. (Another name for the *Pareto Principle* is the 80-20 rule.)

Attribute measurement system studies

When you are measuring attribute data — like pass-fail measurements of an invoice process or categorizing of failed products by failure type — it is important to determine whether your ability to put items into correct categories is consistent and reliable. The risk of a poor attribute measurement system is two-fold: You may falsely accept bad items or you may falsely reject good items. Either way, the risk is that you'll make a decision that is not consistent with reality.

Consider a measurement system that categorizes items — whether it be a characteristic or a process — into categories of "pass" and "fail." How would you begin to study the effectiveness of this type of measurement system? Here's the answer:

1. **Start by setting aside 15 to 30 samples of what is being measured.**

   You want these samples to represent the full range of variation that is typically encountered, with about half of the samples being "passes" and the other half "fails."

2. **Create a "master" standard by designating each of the samples as a "pass" or a "fail."**

   Use a panel of experts to make these distinctions or some standard that you know is absolutely correct.

3. **Pick two or three inspectors.**

   Have them review the sample items in a random order and record their conclusions — whether each item is either a "pass" or a "fail."

4. **Have each inspector repeat their measurements of the samples after mixing them up into a new random order (or spin the inspectors around in place until they are very dizzy). Record the repeated measurements.**

   Note: It is important that each inspector's second measurements are fair, as if they were happening for the first time. You may need to wait for a day before performing the second measurements. Randomizing the samples before the second measurements is critical.

5. **For each inspector, calculate the percentage of their first and second measurements that agreed with each other. This is the *repeatability* for each inspector.**

   You can also calculate an overall measurement system repeatability by averaging the repeatabilities of the individual inspectors.

   Note: The calculated repeatability for the individual inspectors needs to be as close to 100 percent as possible. Calculated individual repeatabilities less than this mean that the inspector is not consistent in distinguishing between good and bad items. Training helps inconsistent inspectors become consistent in their measurements.

6. **For each of the sample items, calculate the percentage of the recorded measurements where each of the inspectors agreed with themselves and all inspectors agreed with each other. This is the *reproducibility* for the measurement system.**

   The calculated measurement system reproducibility tells you how precise the measurement system is over the long-term — over different inspectors, different set-ups, and different environmental conditions.

7. **You can also calculate the percent of the time individual inspectors and the group of inspectors agree with themselves *and* agree with the "master" standard created in Step 2.**

This tells you how consistently your measurement system detects what your experts have decided really is pass and fail.

As an example, a calculated 63 percent agreement between all inspectors for all samples with the "master" standard in a measurement system study means that there is a 63 percent likelihood that this measurement system will correctly measuring the items and a 37 percent chance of error. Clearly, the goal is to achieve a measurement system with as high an effectiveness as possible, that is as close to 100 percent agreement as possible.

More sophisticated analysis tools are available for situations when an attribute measurement system has more than two categories. These tools, like kappa analysis, can be found in advanced statistical analysis software, like Minitab and JMP.

Gauge or continuous variable measurement system studies

When you are measuring continuous or variable data, there are more tools and analyses at your disposal. In all cases, measurement system studies for continuous data mathematically compare the total observed variation to the portion of the variation stemming from the measurement system itself.

Recalling Figure 7-1, the total observed variation is made up of two parts, the variation of the actual items or process being measured and the variation imparted by the measurement system itself. This make-up of the overall variation is summarized by the following equation of variances (see Chapter 5 for a definition of variance):

$$\sigma^2_{OBSERVED} = \sigma^2_{MEASURE} + \sigma^2_{ACTUAL}$$

In an effective measurement system, the contribution of the measurement system itself will be small compared to the overall observed variation. Table 7-2 provides a summary of measurement-to-observed variance ratio scores and what to do for each situation.

Table 7-2	Measurement-to-Observed Variation Ratio Values and Interpretation	
Calculated Variance Ratio	*Diagnosis*	*Prescription*
$\dfrac{\sigma^2_{MEASURE}}{\sigma^2_{OBSERVED}} \leq 0.1$	Good measurement system. Contribution of the measurement system to the overall observed variation is small enough to enable good decisions from the measurements.	Use measurement system as it is. Look for opportunities to simplify or make the measurement system less expensive or more efficient.

Calculated Variance Ratio	Diagnosis	Prescription
$0.1 \leq \dfrac{\sigma^2_{MEASURE}}{\sigma^2_{OBSERVED}} \leq 0.3$	Marginal measurement system. Contribution of the measurement system to the overall observed variation is beginning to cloud results. There is a significant risk of making a wrong decision from the measurements.	Use with caution only if no better measurement alternative exists. Begin to improve the measurement system by training operators, standardizing measure-ment procedures, and investigating new mea-surement equipment.
$\dfrac{\sigma^2_{MEASURE}}{\sigma^2_{OBSERVED}} \geq 0.3$	Unacceptable measurement system. Guessing is probably just as precise. Do not base important decisions off of information from a measure-ment system in this condition.	Measurement system needs to be corrected before any valid infor-mation can be derived from the system. Investigate causes of gross inconsistency.

Mathematically comparing measurement system variation to the overall observed variation is not difficult. The difficult part, rather, is obtaining a good estimate of the measurement system variation from which to make the comparison.

Valid estimates of the variance of the measurement system usually involve two to three inspectors and five to ten process outputs or characteristics to measure. Each inspector also measures each process output or characteristic two to three times. From this, advanced statistical analysis tools, like Minitab or JMP, can be used to automatically perform the gauge analysis calculations and you can begin to diagnosis and improve, if required, your measurement system.

Filling the Funnel

To get a concentrated stream out of the bottom of a funnel, you first must fill the top abundantly. Six Sigma is no different. You start by dispassionately car-rying all possible causes into your project. But as you progress, you let your analyses of the data itself tell you which variables to keep along for the ride and which ones you can safely cast aside as excess baggage.

Let the data do the talking

One of the hallmarks of maturity in Six Sigma is an unwavering reliance on data. Data is used to understand what happened in the past. Data is used to decipher and improve the current situation. And data is the basis for predicting how things will perform in the future.

In Six Sigma, data trumps the usual fare of opinion, speculation, guesswork, and politics. Data-driven decision-making is the culture of Six Sigma. People say, "In God we trust; all others must have data."

In a pure application of Six Sigma, you simply "let the data do the talking." You almost withhold judgment regarding what it is that is wrong or what the solution will be and instead quietly listen to what the data is telling you about the situation and what should be done. This new way of operating stems from an acquired confidence in the science and power of Six Sigma — that gathering and querying data from a process more efficiently reveals the real, unbiased truth of its performance as well as the most effective and lasting improvement solution.

Cast a big net

A corollary of "let the data do the talking" is exposing yourself to the voice of the data in many different ways. In Chapter 4, you discover tools like processing mapping, fishbone diagrams, *X-Y* matrices, and failure mode effects analysis (FMEA). These are very powerful tools for querying a process to discover what potential factors may be contributing to its performance. In the remainder of this chapter, you discover graphical tools that you can use to mine data for evidence of factors influencing process or characteristic performance. In Chapter 8, you find out how to employ statistical hypothesis tests; Chapter 9 discusses designed experiments. Figure 7-4 shows how all these tools are used progressively to identify — and then narrow — the field of potential input *X*s in the equation $Y = f(X)$.

To be successful, it is important to cast a big net, to start your improvement effort by capturing as many potential *X*s as possible. Then, you allow the Six Sigma tools — not your pre-judgment or your opinion — to naturally weed out the *X*s that are not critical and retain those that in fact are. That is one of the beauties of Six Sigma: Its formulaic application guides you to the solution of your improvement task.

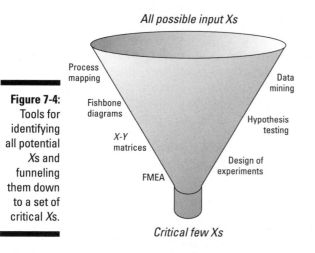

All possible input Xs

Figure 7-4:
Tools for identifying all potential Xs and funneling them down to a set of critical Xs.

Process mapping

Fishbone diagrams

X-Y matrices

FMEA

Data mining

Hypothesis testing

Design of experiments

Critical few Xs

Mining Data for Insight

Data mining is just what its name implies — it is the labor of digging and sorting through data for clues to where the improvement gems may lie. Sometimes you have to go through a lot of dirt to find the gems. Searching for clues in data is not much different.

Go with what you have: Observational studies

Where do you begin your search for improvement gems? And what are the tools of the trade? Six Sigma practitioners have refined the data mining process to an efficient, powerful set of tools.

Data, data everywhere

A world of potential data exists all around you:

✔ You fill the gasoline tank of your car up to a different amount two or three times a month.

✔ The number of reams of paper your company uses in its copy center varies from day to day.

✔ There are different numbers of students in each classroom.

✔ Different people work on a single process step depending on their daily assignment.

✔ The feed rate of a milling machine is adjusted depending on the task.

✔ The list goes on and on.

One way to immediately tap into this cache of information is to simply begin to observe all the potential input and output variables in your improvement project and record them.

Record the data surrounding your project in tabular form — with a column for each X or Y variable and a new row for each point of observation, as shown in Table 7-3.

Table 7-3	Observational Study Data Recording Template				
Obs. No.	Dept. (X_1)	Hour (X_2)	System (X_3)	Processor (X_4)	Items/ Hour (Y)
1	B	8	Web	Sally	43
2	A	5	Web	Sally	37
3	B	4	Web	Bob	44
4	B	8	Desktop	Sally	35
5	B	4	Web	Sally	42
6	A	5	Web	Sally	39
7	B	3	Mainframe	Sally	41
8	A	8	Mainframe	Joan	36
9	A	1	Web	Sally	39
10	B	4	Mainframe	Joan	40

The curious mind: Observational studies

Thinking about, pondering over, and probing your recorded observations is a proven path to increased understanding. In Six Sigma, these activities are called *observational studies*. Observational studies revolve around analyzing the variation in the observed critical output or outputs and investigating which input variables it is linked to. What you are looking for are potential sources of the variation.

Observational studies are different from planned experiments. In an observational study, you simply investigate the variation and data as it happens naturally — whatever the values may be. In an experiment, however, you actively control the variable values to see what the output will do under certain input condition. Experiments provide greater insight and resolution than observational studies do. (You find out about the design and execution of experiments in Chapter 9.) But sometimes, it is not possible or ethical to perform a more powerful experiment. For example, it wouldn't be right to purposely overcrowd a kindergarten classroom with 75 students to see what the effect on learning would be. Instead, education researchers gather naturally occurring data on classroom size, and then perform observational studies.

Usually the results of your observational study are a list of likely suspects. This narrowed list of variables is then investigated further for confirmation and for conclusive evidence using the techniques covered in Chapters 8 and 9. Sometimes, however, your observational study immediately reveals the real set of culprits. So always be on the lookout.

Digging in: Identifying potential sources of variation through graphical analysis

To study whether an observed input has an effect on an observed output, you create a set of box and whisker plots of the critical output — with each box and whisker plot corresponding to a different condition of the input variable (See Chapter 5 for an explanation of box and whisker plots.) Several computer programs — including Minitab, JPM, or Excel — automatically create these plots (see Chapter 11).

Looking at an example

For example, Table 7-3 is a partial list of the data collected for a transactional process. The key output (Y) is how many items per hour are produced. The "big net" of possible input variables includes the department performing the transaction (X_1), the hour of the day in which the transaction was processed (X_2), the processing system used (X_3), and the actual person performing the transaction (X_4). In this example, over 200 historical observations were collected.

What effect does the processor (X_4) have on the items per hour output (Y)? Figure 7-5 shows a set of box and whisker plots of Y for each condition of the X_4 input.

Again, does either Bob, Joan, or Sally have much influence on the items transacted per hour? From the graphical view in Figure 7-5, it is clear that the items transacted per hour is about the same for each operator — they have about the same average level and about the same amount of variation. This tells you that the processor variable (X_4) is not a key contributor to the output variation.

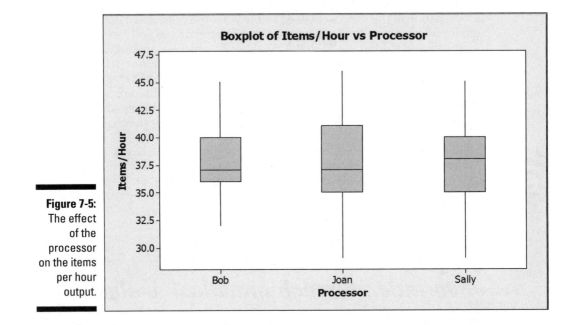

Figure 7-5:
The effect
of the
processor
on the items
per hour
output.

Statisticians using advanced techniques look at the data for Figure 7-5 and numerically compute the variation between the centers of variation for each of the different X_4 conditions and call this the *between group variation.* They then perform a similar calculation to quantify the average width of variation of all the conditions and call this the *within group variation.* If the between group variation is large compared to the within group variation, they conclude that the investigated variable does indeed influence the output. The graphical method outlined previously is just a simple, intuitive way to accomplish the same thing while bypassing all math and technicalities.

Returning to the example, what about the department performing the transaction (X_3)? Does it contribute to the output? Figure 7-6 is another box and whisker plot of the output versus the department doing the transaction.

Graphically, you can quickly see that the difference between the centers of variation from department A and department B is significant compared to the average width of variation within the departments. This tells you that whichever department performs the transaction does have some influence on the output. This variable will pass through your funnel and be investigated further for conclusive evidence.

Another way to perform observational studies is through correlation calculations (covered in Chapter 8). These give you the same insight, but are not graphical, so they're harder to use and interpret.

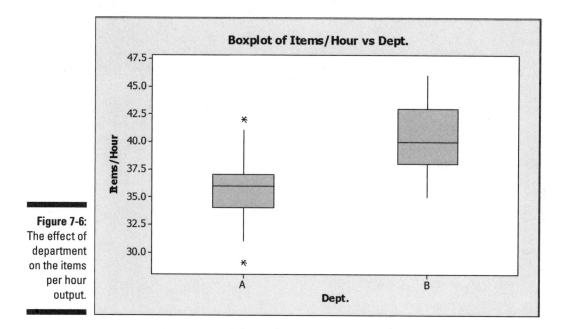

Figure 7-6:
The effect of department on the items per hour output.

Considering additional studies

There are many other tools at your disposal when performing observational studies, including:

✔ **Multi-variable studies:** *Multi-vari* studies, as the name is often shortened, allow you to investigate the effect of several input variables at a time on a critical output.

✔ **Main effects plots:** *Main effects plots* are introduced as a basic graphical technique in Chapter 5. They are an extremely easy and powerful way to explore the principle effect of a variable and its different levels on a critical output.

✔ **Interaction effects plots:** Sometimes, one variable by itself doesn't have a major impact on an output. But when you combine it with other variables, it has a significant influence. This is called an *interaction effect.* For example, adding eggs by themselves to a cake batter doesn't immediately impact the cake's texture. But adding eggs *together* with oven heat to the batter produces a yummy dessert.

Each of these additional observational studies is available in most off-the-shelf Six Sigma software packages (see Chapter 11). This makes it much easier today to perform these analyses automatically, giving you a big advantage over your predecessors.

Chapter 8

Quantifying the Critical Few

. . . .

In This Chapter

▶ Sampling distributions and the central limit theorem

▶ Establishing confidence intervals for means, variances, and proportions

▶ Understanding correlation and curves

▶ Fitting curves

. . . .

Several chapters of this book show you how to identify the potential variables that influence a critical outcome. Process mapping, fishbone diagrams, brainstorming, SIPOC diagrams, and failure mode effects analysis are only some of the tools that help you identify Xs (inputs) that are influencing the critical Y or Ys (output). You may even have a very healthy collection of potential Xs for your improvement project.

Now it is time to begin to prune, to begin to weed out the identified input variables that are not worth carrying along. Your resources are limited, so setting aside insignificant or trivial variables that don't allow you the greatest leverage helps you focus and get to the results of your improvement sooner. In this chapter, you discover how to separate and quantify the critical few variables from the trivial many.

Finding the Best Partner

Six Sigma demands that you use data to make better decisions. So how is it that you go about using data to accomplish this? At the heart of the matter is the ability to distinguish between real and claimed differences. Are Chevy trucks really better than Fords? Are last year's sales figures no different than this year's? Six Sigma gives you tools to quantify the real differences between factors and to investigate your confidence in these measurements.

Viva Las Vegas: The central limit theorem

Imagine flipping a coin ten times and counting the number of heads that you get. The laws of probability say that there's a 50-50 chance of getting heads on any single toss. So if you toss the coin ten times, you'd expect to get five heads, right?

Go ahead and pull a coin out of your pocket and try this if you'd like. You may not get the expected five heads after flipping the coin ten times. You may only get three heads. Or maybe you get six. If you keep repeating the ten-flip experiment over and over again, the distribution of the number of heads that you get in each set of ten flips will look something like Figure 8-1. After each experiment repetition, the number of heads out of the ten flips was counted. The experiment was repeated 10, then 100, and finally 1,000 times.

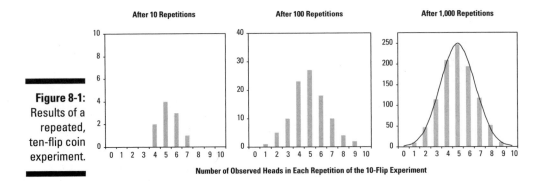

Figure 8-1: Results of a repeated, ten-flip coin experiment.

This imaginary coin flip experiment is analogous to any other measurement or sampling event that is repeated more than once — like taking a sample of measurements from a process and calculating the average. Two important facts arise from Figure 8-1 that can be generalized to any measurement situation:

 ✔ **Repetitions of the measurement event produce different outcome results (variability).** Like in the coin-flipping experiment, not every repetition of the ten-flip series produced the expected five heads. The same is true if you repeatedly take a five-point average of the thickness of paper coming out of a paper mill.

 ✔ **This resulting measurement, or *sampling distribution,* is normally distributed.** The variation is also centered on the expected outcome. And the more repetitions you make, the closer and closer the sampling variation gets to a perfectly normal distribution.

Statisticians call repeated measurements of a characteristic or a process *samples*. So the variation that occurs in repeated sampling events they call its sampling distribution.

Statisticians have refined and honed technical definitions of what is called the *central limit theorem*. Although each definition is equally mysterious, they all say the same thing: When you repeatedly calculate statistics (like the average of a sample) for a process or characteristic, the repeated sample statistics have variation themselves. This sampling variation follows a normal distribution centered on the variation of the process or characteristic itself. Further, the width of the sampling distribution depends on how many measurements you take.

Although statisticians have a difficult time explaining the central limit theorem (and perhaps we authors do, too!), its power and utility are nevertheless remarkable. The results of the central limit theorem allow you to predict the bounds of the future and to quantify the risks of the past.

How sure are you? Confidence intervals

Confidence intervals use the central limit theorem to tell you how much confidence you can place in any of your measurements or statistical conclusions.

Do not confuse confidence in your measurements, the topic of this chapter, with measurement system capability, the topic of Chapter 7. The measurement confidence we talk about here does not address the capability of your system for acquiring measurements. Instead, measurement confidence assumes you have a perfect, ideal system for acquiring your measurements. This should serve as another reminder to you of how important it is to validate the capability of your measurement system.

For example, say your factory has just produced 5,000 ballpoint pens. You want to know the average diameter of this population. (*Population* is a term that means any full set of something, like all the people in your hometown, or all the pens you've produced, or all the invoices sent out over the last year. A *sample*, on the other hand, is any subset of a population.) To determine the average pen diameter, you randomly select 30 pens from the population and measure each of their diameters and calculate the average to be 0.120 inches (see Chapter 5 for details of calculating averages).

Rushing into your office your boss asks, "What's the average diameter of our latest pens? Our customer just called and said they will reject the whole batch if the average is higher than 0.125 inches!" Your sweaty boss waits for your response. What do you say? How confident are you in your calculated average?

The central limit theorem says that if you went out and repeated your 30-sample measurement, you'd get a slightly different average. When your customer measures a sample of the delivered pens, they will, too. But how different will each calculation of the average be?

Confidence intervals, the subject of this chapter, give you a way of quantifying how much variation there will be in repeated measurements and statistical calculations. Knowing how to create confidence intervals, you'll be able to respond to your boss, "With 99.7 percent certainty, our average pen diameter will be within our customer's requirement."

Confidence intervals for means

You see averages every day. Very few of them are communicated with a confidence interval.

How big is it

When your sample size has more than 30 data points, the confidence around your calculated sample average $\bar{x}$ can be calculated as

$$\bar{x} \pm Z \frac{\sigma}{\sqrt{n}}$$

Where

- Z is the sigma value corresponding to the desired level of confidence you want to have
- σ is the calculated standard deviation from your sample
- n is the number of data points in your sample.

Figure 8-2 illustrates what this confidence interval is for $\bar{x}$.

From Figure 8-2, you can see that most sample calculations will be close to the real population average. In fact, 68 percent of calculated $\bar{x}$'s will be within

$$\pm \frac{\sigma}{\sqrt{n}}$$

of the real population average. Further, 95 percent of calculated $\bar{x}$'s will be within

$$\pm 2 \frac{\sigma}{\sqrt{n}}$$

of the real population average. And 99.7 percent of calculated $\bar{x}$'s will be within

$$\pm 3 \frac{\sigma}{\sqrt{n}}$$

of the real population average.

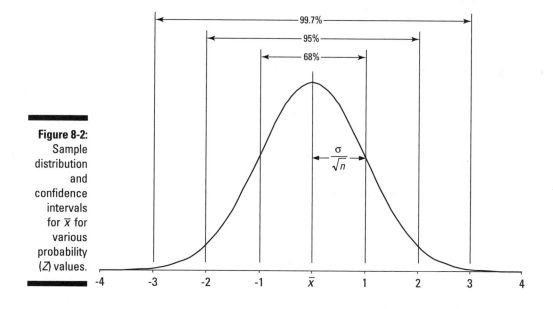

Figure 8-2:
Sample
distribution
and
confidence
intervals
for $\bar{x}$ for
various
probability
(*Z*) values.

This formula works any time you have more than 30 measurements in your sample.

Any time you calculate a confidence interval, there is also an associated risk of being incorrect. This risk is simply the compliment of the calculated confidence. So for a 95 percent confidence interval, there is also a 5 percent risk of the actual population average being outside your calculated confidence interval.

The risk of incorrectly concluding that the population average is within your calculated confidence interval when, in reality, it is not, is called *alpha (α) risk.*

When you have only a few data points in your sample, you're not able to get an accurate estimate of the population standard deviation σ. When your sample has anywhere from two to 30 data points, you have to use a different factor instead of *Z*. Statisticians call this new factor for small samples *t. t* is more conservative, because your smaller sample size lessens the accuracy of your calculated value for σ. In fact, for each desired confidence level, *t* is adjusted depending on how many data points are in your sample. Table 8-1 provides values for *t* for selected confidence percentages and sample sizes.

Table 8-1			*t* Values		
Confidence	*n=2*	*n=5*	*n=10*	*n=25*	*Z*
68%	1.837	1.142	1.059	1.021	1
95%	13.968	2.869	2.320	2.110	2
99.7%	235.811	6.620	4.094	3.345	3

Using *t,* the formula for the confidence interval becomes

$$\bar{x} \pm t \frac{\sigma}{\sqrt{n}}$$

Where the value for *t* depends on your desired level of confidence and the number of data points in your sample.

Which is better?

Very often, you need to determine whether two or more items are different and, if so, by how much. Examples include:

✔ Is there a difference between operators of a process?

✔ Do two alternative manufacturing processes lead to significantly different outputs?

✔ Is the gas mileage of Car A better than Cars B and C?

✔ Are the marketing collateral materials with color graphics really better at generating leads than black and white equivalents?

Confidence intervals for sample averages ($\bar{x}$'s) can be used to verify differences between any two or more versions of the same outcome. Here is the process for doing this:

1. **Take samples and perform measurements of each of the different versions or conditions you are analyzing.**

2. **Calculate the appropriate confidence interval for each different version or condition of the characteristic.**

   Remember, if your sample has less than 30 data points, you need to use the *t* formula to calculate the confidence interval. Also remember to use the same confidence level for each condition or version you are comparing.

3. **Graphically or numerically determine if there is any overlap of the confidence intervals of the different versions or conditions.**

   If there is overlap between any of the confidence intervals, you can say with the decided level of confidence that there is no difference between the overlapping versions.

   On the other hand, if there is no overlap, you can know right away that there is a difference between the different versions of the output.

As an example, Figure 8-3 shows a graphical comparison of the confidence intervals for three different types of computer systems used in an invoicing process.

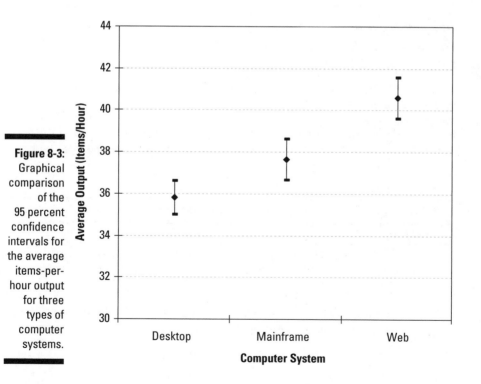

Figure 8-3: Graphical comparison of the 95 percent confidence intervals for the average items-per-hour output for three types of computer systems.

Graphically comparing the confidence intervals for the average performance makes it easy to see that there is no overlap in the intervals. So, with 95 percent confidence, you can say that the "Web" computer system is better than the "mainframe" computer system (better on average by 3 items per hour) and that the "Web" computer system is better than the "desktop" computer system (better on average by almost 5 items per hour.) If there had been an overlap between any of the three computer system options, you would have concluded (with 95 percent confidence) that there was no significant difference between the overlapping versions.

Confidence intervals for standard deviations

Not surprisingly, your calculations of the standard deviation σ of a process or characteristic have sampling variability in them, just like your calculations of the mean do. That means that confidence intervals can be created for standard deviations, too.

How much variation is there?

To construct a confidence interval around your calculated standard deviation, you have to use a new factor invented by statisticians called χ^2. (This factor is named after the 22nd letter of the Greek alphabet χ and is pronounced kye-squared.) Like the t value used to create confidence intervals for averages, the value of χ^2 depends on how many data points are in your sample — the more data points in your sample, the more confident your estimate. Another twist is that there are different values of χ^2 for the lower and upper limits of the confidence interval. Table 8-2 shows upper and lower values of χ^2 for common 1-, 2-, and 3-sigma confidence values.

Table 8-2			χ^2 Values		
Confidence	**n=2**	**n=5**	**n=10**	**n=25**	**Z**
68%	1.987	6.599	13.088	30.833	1
	0.040	1.416	4.919	17.169	
95%	5.187	11.365	19.301	39.749	2
	0.001	0.460	2.628	12.225	

Confidence	n=2	n=5	n=10	n=25	Z
99.7%	10.273	17.800	27.093	50.163	3
	0.000	0.106	1.241	8.382	

Note: First value listed in each table cell is χ^2_{LOWER}. Second value listed in each cell is χ^2_{UPPER}.

The χ^2 values from Table 8-2 are used together with the formula below to calculate the confidence interval for a measured standard deviation.

$$\left[\sqrt{\frac{(n-1)\sigma^2}{\chi^2_{LOWER}}}, \sqrt{\frac{(n-1)\sigma^2}{\chi^2_{UPPER}}} \right]$$

As an example, suppose your sample of five data points leads to a standard deviation of 3.7. To create a 95 percent confidence interval for this standard deviation, you use the values in Table 8-2 corresponding to a 95 percent confidence and $n = 5$. So $\chi^2_{LOWER} = 11.365$ and $\chi^2_{UPPER} = 0.460$. Plugging these values into the equation, you get

$$\left[\sqrt{\frac{(5-1)3.7^2}{11.365}}, \sqrt{\frac{(5-1)3.7^2}{0.460}} \right] \text{ or } [2.195, 10.907]$$

Another way to say this is that, with 95 percent confidence you know that the real standard deviation lies somewhere between 2.195 and 10.907.

Confidence intervals for standard deviations are usually very wide unless you have a lot of data points in your sample. This is because an estimate of the standard deviation is always less accurate than an estimate of the average.

Which has less variation?

Sometimes, you need to compare the variability of two distributions to find out whether one distribution has more variation than the other. You do this by creating a confidence interval for the ratio of the variances of the two distributions. If the ratio confidence interval includes the value 1 within its limits, you know that the two distributions have equal variability. If, on the other hand, the confidence interval doesn't contain the value of 1 within its limits, you know that the two distributions have different amounts of variation.

Constructing a confidence interval around this ratio of variances requires yet another statistical factor. This one is called F by statisticians. Its value depends on three things: the desired level of confidence, the number of data points in the numerator distribution (n_1), and the number of data points in the denominator distribution (n_2). Table 8-3 is a list of F values for 95 percent confidence intervals and various sample sizes.

Table 8-3	F Values for 95% Confidence			
	$n_1 = 2$	$n_1 = 5$	$n_1 = 10$	$n_1 = 25$
$n_2 = 2$	161.446	224.583	240.543	249.052
$n_2 = 5$	7.709	6.388	5.999	5.774
$n_2 = 10$	5.117	3.633	3.179	2.900
$n_2 = 25$	4.260	2.776	2.300	1.984

The F values from Table 8-3 are used together with the formula below to calculate the confidence interval for a ratio of variances:

$$\left[\frac{1}{F(n_2, n_1)} \frac{\sigma_1^2}{\sigma_2^2}, F(n_1, n_2) \frac{\sigma_1^2}{\sigma_2^2} \right]$$

As an example, suppose you have ten data points from distribution A and their variance $\sigma_A^2 = 4$. Another distribution, called B, has five points and its variance $\sigma_B^2 = 7.5$. The 95 percent confidence interval for the ratio of σ_A^2 to σ_B^2 is calculated as:

$$\left[\frac{1}{F(5, 10)} \frac{\sigma_A^2}{\sigma_B^2}, F(10, 5) \frac{\sigma_A^2}{\sigma_B^2} \right] = \left[\frac{1}{3.633} \frac{4.0}{7.5}, 5.999 \frac{4.0}{7.5} \right] = [0.147, 3.199]$$

This confidence interval contains the value of 1 within its limits, so all you can say with 95 percent confidence is that there is no evidence that the distributions have different variances.

Confidence intervals for variance ratios are usually very wide unless you have a lot of data points in your sample. This is because an estimate of the standard deviation is always less accurate than an estimate of the average.

Four out of five recommend: Confidence intervals for proportions

When you calculate the number of successes out of a certain number of attempts — like "four out of five dentists recommend sugarless gum" — you can write this proportion mathematically as

$$\frac{y}{n}$$

where y is the number of successes and n is the total number of attempts or trials.

Calculating a proportion creates yet another sampling distribution. The resulting confidence interval around a calculated proportion is:

$$\frac{y}{n} \pm Z \sqrt{\frac{(y/n)(1 - y/n)}{n}}$$

So, as an example, if you wanted to be 90 percent sure of the calculated proportion for the four out of five dentists, you would calculate the confidence interval in this way:

$$\frac{4}{5} \pm 1.645 \sqrt{\frac{(4/5)(1 - 4/5)}{5}} = \frac{4}{5} \pm 0.294$$

This means that, with 90 percent confidence, the proportion of four out of five dentists really could be as small as one-half or as large as one.

In reality, proportions can never be less than zero or greater than one. So if your confidence interval for your proportion exceeds these natural limits, just adjust the confidence interval to the natural limit.

If you are comparing the *difference* between two proportions

$$\frac{y_1}{n_1} \text{ and } \frac{y_2}{n_2}$$

the confidence interval for this difference becomes

$$\frac{y_1}{n_1} - \frac{y_2}{n_2} \pm Z \sqrt{\frac{(y_1/n_1)(1 - y_1/n_1)}{n_1} + \frac{(y_2/n_2)(1 - y_2/n_2)}{n_2}}$$

To illustrate this confidence interval, imagine you are part of a company with two production lines. You suspect that your Toledo plant produces a higher proportion of good items (yield) than your Buffalo plant. You select samples of size $n_1 = n_2 = 300$ from each plant and find that the number of good items from the Toledo plant (y_1) is 213 while the number from the Buffalo plant (y_2) is 189. That means that a 95 percent confidence interval for the difference between the Toledo and the Buffalo yields is

$$\frac{213}{300} - \frac{189}{300} \pm 2 \sqrt{\frac{(213/300)(1 - 213/300)}{300} + \frac{(189/300)(1 - 189/300)}{300}} = 0.08 \pm 0.076$$

or, equivalently [0.004, 0.156]. Because this confidence interval does not include zero, you can conclude — with 95 percent confidence — that the Toledo plant produces, on average, a higher proportion of good items than the Buffalo plant.

Table 8-4	Confidence Interval Summary	
Name	**Equation**	**Look-Up Factor**
Average with large (> 30) sample size	$\bar{x} \pm Z \dfrac{\sigma}{\sqrt{n}}$	Z
Average with small (< 30) sample size	$\bar{x} \pm t \dfrac{\sigma}{\sqrt{n}}$	t
Standard deviation	$\left[\sqrt{\dfrac{(n-1)\sigma^2}{\chi^2_{LOWER}}}, \sqrt{\dfrac{(n-1)\sigma^2}{\chi^2_{UPPER}}} \right]$	χ^2
Ratio of variances	$\left[\dfrac{1}{F(n_2, n_1)} \dfrac{\sigma_1^2}{\sigma_2^2}, F(n_1, n_2) \dfrac{\sigma_1^2}{\sigma_2^2} \right]$	F
Proportion	$\dfrac{y}{n} \pm Z \sqrt{\dfrac{(y/n)(1-y/n)}{n}}$	Z
Difference of proportions	$\dfrac{y_1}{n_1} - \dfrac{y_2}{n_2} \pm Z \sqrt{\dfrac{(y_1/n_1)(1-y_1/n_1)}{n_1}}$ $+ \sqrt{\dfrac{(y_2/n_2)(1-y_2/n_2)}{n_2}}$	Z

Understanding Relationships

Y is a function of X. To get to the next level of understanding, you need to be able to quantify the relationships between the input variables and the critical outputs.

Correlation

Scatter plots (explained in Chapter 5) are a great way to visually discover and explore relationships between variables — both between Ys and Xs and between Xs and Xs. In a scatter plot, you graph the values of one variable against paired values of another variable. As an example, Table 8-5 is a list of paired data for the curb weight (lbs.) of some common automobiles and their corresponding fuel economy (mpg).

Table 8-5	Automobile Curb Weight versus Fuel Economy	
Make/Model	*Curb Weight (lbs.)*	*Fuel Economy (mpg)*
Toyota Camry	3,140	29
Toyota Sequoia	4,875	17
Honda Civic	2,449	35
Land Rover Discovery	4,742	16
Mercedes-Benz S500	4,170	20
VW Jetta Wagon	3,078	27
Chrysler 300	3,715	22
Chevrolet Venture	3,838	23
Hyundai Tiburon	2,940	27
Dodge Ram 2500 Quad	6,039	11

A data point for each automobile in the study is plotted in Figure 8-4.

The scatter plot in Figure 8-4 shows that there is a negative relationship between the curb weight of the vehicle and its fuel economy — the heavier the car, the lower its fuel economy. The scatter plot also shows that the relationship between the two variables is approximately linear, meaning that its shape approximately follows a straight line. Finally, the relationship between the variables is fairly strong, as evidenced by the tight clustering of the plotted data points around the drawn line approximating the relationship.

But how do you quantify this relationship? How do you put numbers to it? Correlation offers such a measure. It tells you how closely the relationship between the two variables follows a linear pattern.

Correlation tells you only how linear the relationship between the variables is. There is a chance it will miss more complicated relationships where the variables follow a non-linear pattern. Always include a graphical scatter plot when doing a correlation analysis. That way you can visually check to make sure the variable relationship really is linear.

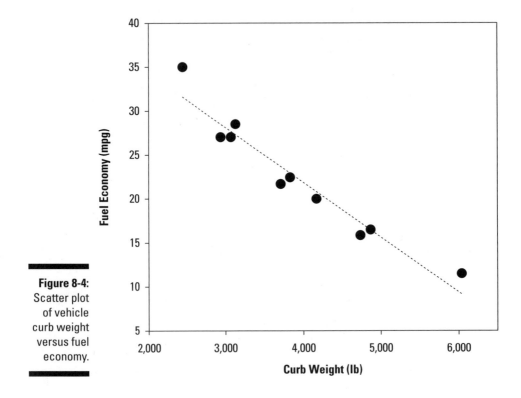

Figure 8-4:
Scatter plot
of vehicle
curb weight
versus fuel
economy.

To quantify how linear the relationship is between two variables, you use the following formula to calculate the *correlation coefficient (r):*

$$r = \frac{1}{n-1} \sum_{i=1}^{n} \left(\frac{x_i - \overline{x}}{\sigma_x} \right) \left(\frac{y_i - \overline{y}}{\sigma_y} \right)$$

where n is the number of data pairs,

x_i and y_i are the individual x-variable and y-variable measurements,

$\overline{x}$ and $\overline{y}$ are the averages of the X and Y measurements, respectively,

σ_X and σ_Y are the standard deviations of the X and Y measurements, respectively, and

Σ is a capital Greek letter telling you to add up all the $\left(\frac{x_i - \overline{x}}{\sigma_x} \right) \left(\frac{y_i - \overline{y}}{\sigma_y} \right)$ terms, from 1 to n.

The calculated correlation coefficient will always be between –1 and 1.

✔ The sign of r tells you the direction of the relationship between the variables.

If r is greater than zero (positive), that means that the variable relationship is *positive;* if the value of one variable is increased, the other variable also increases.

If r is less than zero (negative), the variable relationship is *negative;* if the value of one variable is increased, the value of the other variable decreases, and vice versa.

✔ The absolute value of *r* tells you how strong the relationship is.

The closer *r* gets to −1 or 1, the *stronger* the variable relationship is.

An *r* equal to 1 or −1 indicates a perfect linear relationship, with all points being exactly on the line.

An *r* close to 0 indicates that there is an absence of a linear fit to the data.

For the automobile fuel economy example introduced earlier, the calculated correlation coefficient *r* then is

$$r = \frac{1}{10-1}\sum_{i=1}^{10}\left(\frac{x_i - 3{,}899}{1{,}087}\right)\left(\frac{y_i - 23}{7}\right) = \frac{1}{9}(-8.738) = -0.971$$

An *r* of −0.971 verifies that the relationship between the two variables is indeed linear and is negative. Also, an *r* of magnitude −0.971 is very close to -1, telling you that the relationship is very strong.

Correlation basically just confirms that there is a linear relationship between two variables and it quantifies how linear that relationship is. What correlation does *not* tell you is how much a given change in one variable will change a related variable. To get that kind of information, you need to become acquainted with some predictive tools.

Even though two variables are correlated, it does not mean that one *causes* the other. For example, studies show that a person's reading comprehension ability (*Y*) is correlated with their height (*X*). Does this mean that height *causes* reading comprehension? Think about it for a second. Young children have not yet developed cognition and reading skills. In the teenage years, physical growth continues along with maturation of mental and reading abilities. By the time you're a full-grown adult, your brain and mental abilities have fully developed. Clearly, a person's height does not *cause* his or her reading ability. Rather, height is an indirect indicator of overall maturation and growth, including cognitive abilities. So be very careful: Don't assume there is a causal link when there is correlation.

Curve fitting

A step beyond correlation is curve fitting. In curve fitting, you actually determine the equation for the curve that best fits your data. Armed with this information, you know quantitatively what effect one variable has on another. You also know which variables are significant influencers and which ones are just in the noise. Finally, you know how much of the system behavior your equation does *not* explain.

In some rare cases, the exact details of the $Y = f(X)$ equation relating the Xs to the Y is known without having to do any curve fitting — either from a very mature understanding of the physics of the process or system, or from some other source of knowledge. These situations are called *deterministic* because you know with certainty that setting the input Xs to certain values will always lead to the exact same value for the output Y, even when the process is repeated.

For the vast majority of cases, however, the exact relationship between the Xs and the Y or Ys is *not* known. This is due to the complexity of the system and the human inability to address all the factors that truly exert influence on the output. Because of this natural limitation, repetitions of the system with the same input values will not always produce the same output performance. These situations are called *statistical*.

The goal of curve fitting is to develop an approximate equation that describes the system or process statistical behavior as much as possible. When you work to create an approximate equation for a system that has a single output Y and a single input X, this type of curve fitting is called *simple linear regression*. When you work to create an equation that includes more than one variable it is called *multiple linear regression*.

Finding the line: Simple linear regression

In simple linear regression, you assume that each observed output point Y_i can be described by a two-part equation:

$$Y = \beta_0 + \beta_i X + \varepsilon$$

The first part of this equation is $\beta_0 + \beta_1 X$. The second part is ε. Graphically, the decomposition of this equation is shown in Figure 8-5.

Time warping back to your high school algebra days, you may recall that the $\beta_0 + \beta_1 X$ part of the equation for Y is just an equation for a straight line: β_0 by itself tells you at what value the fitted line crosses the Y axis; and β_1 tells you the line's slope. The ε part of the equation is a normal, random distribution with a center value equal to zero.

In simple linear regression, you mathematically determine values for β_0 and β_1 so that the resulting line fits your observed $X - Y$ data as closely as possible with the minimum amount of error. Then you determine how wide the ε portion needs to be so that it accounts for all the extra Y variation that isn't already captured by the line.

You calculate β_0 and β_1 from the equations:

$$\beta_1 = \frac{\sum (x_i - \overline{x})\, y_i}{\sum (x_i - \overline{x})^2}$$

where x_i and y_i are the paired data points and $\overline{x}$ and $\overline{y}$ are the calculated averages for all the X points and all the Y points, respectively.

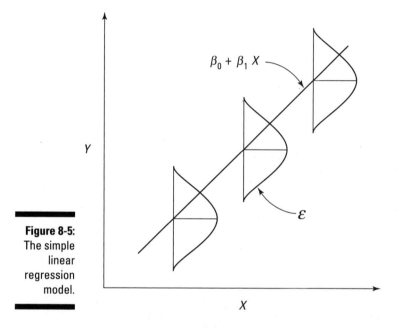

Figure 8-5:
The simple
linear
regression
model.

Going back to the previous automobile weight versus fuel economy example, the calculated value for β_1 turns out to be –0.00624, and β_0 comes out to be 46.9. So the equation for the line that best fits the data is

$$\hat{Y} = 47.3 - 0.00632X$$

where the Y with the pointed hat "^" over it, $\hat{Y}$, represents the estimate or prediction for Y, not an actual observed value for Y. You are now armed with a powerful, predictive tool. If, say, you found that a car you were interested in had a curb weight of 5,000 pounds, you can plug that X value right into your equation to predict its fuel economy:

$$\hat{Y} = 47.3 - 0.00632(5,000) = 15.7\, \text{mpg}$$

All without ever test driving the car!

There are a couple of points of caution you need to be aware of in using your new-found Six Sigma powers:

✔ **Be careful not to extend your predictions very far beyond the range of the data in your study.** For example, you don't want to use your equation to predict the fuel economy of a vehicle weighing 25,000 pounds, like a locomotive. Vehicles in this weight class are so much heavier than the automobiles of the study that they use very different mechanisms and technology and don't fit the line.

The general rule is not to extrapolate any predictions beyond the range of your study data.

✔ **Remember that the derived equation for the line is missing the ε component.** The line predicts only the expected *average* performance. In reality, the actual performance level varies from the predicted value. This is the effect of the ε component. For some situations, this random variation component dominates, leaving little room for effective predictions. In other cases, your derived line equation gets you very close to actual, real-world values.

Your next step is to understand and quantify the ε component of your regression equation.

If the shoe fits, wear it: Residuals and adequacy of the fitted model

For each of the *i* data points in your study, you can calculate an error term e_i — how far off the predictive equation line is from the observed data. For example, referring to Table 8-5, the data for the Toyota Camry shows that its curb weight is 3,140 pounds and its fuel economy is 29 mpg. But plugging an *X* value of 3,140 pounds into the derived regression equation, you get a predicted fuel economy of

$$\hat{Y} = 47.3 - 0.00632(3,140) = 27.49\,\text{mpg}$$

The difference between the observed and the predicted fuel economy is

$$e_1 = Y_1 - \hat{Y}_1 = 29 - 27.49 = 1.51\,\text{mpg}$$

Similar error e_i terms can be calculated for each of the nine other data points in your regression study. These e_i terms are called *residuals* — or what's left over after using the predictive equation.

The beginning assumption of the predictive linear equation is that there is a secondary ε part of the equation that is a normal, random distribution with a center value equal to zero. This variation is manifest in the residuals and is the bell-shaped variation identified back in Figure 8-5.

The most efficient way to check the validity of your predictive linear equation is to graphically review the residuals to make sure they are behaving as you've assumed. You may need to create up to four different types of graphical checks of the residuals.

- A scatter plot of the residuals e_i versus the predicted $\hat{Y}$ values from the derived equation.
- A scatter plot of the residuals e_i versus the observed X data.
- Additional scatter plots of the residuals e_i versus any other X variables that you didn't include in your equation.
- A run chart of the residuals e_i versus the previous residuals e_{i-1} if you collected your study data sequentially over time.

In each of these graphical residual checks you are looking for:

- The variation has no obvious patterns and is truly random, like a cloud of scattered dots.
- The residual variation is centered around the value of zero.

Figures 8-6, 8-7, and 8-8 are examples of residual-checking plots for the previous automobile weight-fuel economy study.

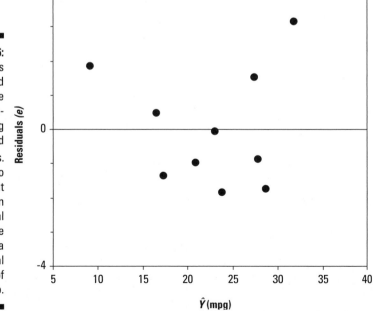

Figure 8-6: Residuals plotted versus the corresponding predicted $\hat{Y}$ values. Review to verify that the variation is normal over time with a central value of zero.

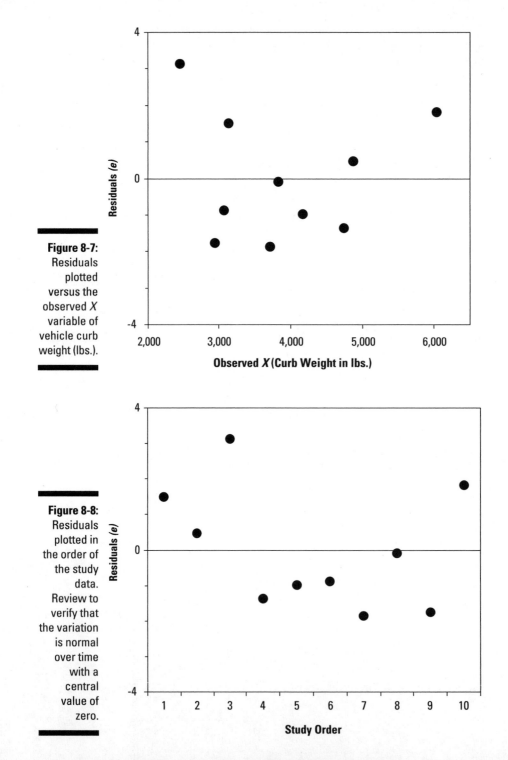

Figure 8-7:
Residuals plotted versus the observed *X* variable of vehicle curb weight (lbs.).

Figure 8-8:
Residuals plotted in the order of the study data. Review to verify that the variation is normal over time with a central value of zero.

Figures 8-6, 8-7, and 8-8 appear valid. In each case, the residuals show evidence of being truly random, normal, and centered over time around zero. You can now conclude that your derived linear predictive equation is valid.

What do residual plots look like when you have data that is not valid? Figure 8-9 shows two examples of an inappropriate simple linear regression model. In (a), the variation of the residuals is not centered on zero. Instead it shows a curved pattern. In (b), the residual variation is not consistent — lower values of variable X produce larger residual variation then higher values of variable X.

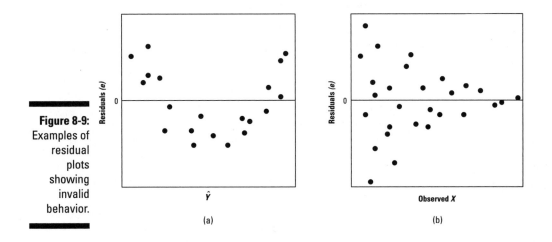

Figure 8-9: Examples of residual plots showing invalid behavior.

(a)   (b)

There is another way to investigate how good your derived regression model is. It involves looking at the variation of the output variable Y. This new assessment is done on a squared error basis.

The total sum of the squared error (*SSTO*) in the output variable Y can be written as

$$SSTO = \sum_{i=1}^{n}\left(Y_i - \overline{Y}\right)^2$$

where Y_i are the n observed output values.

In a similar way, the squared error from just the derived regression equation (SSR) can be stated as

$$SSR = \sum_{i=1}^{n}\left(\hat{Y}_i - \overline{Y}\right)^2$$

where $\hat{Y}_i$ are the predicted estimates for the n data points.

Finally, the squared error from the remaining ε variation (SSE) can be expressed as

$$SSE = \sum_{i=1}^{n} e_i^2 = \sum_{i=1}^{n} \left(Y_i - \hat{Y}_i \right)^2$$

Together, these three squared error terms can be related with the simple sum

$$SSTO = SSR + SSE$$

You can do three important tests using these squared error terms.

1. **Calculate the *coefficient of determination, R^2*, for your predictive model.**

   The coefficient of determination is simply the ratio of the squared regression error (SSR) and the total squared error ($SSTO$), like this

   $$R^2 = \frac{SSR}{SSTO}$$

   What R^2 tells you is how much of the total observed variation is determined or explained by your linear model. You want this number to be 80 percent or higher. This means that the unexplained variation ε accounts for the remaining 20 percent or less.

   With a high R^2 value, you can know that your predictions will be close — and not dominated by the unexplained variation.

   For the automobile curb weight versus fuel economy study introduced earlier in this chapter, the R^2 value is

   $$R^2 = \frac{424.2}{450.1} = 0.94$$

   This is very good. Ninety-four percent of the observed variation is explained by your derived linear model. That leaves only six percent that is unexplained and left to random chance.

2. **Quantify the unexplained ε variation in terms of its standard deviation.**

   Remember that ε represents a random, normal distribution centered at a value of zero. This value is an inherent part of your predictive linear equation. But how big is its variation?

   An estimate of the standard deviation of the ε distribution can be calculated using the surprisingly simple equation

   $$\hat{\sigma}_\varepsilon = \sqrt{\frac{SSE}{n-2}}$$

   This estimate comes in handy when you want to mimic what may happen in reality. You use your derived linear model to predict the average or expected performance of the output $\hat{Y}$, and then add to it a random number generated from the ε distribution — with mean of zero and standard deviation equal to $\hat{\sigma}_\varepsilon$. In this way, you can simulate what would happen if your process or characteristic were repeated over and over again.

For the automobile curb weight versus fuel economy study, you can estimate the standard deviation of the unexplained variation as

$$\hat{\sigma}_\varepsilon = \sqrt{\frac{25.9}{10-2}} = 1.80 \, \text{mpg}$$

3. **Perform an *F* test to quantify your confidence in the validity of your regression model.**

   Another test of validity for your derived linear equation is to statistically compare the variation explained by your regression model to the unexplained variation.

   Yet another way to mathematically represent the variation in the regression model is by an estimate of its variance

   $$\hat{\sigma}^2_{REG} = SSR$$

   You also already know — from Step 2 — that

   $$\hat{\sigma}^2_\varepsilon = \frac{SSE}{n-2}$$

   Creating a ratio of $\hat{\sigma}^2_{REG}$ to $\hat{\sigma}^2_\varepsilon$ is just like the confidence intervals covered in the "Which has less variation?" section earlier in this chapter for comparing the size of two different distributions. So if

   $$\frac{\hat{\sigma}^2_{REG}}{\hat{\sigma}^2_\varepsilon} \geq F(2, n-1)$$

   you can say with 95 percent or 99 percent confidence — whichever level of confidence you select — that your derived predictive model is, in fact, valid.

   For the automobile curb weight versus fuel economy study, if you want to be 99 percent confident with your $n = 10$ data points, the F test of the variances becomes

   $$\frac{424.2}{25.9} = 16.4 \geq 11.259 = F(2, 9)$$

   Because the calculated ratio value of 16.4 is greater than the critical 99 percent F value, you can conclude with 99 confidence that there is something to your derived model.

Tools for fitting lines

Simple linear regression is becoming a commonplace activity. Anyone with Microsoft Excel, for example, can take data from an X and a Y variable and almost immediately create a scatter plot of the two. Then, with just a couple of clicks, the program will automatically derive the fitted line for your data.

If you have Excel, try this on the automobile weight versus fuel economy study introduced in this chapter.

1. **Enter the data from Table 8-5 into Excel as two columns of data — one for the curb weight (X) data and another for the fuel economy (Y) data.**

2. **Select the entered data in the spreadsheet and create what Excel calls an XY (scatter) plot.**

3. **Right click on the plotted data in the graph and select Add Trendline from the menu that pops up. Select the Linear option and click OK.**

   The best fit line with the right β_0 and β_1 parameters is automatically added to your graph!

4. **If you double-click on this fitted line, you are given options to display the equation for the line and also to display the coefficient of determination R^2, if you'd like.**

   The results of these display options are shown in Figure 8-10.

Minitab, JMP, and other statistical analysis software tools provide tremendous detail and options and make simple linear regression almost fun!

Figure 8-10:
A simple linear regression model automatically fitted by Microsoft Excel. Notice that you can also choose to display the equation and the calculated R^2 value.

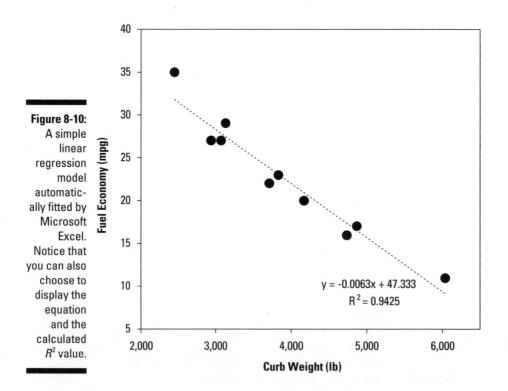

$y = -0.0063x + 47.333$

$R^2 = 0.9425$

Fancy curve fitting: Multiple linear regression

You now understand how to generate and validate a predictive model linking a single X to a Y. But what about all the situations where there is more than one X influencing a Y? Surely there must be many more situations like this than there are with just a single influencing variable.

When you generate a $Y = f(X)$ equation with multiple Xs, like

$$Y = f(X_1, X_2, \ldots, X_n),$$

it is called multiple linear regression.

The general form of the multiple linear regression model is simply an extension of the simple linear regression model. For example, if you have a system where *X1* and *X2* both contribute to *Y,* the multiple linear regression model becomes

$$Y_i = \beta_0 + \beta_1 X_1 + \beta_{11} X_1^2 + \beta_2 X_2 + \beta_{22} X_2^2 + \beta_{12} X_1 X_2 + \varepsilon$$

There are five different distinct kinds of terms in this equation.

1. $\boldsymbol{\beta_0}$: This is the *overall effect*. It sets the starting level for all the other effects, regardless of what the X variables are set at.

2. $\boldsymbol{\beta_i X_i}$: These are the *main effects* terms in the equation. Just like in the simple linear regression model, these terms capture the linear effect each X_i has on the output Y. The magnitude and direction of each of these effects is captured in the associated β_i coefficients.

3. $\boldsymbol{\beta_{ii} X_i^2}$: These are the *second-order* or *squared effects* for each of the Xs. The effect here will not be linear. Instead it is quadratic, because of the variable being raised to the power of two. Again, the magnitude and direction of each of these second-order effects is captured in the associated β_{ii} coefficients.

4. $\boldsymbol{\beta_{12} X_1 X_2}$: This called the *interaction effect.* This term allows the input variables to have an interactive or combined effect on the outcome Y. Once again, the magnitude and direction of the interaction effect is captured in the β_{12} coefficient.

5. ε: This is the term that accounts for all the random variation that can't be explained by all the other terms. ε is a normal distribution with its center at zero.

The equation for multiple linear regression can fit much more than a simple line. It can accommodate curves, three-dimensional surfaces, and even abstract relationships in *n*-dimensional space! Multiple linear regression can handle about anything you throw at it.

The process for performing multiple linear regression follows the same pattern you used when doing simple linear regression.

1. **Gather the data for the *X*s and the *Y*.**

2. **Estimate the multiple linear regression coefficients.**

   When you have more than one *X* variable, the equations for deriving the β's become very complex and very tedious. You definitely want to use a statistical analysis software tool to calculate these automatically for you. The β's just pop right out. Otherwise, go buy a box of Number 2 pencils and roll up your sleeves!

3. **Check the residual values to confirm that the upfront assumptions of the multiple linear regression model are met.**

   Checking that the residuals are normal is critically important. If the variation of the residuals is not centered around zero and if the variation is not random and normal, the starting assumptions of the multiple linear regression model haven't been met and the model is invalid.

4. **Perform statistical tests to see which terms of the multiple linear regression equation terms are significant (and should be kept in the model) and those that are insignificant (and need to be removed).**

   Some terms in the multiple regression equation will not be significant. You find out which ones by performing an *F* test for each term in the equation. When the variation contribution of an equation term is small compared to the residual variation, that term will not pass the *F* test and you can remove it from the equation.

   Your goal is to simplify the regression equation as much as possible while maximizing the R^2 metric of fit. As a general rule, simpler is always better. So if you find two regression equations that both have the same R^2 value, you want to settle on the one with the fewest, simplest terms.

   Usually, the higher order terms are the first to go. There's just less chance of a squared term or an interaction term being statistically significant.

   Many of the more sophisticated statistical analysis software tools even have automated algorithms that will search through the various combinations of equation terms while maximizing R^2.

5. **Calculate the final coefficient of determination R^2 for the multiple linear regression model.**

   Use the R^2 metric to quantify how much of the observed variation your final equation explains.

With good analysis software becoming more and more accessible, the power of multiple linear regression is becoming available to a growing audience.

Chapter 9

Achieving the Objective

In This Chapter

▶ Looking at the advantages of planned experimentation

▶ Examining experimental considerations and terminology

▶ Exploring the 2^k full factorial experiments

*T*he point of Six Sigma is improvement, and you are now at the point in the DMAIC roadmap where you synthesize improvements and/or reconfigure your system or process to be better. Six Sigma offers extremely powerful tools to aid you in your improvement efforts. Chief among these tools is experimentation. In Six Sigma, you first design an experiment before you carry it out. Then you follow it up with analysis to uncover previously hidden knowledge.

Design of Experiments (or *DOE* for short) has always been at the technical heart of Six Sigma. As necessity is the mother of invention, the field of DOE has matured due to the need to understand, and then improve, the world around you. This chapter gives you the lowdown.

Why Experiment? The Improvement Power of Six Sigma Experiments

How is improvement achieved? The spark of improvement comes from a curious mind, trying to figure out what it is that makes things tick.

What is an experiment, anyway?

In an *observational study* (covered in Chapter 7), you simply act as an outside observer, recording data as it happens, trying to glean understanding from careful review of the world around you. In these types of studies, you just let the Xs (inputs) of the system or process you are working on take whatever values they do. And as this plays out, you record the corresponding process output Y values.

Experiments, on the other hand, are different from observational studies in one fundamental way: In experiments, instead of just letting the Xs of the process you are studying take on whatever values they do, you purposely set and control the values that the Xs take on. In an experiment, you actively control and modify the process being studied.

Experiments offer a greater level of insight and knowledge than observational studies do. Think of the many observational studies performed for decades in fields like medicine, education, economic policy, diet, and so on. Dozens upon dozens of observational studies have only added incremental knowledge to these areas; there is, for example, still a lot of debate about what specific foods are part of a healthy diet. Because you purposefully control the factors, the amount of specific knowledge you get out of an experiment almost always exceeds what you gain from observational studies. For that reason, designing and analyzing experiments — in spite of the complexity of the topic — has always been one of the core pillars of Six Sigma breakthrough improvement.

The purpose of Six Sigma experiments

Every experiment in Six Sigma is targeted at better understanding the $Y = f(X)$ relational foundation between the inputs and outputs of the process or system being improved. Better understanding from experimentation includes

- ✔ Knowing which input Xs have a significant effect on the output Y, and knowing which Xs are insignificant.

- ✔ Formulating and quantifying the mathematical relationship between the significant Xs and the output Y.

- ✔ Statistically confirming that a change or improvement has been made to a process or system.

- ✔ Discovering where to set the values of the significant Xs so that they combine together to produce the optimal output value of Y.

Few activities in Six Sigma offer as much insight and change horsepower as experiments do. That's because properly designed experiments reveal, quantify, and confirm the underlying $Y = f(X)$ relationship of a process or system.

Experimenting with words

The field of planning and analyzing experiments is much older than Six Sigma. As a result, a few somewhat unique terms are used. Here are some of the interesting terms you need to know — along with their relation to Six Sigma.

✔ *Response* is the term used for the output of the process that you investigate in the experiment. In Six Sigma terms, the response is synonymous with the Y in the $Y = f(X)$ equation. The whole point of the experiment is to figure out how the Xs combine together to effect the response, or Y.

✔ The input characteristics, or variables you purposely control during the experiment, are called experimental *factors*. Sometimes, they're also called *conditions, variables,* or simply *inputs*. In all cases, the experimental factors are the Xs in the Six Sigma $Y = f(X)$ equation.

✔ In your experiment, you choose two or more values for each of the experimental factors. These values are called the *levels* for that factor. Planning your experiment includes deciding how many levels you need to use for each factor.

✔ Processes and systems have variation. Part of experimentation is repeating your whole experiment, or parts of it, to understand how much variation there actually is. These types of repetitions are called *replications*. Deciding what part of your experiment needs to be replicated and deciding how many replications there will be is part of developing your experiment plan.

✔ Every experiment is made up of a series of *runs*. Each experimental run consists of a unique, predetermined set of values for each of the factors. You then conduct the process or system through one cycle with those input values, and the output is recorded. That is a run in an experiment.

The end game of Six Sigma experiments

It has been said, "Knowledge is power." Six Sigma experiments are a confirmation of that statement.

The power of Six Sigma experiments lies in their ability to formulate, quantify and validate the $Y = f(X)$ relationship of a process or system. Knowing the form and details of $Y = f(X)$ for a system, you literally have a window into the past, present, and — most importantly — the future.

After wrapping up an experiment, you have in your hands a $Y = f(X)$ equation that identifies each critical input X and quantifies its influence on the output Y. For example, if you are working on a marketing plan to improve brand awareness (that's the output Y), a Six Sigma experiment provides an equation that tells you which type of advertisements — newspaper, radio, TV, Internet, and so on — and how many of each type to run (the input Xs) to reach a specified improvement goal. Or if you are managing the production of plastic seals that must meet a minimum tear strength requirement (the Y), after proper experimentation, you have an equation that tells you exactly where to set the mold press temperature (X_1), how much pigment to add (X_2), and the correct operating temperature of the mold press (X_3). In all cases, whether they involve continuous or attribute data, successful experimentation reveals detailed, specific knowledge of which input Xs influence the output Y — and by how much.

With this level of system or process knowledge, your operational focus immediately switches from passively watching the output and hoping for success to actively monitoring and controlling identified key inputs, knowing that your purposeful management and control of these inputs will always lead to the desired process outcome. This is where you open the door to the new world of breakthrough performance.

Look Before You Leap: Experimental Considerations

Trial and error — tinkering with the input knobs of a process or system — is temptingly simple. We all have a desire to jump in and quickly fix a problem. In the long-run, though, careful planning almost universally leads you to a quicker and better solution.

Frankenstein should have planned

How should you approach experimentation? Where do you start?

The trial-and-error approach

Many people approach experimentation by rolling up their sleeves and jumping into an unstructured exploration of the experimental variables and their resulting output: Tweak the knobs, adjust the settings, and observe the results. Often, judgment and intuition are the basis for steering the exploration and interpreting the findings.

For obvious reasons, however, this unstructured, haphazard approach rarely increases knowledge. Every once in a while, you may get lucky, but this approach, is unreliable.

The one-factor-at-a-time approach

At the other end of the spectrum, there's a structured approach: Isolate a single input variable and study its effect on the output; carefully hold all other factors constant while the selected input variable is incremented across an exploratory range of operation. Then repeat this meticulous scan for each of the input variables.

The downfall of this method is twofold:

- ✔ **The one-factor-at-a-time approach is inefficient and expensive.** A scan, conducted one factor at a time, of the possible operating range for each input variable leads to a huge amount of experimental runs. Unless you have only one variable in your system, this approach becomes unwieldy and wastefully expensive.

- ✔ **The results of one-factor-at-a-time experiments are often misleading.** When you isolate individual variables, you automatically negate the possibility of two or more factors combining together to affect the outcome. But these types of interaction effects are an unavoidable part of reality. Think of baking a cake. A delicious-tasting outcome (the Y) is a function of several input Xs — like "amount of flour," "number of eggs," "oven temperature," "baking time," and so on. Obviously, the right value for the variable of "baking time" depends on the setting for "oven temperature." How hot the oven is and how long you leave the cake in the oven are two input variables that interact with each other. One-factor-at-a-time experiments will never uncover this essential relationship. The danger is that you draw unfounded conclusions from your experiment — or miss important information altogether.

Use the one-factor-at-a-time approach only when you have a process or system with a single input variable. This approach works with a single-X system because there is no possibility of an interaction effect.

The Six Sigma approach — doing more than one thing at a time

Now you know the drawbacks of the haphazard approach and the one-factor-at-a-time approach. Is there a better way? Six Sigma uses a reliable approach to experimentation that:

- ✔ Efficiently accumulates information about a process or system
- ✔ Provides valid insights, including knowledge regarding variable interactions
- ✔ Quantifies the amount of knowledge discovered about a system as well as the amount of knowledge that remains unknown

The experimental approach you use in Six Sigma incorporates the best practices from the various disciplines of science. Over the years, scientists have developed experiment plans that return a vast amount of knowledge in a very efficient way. The key elements of the Six Sigma approach include:

- **Planning out the experiment before you conduct it.** "Look before you leap" is a mantra of every good experimenter. Careful planning always increases the value of your experiment results while minimizing the amount of work and money you have to invest.

- **Exploring the effect of more than one input variable at a time.** This allows you to be efficient while at the same time capturing unsuspected and sometimes hard-to-find interaction effects.

- **Minimizing the number of required runs in your experiment.** It's surprising how much you can get out of a small number of properly planned experimental runs.

- **Replicating key experiment conditions to assess variation.** A part of every experiment is understanding how much of your system's or process's behavior is deterministic and how much is random variation.

- **Accounting for known and unknown factors that you are not directly including in your experiment.** You can never take everything into consideration in your experiment. There are ways, however, to keep these nuisance factors from clouding the results of your experiment.

Simple, sequential, and systematic is best

Rome wasn't built in a day. Properly planned experiments fit into a larger strategy of iteratively converging to an ideal improvement solution.

The problem with boil-the-ocean super-experiments

The power of designed experiments is intoxicating. Be careful, though, not to get carried away. There is a temptation to try to solve everything in one fell swoop, using a big, well-designed super-experiment. But putting all your eggs into one experimental basket has some definite drawbacks.

- Creating a single super-experiment based only on the knowledge you have *before* the experiment begins necessitates that you include all the variables that you suspect are contributing to the situation. This always leads to a long list of potential Xs, and consequently, always results in a long, expensive, unwieldy experiment.

✔ As a large super-experiment is carried out over a protracted period of time, there is a greater chance of unknown factors creeping in, confounding the experimental conditions and results.

✔ With no prior knowledge, it is difficult to know what values and ranges to assign to each experimental X input.

✔ Conducting an experiment takes time and money. If something goes wrong in your one super-experiment or if new information is revealed that requires a change to your initial assumptions, you will have already consumed your experimental budget and resources.

The progressive, iterative approach

An efficient and consistently successful approach to experimentation follows a progressive and iterative approach.

✔ **Screening experiments:** At this first stage, experiments are designed to handle a large number of factors or variables. When you first start investigating a process or system, you identify all the possible Xs that may be influencing the output Y. The whole point of screening experiments is to quickly verify which of these factors has a significant effect on the output.

✔ **Characterizing experiments:** When you have screened out the unimportant variables, your experiments focus on characterizing and quantifying the effect of the remaining critical few. These characterization experiments reveal what form and what magnitude the critical factors take in the $Y = f(X)$ equation for your process or system.

✔ **Optimization experiments:** After characterizing your process or system, the final step is to conduct experiments that teach you what the best settings are for the input variables to meet your desired outcome goal. Your goal may be to maximize or to minimize the value of the output. Or it may be to hit a certain target level. More often, your goal is simply to minimize the amount of variation in the output Y. Optimization experiments find the best settings of the Xs to meet your Y goal.

The purpose of each of these types of experiments — screening, characterizing, and optimizing — are very different. The form and plan of the experiments you conduct at each of these stages, therefore, are necessarily different from each other.

Figure 9-1 shows the progressive and iterative approach used in Six Sigma experiments.

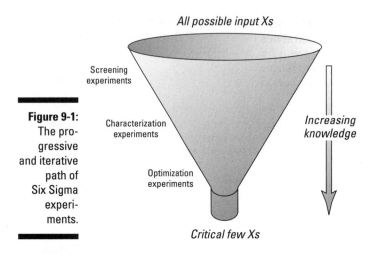

All possible input Xs

Screening experiments

Figure 9-1:
The progressive and iterative path of Six Sigma experiments.

Characterization experiments

Increasing knowledge

Optimization experiments

Critical few Xs

2^k *Factorial Experiments*

Design and analysis of experiments is a topic large enough for a whole *For Dummies* book by itself. To get you quickly up to speed, however, the following section of this book shows you how to plan, conduct, and analyze the most common type of experiment in Six Sigma — the 2^k factorial (pronounced two to the k). 2^k factorial experiments can be easily adapted to provide screening, characterization, or optimization information. Insights into other types of experiment designs and variations used in Six Sigma are offered along the way.

Plan your experiment

Like in almost all other endeavors, time spent in planning is rewarded with better results in a shorter period of time. Planning 2^k factorial experiments follows a simple pattern that is outlined in the following sections.

Select the experiment factors

The first thing to do in your planning is to identify the input variables, the *X*s, that you will include in your experimental investigation. The factors you include should all be potential contributors to the output *Y* you are investigating.

How many factors you want to include in your experiment guides you in choosing the right experimental design. 2^k factorial experiments work best when you have between two and five Xs. But if you have over five Xs in your experiment, full 2^k factorial experiments become relatively inefficient and can be replaced with pared down versions called *fractional factorials,* or with other screening designs.

One good strategy is to include all potential Xs in a first screening experiment — even the ones you are skeptical about. You then use the analysis of the experiment results to tell you objectively, without any guessing, which variables to keep pursuing and which ones to set aside. Remember, in Six Sigma, you let the data do the talking.

Experience with experiments verifies the *Pareto Principle* introduced in Chapter 7 — that even if you include dozens of contributing factors in your experiment, only a small number of these Xs have a significant effect on the output response. When you initially have more than four or five factors, your experiment purpose is to screen out the "trivial many" factors from the "critical few." After that, you then run characterization experiments to provide the detailed knowledge about the remaining critical few.

Plackett-Burman experiment designs are an advanced method you may hear about for efficiently screening dozens of potential Xs. Although they don't reveal all the detailed knowledge provided by a 2^k factorial design, Plackett-Burman experiments quickly identify which experimental variables are *active* in your system or process. You then follow these screening studies up with more detailed characterization experiments.

Set the factor levels

2^k factorial experiments all have one thing in common — they use only two levels for each input factor. (That's what the "2" in 2^k stands for! The k represents the number of factors included in your experiment.) For each X in your experiment you select a "high" and a "low" value that bounds the scope of your investigation.

For example, suppose you are working to improve an ice cream carton filling process. Each filled half-gallon carton needs to weigh between 1,235 and 1,290 grams. Your Six Sigma work up to this point has identified ice cream flavor, the time setting on the filling machine, and the pressure setting on the filling machine as possible contributing Xs to the Y output of weight. For each of these three factors, you need to select a "high" and a "low" value for your experiment.

With only two values for each factor, you want to select high and low values that bracket the expected operating range for each variable. For the ice cream flavor variable, for example, you may select Vanilla and Strawberry to book-end the range of possible ice cream consistencies. Table 9-1 provides a summary of the selected experiment variables and their values.

Table 9-1		Variable Values for the Ice Cream Carton Filler Experiment	
Variable	*Symbol*	*"Low" Setting*	*"High" Setting*
Ice cream flavor	X_1	Vanilla	Strawberry
Fill time (seconds)	X_2	0.5	1.1
Pressure (psi)	X_3	120	140

2^k experiments are intended to provide knowledge only *within* the bounds of your chosen variable settings. Be careful not to put too much credence on information extrapolated outside these original boundaries.

Experimental codes and the design matrix

With the experiment variables selected and their "low" and "high" levels set, you are now ready to outline the plan for the runs of your experiment. For 2^k factorial experiments, there will be 2^k number of unique runs, where k is the number of variables included in your experiment. For the ice cream carton filler example, then, there will be $2^3 = 2 \times 2 \times 2 = 8$ runs in the experiment, because there are three input variables. For an experiment with two variables there will be $2^2 = 2 \times 2 = 4$ runs, and so on.

Each of these 2^k experimental runs corresponds to a unique combination of the variable settings. In a full 2^k factorial experiment, you conduct a run or cycle of your experiment at each of these unique combinations of factor settings. In a two-factor, two-level experiment, the $2^2 = 4$ unique setting combinations are with:

- Both factors at their "low" setting
- The first factor at its "high" setting and the second factor at its "low" setting
- The first factor at its "low" setting and the second factor at its "high" setting
- Both factors at their "high" setting

There are no other ways that these two factors can combine with their two levels. For a three-factor experiment, there are eight such unique variable setting combinations.

A quick, shorthand way to create a complete table of an experiment's unique run combinations is to create a column for each of the experiment variables and a row for each of the 2^k runs. Then, using –1s as a code for the "low" variable settings and +1s as a code for the "high" settings, start with the left-most variable column, and fill in the column cells with alternating –1s and +1s. With the left-most column filled in, move on to the next column to the right and repeat the process — but this time with alternating *pairs* of –1s and +1s. Fill in the next column to the right with alternating *quadruplets* of –1s and +1s, and so on, repeating this process from left to right until, in the right-most column, you have the first half of the runs marked as –1s and the bottom half listed as +1s. This table of patterned +1s and –1s is called the *coded design matrix*. Table 9-2 shows the coded design matrix for a three-factor experiment, such as the ice cream carton filler.

Table 9-2	Coded Design Matrix for a Three-Factor Experiment		
Run	*X_1*	*X_2*	*X_3*
1	–1	–1	–1
2	+1	–1	–1
3	–1	+1	–1
4	+1	+1	–1
5	–1	–1	+1
6	+1	–1	+1
7	–1	+1	+1
8	+1	+1	+1

Remember that these three factors are coded values in the table; when you see a "–1" under the X_1 column, it really represents a discrete value, such as "Vanilla" in the ice cream experiment; and a "+1" really represents the other value, like "Strawberry."

Conduct your experiment

With your experiment well planned, the act of carrying it out is easy — it's like falling off a log. Now it's time to roll up your sleeves and get into the scientific trenches.

Randomize: Safeguard against unknown nuisance factors

Despite your best efforts, external factors beyond the control of your selected experiment variables may creep in and influence the outcome of your experiment. These are factors (called *nuisance factors*) that you haven't foreseen, but they have the potential to blur the clarity of your analysis and insights. For example, in the ice cream carton filling process discussed in the preceding section, a rise in the ambient factory temperature during the duration of the experiment may affect the experiment outcomes and be falsely construed as a real effect from your selected experimental factors.

One way to compensate for these unknown nuisance variables is to *randomize* the order of your experimental runs. This spreads out the otherwise concentrated or confounding potential for nuisance effects evenly and fairly over all of the experimental runs and preserves the clarity of your results.

Always randomize the order of your experiment runs. This reduces the risk of extraneous variables skewing the results of your analysis.

Randomize materials being used in your experiment, your personnel, or your equipment. The idea is to guarantee that only the effect of your selected factors is purposely concentrated during your experiment.

Blocking: Safeguard against known nuisance factors

When you know the source of nuisance variation that is not part of your selected experimental factors, you can purposely include this nuisance effect in *all* your experimental runs. In this way, you guarantee that there will be no bias on only a portion of your experimental settings.

In the ice cream carton filling example, you may decide to perform each experimental run at the same time each day. This way, the influences from different times of day are blocked from impacting only some of the experimental runs.

A catchy phrase may help you remember the roles of randomizing and blocking in your experiments: Block what you can and randomize against what you can't block.

Perform the experiment and gather the data

Running the experiment is the fun part. All you have to do is follow your experimental plan, like the one shown in Table 9-3 for the ice cream carton filler project.

Table 9-3		Plan and Results for the Ice Cream Carton Filler Experiment			
Run	Order	X_1: Flavor	X_2: Time	X_3: Pressure	Y
1	7	−1	−1	−1	1,238
2	2	+1	−1	−1	1,252
3	5	−1	+1	−1	1,228
4	8	+1	+1	−1	1,237
5	3	−1	−1	+1	1,223
6	6	+1	−1	+1	1,234
7	1	−1	+1	+1	1,238
8	4	+1	+1	+1	1,250

In Table 9-3, the coded design matrix is augmented with a column showing the random order in which the experimental runs are conducted. Also, on the far right, a column is added to capture the outcome Y variable for each experimental run. In Table 9-3, recorded values for the ice cream carton filling example experiment are provided.

Analyze your experiment

The purpose of analyzing your experiment is to take the experiment results and piece together the $Y = f(X)$ puzzle for your process or system. How much effect does X_1 have on Y? What mathematical form does this relationship take on? These are the questions that your analysis will answer.

Visualize and calculate the main effects

A *main effect* is the quantitative influence a single experiment factor has on the response Y. There will be a main effect for each factor in your experiment. For example, how much effect does ice cream flavor — going from "Vanilla" to "Strawberry" — have on the resulting filled weight of the carton?

The main effect of the X_1 ice cream flavor factor is the average response of the experiment runs with X_1 at its "high" or "Strawberry" setting, minus the average response of the experiment runs with X_1 at its "low" or "Vanilla" setting. To find the answer, refer to the captured values in Table 9-3. Runs 2, 4, 6, and 8 are where X_1 is at its "high" setting. Runs 1, 3, 5, and 7 are where X_1 is at its "low" setting. So the main effect of ice cream flavor (called E_1) can be written mathematically as

$$E_1 = \frac{Y_2 + Y_4 + Y_6 + Y_8}{4} - \frac{Y_1 + Y_3 + Y_5 + Y_7}{4}$$

$$E_1 = \frac{1,252 + 1,237 + 1,234 + 1,250}{4} - \frac{1,238 + 1,228 + 1,223 + 1,238}{4}$$

$$E_1 = 1,243.25 - 1,231.75$$

$$E_1 = 11.5$$

Figure 9-2 shows the main effect of ice cream flavor graphically. You can see that as the ice cream flavor changes from "Vanilla" to "Strawberry," the carton weight changes by 11.5 grams.

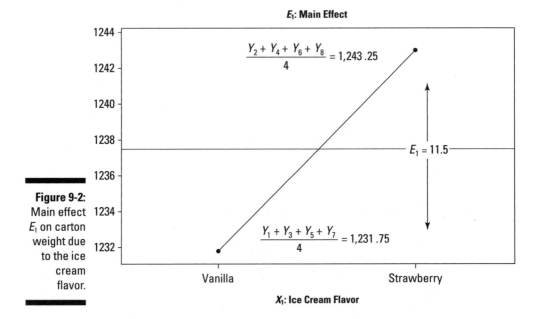

Figure 9-2: Main effect E_1 on carton weight due to the ice cream flavor.

To calculate the main effect E_2 of fill time on the filled carton weight Y, you can leverage the coded setting values for factor X_2 in Table 9-3. Call these coded values $c_{2,1}$, $c_{2,2}$, and so on through $c_{2,8}$, for each of the experimental runs. Another way to write the equation for the main effect of fill time, then, is

$$E_2 = \frac{c_{2,1}Y_1 + c_{2,2}Y_2 + c_{2,3}Y_3 + c_{2,4}Y_4 + c_{2,5}Y_5 + c_{2,6}Y_6 + c_{2,7}Y_7 + c_{2,8}Y_8}{4}$$

$$E_2 = \frac{(-1)\,1{,}238 + (-1)\,1{,}252 + (+1)\,1{,}228 + (+1)\,1{,}237 + (-1)\,1{,}223 + (-1)\,1{,}234 + (+1)\,1{,}238 + (+1)\,1{,}250}{4},$$

$$E_2 = \frac{-1{,}238 - 1{,}252 + 1{,}228 + 1{,}237 - 1{,}223 - 1{,}234 + 1{,}238 + 1{,}250}{4}$$

$$E_2 = 1.5$$

which gives a main effect of fill time of 1.5 grams.

Then using the coded setting values for X_3 — $c_{3,1}$, $c_{3,2}$, ..., $c_{3,8}$ — the same procedure can be used to calculate the main effect of pressure E_3:

$$E_3 = \frac{-1{,}238 - 1{,}252 - 1{,}228 - 1{,}237 + 1{,}223 + 1{,}234 + 1{,}238 + 1{,}250}{4},$$

$$E_3 = -2.5$$

with the main effect of pressure being –2.5 grams.

In fact, the coded setting values can be leveraged to create a generalized equation to compute *any* effect in a 2^k full factorial experiment.

$$E_i = \frac{1}{2^{k-1}} \sum_{j=1}^{2^k} c_{i,j} Y_j,$$

where k is the number of experiment factors and i designates which effect you're calculating.

Figure 9-3 shows all three main effects on a single plot for comparison.

Figure 9-3:
Graphical comparison of main effects for the ice cream carton filling example.

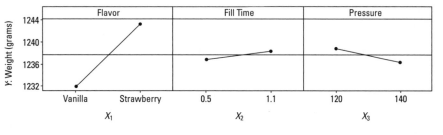

Visually, it is easy to see that X_1, the flavor of the ice cream, has the largest main effect on the filled weight of the cartons. (See Chapter 5 for a more detailed discussion of main effects plots.)

Visualize and calculate the interaction effects

One input variable interacting with another is always a possibility. Are there any of these type of interaction effects in the ice cream carton filling example? How do you find out?

Call the interaction effect between ice cream flavor (X_1) and fill time (X_2) E_{12}. What you do next is create a new column of coded setting variables that represents the interaction of factors X_1 and X_2. You do this by multiplying the coded values of X_1 and X_2 together for each experiment run. For example, $c_{12,1}$ = $c_{1,1} \times c_{2,1}$, $c_{12,2}$ = $c_{1,2} \times c_{2,2}$, and so on up through $c_{12,8}$ = $c_{1,8} \times c_{2,8}$. Table 9-4 shows the new coded setting values for the two-variable and the three-variable interactions possible in the 2^3 ice cream carton filler experiment.

Table 9-4			Interaction Coded Variables for the Ice Cream Carton Filler Experiment					
Run	c_1	c_2	c_3	c_{12}	c_{13}	c_{23}	c_{123}	**Y**
1	−1	−1	−1	+1	+1	+1	−1	1,238
2	+1	−1	−1	−1	−1	+1	+1	1,252
3	−1	+1	−1	−1	+1	−1	+1	1,228
4	+1	+1	−1	+1	−1	−1	−1	1,237
5	−1	−1	+1	+1	−1	−1	+1	1,223
6	+1	−1	+1	−1	+1	−1	−1	1,234
7	−1	+1	+1	−1	−1	+1	−1	1,238
8	+1	+1	+1	+1	+1	+1	+1	1,250

With the coded values for the interaction effects, you can now use the general formula to calculate each of the possible two-variable interaction effects. For example, the interaction effect between ice cream flavor (X_1) and fill time (X_2) is calculated as

$$E_{12} = \frac{1}{2^{k-1}} \sum_{j=1}^{2^k} c_{12,j} Y_j$$

$$E_{12} = \frac{(+1)\,1{,}238 + (-1)\,1{,}252 + (-1)\,1{,}228 + (+1)\,1{,}237 + (+1)\,1{,}223 + (-1)\,1{,}234 + (-1)\,1{,}238 + (+1)\,1{,}250}{4}$$

$$E_{12} = \frac{1{,}238 - 1{,}252 - 1{,}228 + 1{,}237 + 1{,}223 - 1{,}234 - 1{,}238 + 1{,}250}{4}$$

$$E_{12} = -1.0$$

Or –1.0 grams effect when the X_1 and the X_2 factors are combined together.

Using the same procedure, you can calculate interaction effects for E_{13} and E_{23}. You should get values of 0.0 grams and 14.0 grams, respectively. Figure 9-4 shows all three two-variable interaction effects.

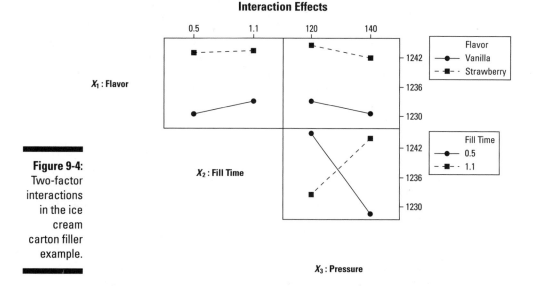

Figure 9-4:
Two-factor
interactions
in the ice
cream
carton filler
example.

In the grid layout of Figure 9-4 for the $X_2 - X_3$ interaction, you can see that the plotted effect lines have very different slopes. This is your graphical clue to know that E_{23} is very strong. The plotted effect lines for $X_1 - X_2$ and $X_1 - X_3$, however, have very similar slopes. It is no surprise that their calculated interaction effects, E_{12} and E_{13}, are rather small.

For a three-factor experiment, there is one more interaction effect you need to compute. It is the possible interaction when all three variables are combined (E_{123}). This may sound tricky, but it's not because you're using the coded setting values and the same general formula for calculating the effects.

$$E_{123} = \frac{1}{2^{k-1}} \sum_{j=1}^{2^k} c_{123,j} Y_j$$

$$E_{123} = \frac{-1{,}238 + 1{,}252 + 1{,}228 - 1{,}237 + 1{,}223 - 1{,}234 - 1{,}238 - 1{,}250}{4}$$

$$E_{123} = 1.5$$

Or 1.5 grams effect when all three factors are combined.

Which effects are significant?

Even though you can calculate all the main and interaction effects of the variables, are they all significant? Are they all necessary? The Pareto Principle (see Chapter 7) tells you that a relatively small subset of all the possible effects explains the vast majority of the output responses. So how do you know which effects to hold on to and which ones to cast aside?

If the factors you select for your experiment have no impact on the outcome Y, the calculated main and interaction effects will just be random — they'll be normally distributed and centered around zero. But if any one of the effects is significant, it will depart from the random cluster of the rest.

The easiest way to detect this departure is graphically, by plotting all the calculated effects against a line representing a normal distribution. If a plotted effect doesn't fit this line, you know that it is *not* part of the random noise, but instead *is* significant.

To create this graph for the ice cream carton filler example, you list all the calculated effects in rank order from smallest to largest and write down the rank i next to each effect. In case of ties, like between E_2 and E_{123}, you assign the average rank to the tied effects. You can see this in Table 9-5.

Table 9-5		Creating the Normal Scores for the Ice Cream Carton Filler Example		
Effect	*Value*	*Rank (i)*	*P*	*Z*
E_3	−2.5	1	0.071	−1.465
E_{12}	−1.0	2	0.214	−0.792
E_{13}	0.0	3	0.357	−0.366
E_2	1.5	4.5	0.571	0.180
E_{123}	1.5	4.5	0.571	0.180
E_1	11.5	6	0.786	0.792
E_{23}	14.0	7	0.929	1.465

As an intermediate step, you have to calculate the expected probability for each rank. This is called P and is in the fourth column of Table 9-5. The formula calculating the P for each row in the table is

$$P_i = \frac{i - 0.5}{2^k - 1}$$

So for the E_{13} effect, its expected probability, P, is

$$P_{13} = \frac{3 - 0.5}{2^3 - 1} = \frac{2.5}{7} = 0.357$$

The final step in creating the values of Table 9-5 is looking up the *Z* value for each intermediate *P* value. Using a look-up table for *Z*, you can see that the *Z* score corresponding to the *P* of 0.357 on E_{13} is –0.366.

Having filled in all the values of Table 9-5, you now simply plot the calculated *Z* value against each of the corresponding effect values. This is shown for the ice cream carton filler example in Figure 9-5.

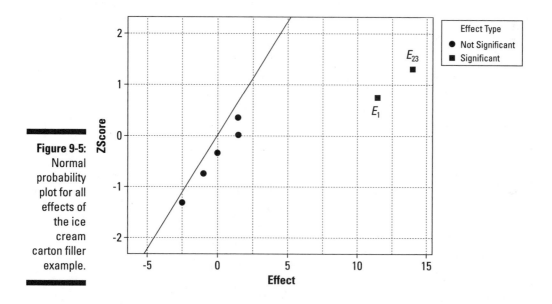

Figure 9-5:
Normal
probability
plot for all
effects of
the ice
cream
carton filler
example.

Looking at Figure 9-5, it is obvious that effects E_1 and E_{23} are very different from the rest of the effects. While E_1 and E_{23} are not centered around zero and clearly don't fit the expected normal probability line, all the others do.

The more complicated a potential interaction is, the less likely it is to be significant in reality. Very often, for example, two-factor interaction effects are found to be significant. Much less often, three-factor interactions are determined to be important. It is a real rarity to uncover a legitimate interaction effect that includes four or more factors. The more complicated an interaction effect is, the more skeptical you should be about it being real.

With just an eight-run experiment, you have determined that there are really only two effects that significantly effect the performance of the ice cream carton filler. The first is the type or flavor of ice cream being produced. Also, the combined, interactive effect of filler time and pressure definitely impacts performance. But filler time and pressure, acting by themselves, don't have a significant effect.

This is the power of Six Sigma. Rather than guessing or fumbling in the dark for the answer, you let the data and the analysis show what is important and what is not. In return, you look like the hero!

The general form of the equation

2^k factorial experiments not only reveal which factors effect the output Y, but they also allow you to understand the form of the $Y = f(X)$ equation for the system or process you are improving. At the onset, a 2^k experiment investigates the possibility of all main and interaction effects being significant. (Subsequent analysis shows you which ones you can safely ignore.)

Picture in your mind a general $Y = f(X)$ equation with a term for each main effect, a term for each interaction effect, and an overall offset effect. For the three-factor ice cream carton filler example, this general equation takes the form:

$$Y = \beta_0 + \beta_1 X_1 + \beta_2 X_2 + \beta_3 X_3 + \beta_{12} X_1 X_2 + \beta_{13} X_1 X_3 + \beta_{23} X_2 X_3 + \beta_{123} X_1 X_2 X_3$$

In this general equation, each combination of the input X variables is prefixed with a multiplier coefficient represented by the β's (the Greek letter beta; pronounced BAY-tah). The little subscripts at the lower right of each β tell you which effect it corresponds to. In stuffy mathematical terms, these β's are called coefficients.

A two-factor system would have a general equation of

$$Y = \beta_0 + \beta_1 X_1 + \beta_2 X_2 + \beta_{12} X_1 X_2$$

while a four-factor system would include additional terms for all the three-variable and four-variable interactions.

The β_0 term in all these equations represents the overall level of the process or system you are working on. No matter what you do to the setting of any of the system variables, the system will take on at least this value. That's why it is often called an *offset* or *constant* term.

Define your Y = f(X) equation

For the system or process you are working on, the only terms of the general equation you need to hang on to are the ones that correspond to the effects you have found to be significant. For example, in the ice cream carton filler process, only the ice cream flavor X_1 and the filler time-pressure interaction $X_2 X_3$ effects were found to be significant. That leads to a simplified equation form of

$$Y = \beta_0 + \beta_1 X_1 + \beta_{23} X_2 X_3$$

But what are the values of the βs? Again, finding these values is easier than you may think.

The value for the offset β_0 is simply the computed average for all the 2^k experiment runs. For the ice cream carton filler example, the average output Y for the eight experiment runs is 1,237.5, so

$$\beta_0 = 1{,}237.5$$

The β value for all other significant factors is found by dividing the corresponding effect value in half. That means that

$$\beta_1 = \frac{E_1}{2} = \frac{11.5}{2} = 5.75$$

$$\beta_{23} = \frac{E_{23}}{2} = \frac{14.0}{2} = 7.0$$

Why are the β coefficients half the effect value instead of the full effect value? It's because the effect value is calculated over a span of +1 to −1 for the variable. That's an effective distance of two, not one. Therefore, to get back to the right equation coefficient, you have to divide the calculated effect value by two.

With these coefficients calculated, you can write the $Y = f(X)$ equation for the ice cream carton filler system:

$$Y = 1{,}237.5 + 5.75\, X_1 + 7.0 X_2 X_3$$

Armed with this equation, you can now go out to the ice cream production line and immediately correct the problem situation of this example.

Suppose that the weight of the filled ice cream cartons is required to be between 1,225 and 1,280 grams. If you are producing a batch of vanilla ice cream, you can plug that coded value into the equation ($X_1 = -1$), and then plug in various coded values for X_2 and X_3 to calculate what your fill time and pressure settings should be on the ice cream filler machine. When you switch over to making strawberry ice cream, you can then pull out your equation again and know exactly how to alter your fill time and pressure settings to maintain the correct filled carton weight.

Be careful to plug only *coded* values into your derived $Y = f(X)$ equation.

You've Only Just Begun — More Topics in Experimentation

2^k full factorial experiments give you a powerful jump start into the world of improvement through DOE. But really, they are just the tip of the iceberg. As you gain experience, you want to discover how to address more advanced topics.

✔ **Curvature:** The assumption of 2^k experiments is that the effects of your experimental factors is linear. Although this is often a good first approximation, there are many times when a line doesn't fit your process or system. For those cases, you need to design your experiment to reveal the curved nature of reality. This is usually done by including more than two levels for each of your experimental factors.

✔ **Replications:** If you repeat your experiment, you get slightly different results. This shouldn't surprise you. Variation, as always, is a part of everything — including your experiment. Repeating runs of your experiment (called *replications*) allows you to estimate how much of the observed variation in your process or system is explained by the derived $Y = f(X)$ equation and how much remains unexplained.

✔ **Analysis of variance (ANOVA):** Almost all experiments involve exploring, investigating, and comparing the sources of observed variations. ANOVA is an advanced method that allows you to categorize and quantify all the various sources of variation.

✔ **Robustness:** The ability of a process or system to perform consistently in the face of variation is called *robustness*. Taguchi and other experiment designs allow you to investigate and optimize your process or system so that it is as immune as possible to the ravages of variation.

✔ **Response surface methods (RSM) and optimization:** The purpose of many experiments is to find out the best values to set the input variables at. A whole branch of the field of DOE focuses on designing and analyzing experiments to find the local or global optimal operation settings.

✔ **Fractional factorial experiments:** 2^k full factorial experiments can be adapted to more efficiently search through a large number of experimental factors. What you give up in increasing the number of experimental factors is analysis accuracy. Fractional factorial experiments teach how and where to adapt your experiment to get the most out of your search efforts.

Chapter 10

Locking in the Gains

In This Chapter

▶ Implementing a strategy for sustainable results

▶ Selecting tools to achieve process control

▶ Examining control charts and statistical process control

▶ Mistake-proofing with Poka-Yoke

▶ Creating the right level of control

A solution that isn't sustained over the long term has little value. That kind of solution can make you feel good for a little while, but if the problem doesn't stay solved, it will end up being a frustrating experience. The Control phase helps you make sure the problem stays fixed, and, if done properly, provides you with additional data to make further improvements to the process.

In this chapter, you find an abundance of easy-to-use and readily available tools and techniques to assure that your problem remains solved for the long-term. These tools range from the use of statistical methods for quantitative control to documented plans and strategies to the use of common-sense approaches for managing process performance.

The Need for Control Planning

Six Sigma emphasizes the Control phase. This is because previous attempts at improving quality and business performance have repeatedly demonstrated that process behavior is complex and fragile and that hard-earned gains slip away if the process is left to itself.

A process is a system of events, activities, and feedback loops. A well designed process exhibits inherent self control, while a poorly designed process requires frequent external control and adjustment to meet requirements. Some people use the terminology *tampering with the process* to describe such adjustments.

A process with control designed-in acts like the heating and cooling system in a house: The system automatically maintains a comfortable temperature at all times. A process without inherent control is like having to get up from the couch to manually turn on the heat, and then, when it gets too hot, you get up again to turn it off. When it's too cold again, you turn the heat back on, starting the cycle all over again. There is a lot of variation in this type of process — and waste comes from excessive variation.

The Six Sigma act of developing a control plan, and the knowledge (the reference documentation and the organizational memory) that you gain from it, virtually guarantees the improved performance you've worked so hard to achieve will stick.

Before Six Sigma came along, developing process controls tended to be like trying to boil the ocean. Some organizations even went to Herculean efforts to have an exhaustive plan for every process and every detail of every process, regardless of the importance of the process. It was like trying to eat the elephant in one bite!

Six Sigma, however, gives you the ability to pick those processes that are most important and to identify the input and output variables of the process that matter most (effectively eating the elephant one bite at a time). This changes the control effort from a broad-swathed flashlight to a focused laser beam. Developing a control plan for a Six Sigma project is a much easier alternative — and it's an absolutely essential activity.

There are two aspects to a control plan. $Y=f(X)$ shows the inputs that must be controlled (see Chapter 2 for details on this equation). The outputs can be monitored only to see whether control has or has not been achieved. Accordingly, there are two aspects of a Six Sigma control plan:

- ✔ *Process monitoring* of outputs uses a tool called a process management summary. The objective of the process management summary is to enable the visibility, review, and action for all critical process outputs in an organization.

- ✔ *Process control* of inputs uses a tool called a process control plan. The objective of the process control plan is to create systematic feedback loops and actions to assure the process has inherent, automatic control. With a good process control plan, you can change out people, equipment, materials, and production rates without significantly altering the performance quality of the process.

The two following sections provide further details.

The process management summary

The *process management summary,* shown in Figure 10-1 is intended to be a collection of all the critical-to-quality outputs, or CTQs, for a process, a department, a division, or even up to an entire company. The summary rolls up to whatever level an organization needs for monitoring, reviewing, and taking action to assure acceptable process and business performance. Each time a Six Sigma project is completed, that project's CTQs are added to the summary, building a complete process management system.

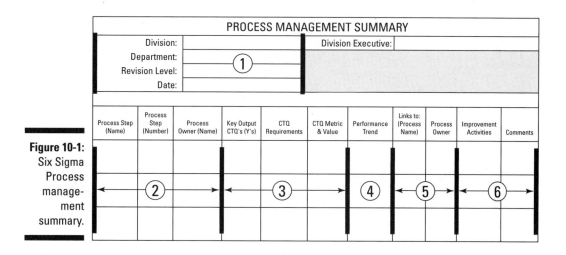

Figure 10-1:
Six Sigma
Process
manage-
ment
summary.

The administrative section of the summary (Section 1) provides identification of the organizational areas involved, plus the revision level and date of the information. The main body of the summary (Sections 2 through 6) provides enough information so that anyone can readily see the current status of the CTQs, how they relate to downstream processes, and what actions, if any, are currently being taken.

The process control plan

The *process control plan,* shown in Figure 10-2, is the companion to the process management summary. The process control plan is focused on the *X*s, the inputs to the process. The inputs, by definition in the formula of $Y = f(X)$, are the critical *X*s that are determined from the Six Sigma project. But it is okay to place process outputs, the *Y* (the CTQs), on a process control plan, too. When done correctly, the process control plan creates a complete picture of all possible inputs, outputs, and activities for a single process.

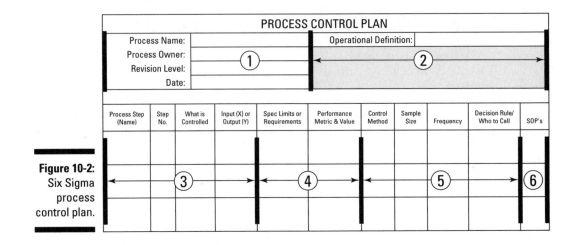

Figure 10-2:
Six Sigma
process
control plan.

The administrative section of the process control plan (Section 1) provides key information for identifying the process, including the owner. It also includes revision control information. Section 2 is a larger space for writing an operational definition of the control plan. This helps people understand why the process exists — that is, what its value proposition is — and helps put the control activities into proper context. Section 3 identifies what is specifically being controlled. Section 4 is the requirements and current performance levels of the requirements. In this section, you can quickly see how well the process is performing and how the control activities are going.

The method of control, and the actions to be taken if the process goes out of control, are in Section 5. This is where the rubber meets the road. The control methods may include checklists, mistake-proofing methods, statistical process controls, or any other appropriate procedure. More and more, control methods include the use of automated data collection and process execution technologies. This section also contains the size of the sample required and the frequency of sampling in order to provide the proper feedback to the process. Feedback is important, just like it is when you are driving a car. If you don't have the right amount of feedback at the right time to keep your car going down the center of the road, you may suddenly find yourself in the ditch. The same is true for keeping a process on track. Section 5 documents the action to be taken if the controlled parameter does not meet its requirements. This is analogous to calling 911 — it's what will be done and who will do it. A sense of emergency exists, always, when an input X or an output Y (or CTQ) goes out of control.

Section 6 contains the names of any governing documents for the process and any standard operating procedures (SOPs). With a good process control plan in place, you're ready to hand your project off to the process owner and process workers, highly confident that they will be able to sustain the improvement your Six Sigma efforts have made.

Creating a process control plan requires some thinking about what needs to be done, but it is worth the effort. Without a good control plan in place, your Six Sigma project is not complete.

Statistical Process Control

Statistical process control (SPC) involves the use of statistical techniques to monitor and control the variation in processes. SPC is used first to stabilize out-of-control processes. But it is also used as a follow-on, to monitor the consistency of product and service processes.

The primary SPC tool is the *control chart* — a graphical tracking of a process input or an output over time. In the control chart, these tracked measurements are visually compared to decision limits calculated from probabilities of the actual process performance.

The visual comparison between the decision limits and the performance data allows you to detect any extraordinary variation in the process — variation that may indicate a problem or fundamental change in the process. There are several different types of control charts, depending on what type of process measurement you are tracking.

These different types of control charts are separated into two major categories: continuous data control charts and attribute data control charts. Here is a list of some of the more common control charts used in Six Sigma:

- ✔ **Continuous data control charts:**
  - Averages and ranges $(\overline{X} - R)$
  - Averages and standard deviations $(\overline{X} - S)$
  - Individual values and moving ranges $(I - MR)$
- ✔ **Attribute data control charts:**
  - p chart
  - u chart

The control chart you choose is always based first on the type of data you have, and then on your control objective. The control chart decision tree in Figure 10-3 aids you in your decision.

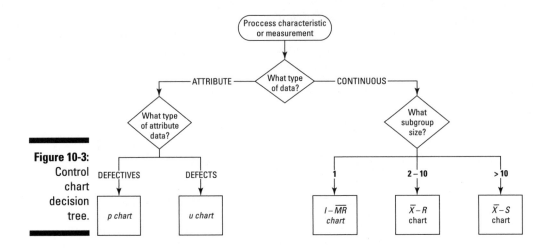

Figure 10-3:
Control
chart
decision
tree.

Control charts provide you information about the process measure you are charting in two ways: the *distribution* of the process and the *trending* or change of the process over time. Control charts are used to:

✔ Provide a simple, common language for discussing the behavior and performance of a process input or output measure

✔ Control the performance of a process by knowing when and when not to take action

✔ Reduce the need for inspection

✔ Understand and predict process capability based on trends and other performance insights

✔ Determine whether changes made to the process are having the desired result

✔ Provide an ongoing, continual view of the performance of the process

✔ Create a repository of data for follow-on improvement activities

Monitoring the Process: Control Chart Basics

What gets measured gets managed. Deciding what to measure and manage in Six Sigma is determined by your define, measure, analyze, and improve project activity (see Chapter 3) before you get to the control phase. Simply stated, they are the critical input *X*s and the output CTQs (the *Y*s) you discover in your project. These are the movers and shakers in your process that align to the needs of your customer. In the control phase, you monitor the outputs — the CTQs — and you control the inputs, the critical *X*s. When done properly, this monitoring allows you to consistently reap the fruits of your efforts.

Control charts are two-dimensional graphs plotting the performance of a process on one axis, and time or the sequence of data samples on the other axis. These charts plot a sequence of measured data points from the process. You can also view the sequence of points as a distribution. Figure 10-4 demonstrates how a distribution can be displayed from a sequence of data points.

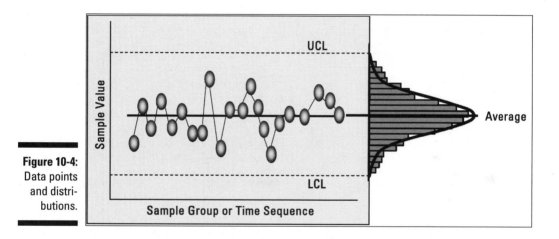

Figure 10-4: Data points and distributions.

Control charts have the following attributes determined by the data itself:

✔ **There is an average or center line for the data:** The sum of all the input data divided by the total number of data points.

✔ **There is an upper control limit (UCL):** It's typically three process standard deviations above the average.

✔ **There is a lower control limit (LCL):** It's typically three process standard deviations below the average.

Understanding control limits

You may ask, "What is the significance of a control limit and where does it come from?" The simplicity of control limits, yet their powerful implications, will surprise you.

Control limits come from probability, or the likelihood of an event occurring. Control charts use probability, expressed as control limits, to help you determine whether an observed process measure would be expected to occur (in control) or not expected to occur (out of control), given normal process variation.

The likelihood that a specific event or measurement value will occur is the ratio of the number of times that event or measurement value occurs compared to the total number of times all other possibilities occur. This is demonstrated using Figure 10-5, which is a population of data that contains 100 data points, plotted in a *histogram* (see Chapter 5).

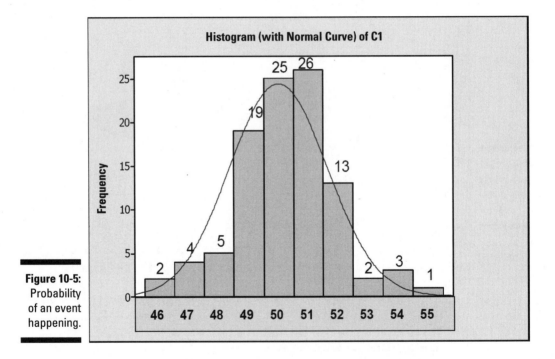

Figure 10-5:
Probability
of an event
happening.

In Figure 10-5, there are 25 data points out of 100 with a value of 50. You then estimate that the probability of getting an event with a value of 50 is 25 out of 100, or 25 percent. Similarly, the probability of getting an event with a value of 52 is approximately 13 percent, and for values of 55 and above, the probability is much less.

Figure 10-6 takes the data from the histogram in Figure 10-5 and plots the data in a chronological sequence as a control chart for individual measurements.

The upper control limit of 58.7 is 3 standard deviations above the average. The lower control limit of 41.3 is 3 standard deviations below the average. Plus or minus three standard deviations from the mean includes 99.7 percent of all the data in a normally distributed population. Therefore, there is a 99.7 percent probability that a data point will fall between these two limits. That means there is only a 0.3 percent chance that a measurement will be above the UCL or below the LCL.

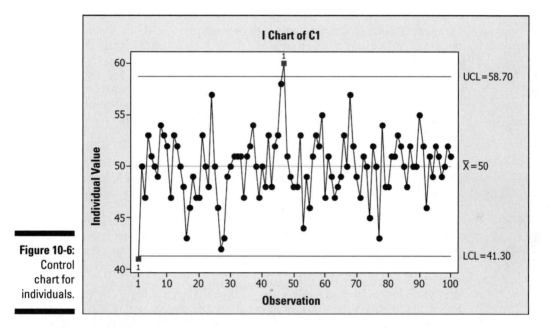

Figure 10-6:
Control
chart for
individuals.

In the early 20th century, Walter Shewhart, one of the founders of the modern quality movement, formalized the ideas used in control charts. He defined that if a measurement falls within plus or minus three standard deviations of its average, it is considered "expected" behavior for the process.

This is known as *common cause variation* (see Chapter 5). Common cause variation results from the normal operation of a process and is based on the design of the process, process activities, materials, and other process parameters.

However, if a data point falls outside of the control limits, something special has happened to the process. In other words, something out of the ordinary has caused the process to go out of control. This is known as *special cause variation* (also discussed in Chapter 5). What this says is, "The probability that a process measurement could be that far from the average, based on the behavior of the process up to that point, is less than 0.3 percent." A measurement with such a low probability of occurrence suggests that there was special circumstances affecting the process. This simple, quantitative approach using probability is the essence of all control charts.

Using control charts to keep processes on track

If you apply control charting as a part of your process control plan, you can use the control chart itself to trigger action or to leave things as they are, based on what the control chart tells you.

Sample data, also called *subgroup data,* is collected from the process characteristic (an input or an output) in which you are interested. The process must be allowed to operate normally while you're taking a sample.

How often you sample depends on how sensitive you want your chart to be to detect trends or other special-cause patterns in the process behavior. At first, error on the side of taking samples very often, and then, if the process demonstrates that is stable and in control, you can take samples less often.

If you treat the process you're charting with out-of-the-ordinary care or with any special treatment, the information from the control chart is invalid. You must allow the process to act as it normally does while you're creating a control chart for it.

After you have collected a minimum of 25 subgroups of data (with 2 to 5 measurements in each subgroup), you can calculate the statistics and control limits using statistical software like Minitab or JMP (see Chapter 11). If you already have historical data, it is useful to include this data in the analysis to form a strong baseline of information.

If the sample observations are normally distributed around the average and lie within the control limits then the process is said to be *stable* and *in control.* Further, the sequence of measurements will not show any trends or shifts in centering. This type of behavior is what is expected from a normally operating process, and that is why it is called common cause variation.

Never confuse control chart limits with specification limits! Specification limits — like the USL and LSL introduced in Chapter 6 — represent the voice of the customer. Control charts, however, represent only the voice of the process, something totally different. Discovering how the process performs naturally, apart from whatever its specifications may be, is the purpose of control charts. Another way of saying this is that control charts only determine whether the process is *stable* and *predictable.* They do not tell you whether the process is capable of meeting customer requirements. To assess a process's capability, refer to the capability material in Chapter 6. Always resist the temptation to interpret control chart limits as specifications, and avoid overlaying specification limits onto your control charts.

A process should be left as it is, if it is stable and predictable (in control) and if it is capable of meeting customer requirements (see Chapter 6). If special cause variation occurs, however, you must investigate what caused this extraordinary variation and find a way to prevent it from happening again. Some form of action is always required to make a correction and to prevent future occurrences.

Using control charts to detect patterns, shifts, and drifts

Besides control chart points that lie beyond the control limits, there are other visual patterns that tell you that something out-of-the-ordinary is happening to your process. These other patterns also indicate special cause variation.

Detecting special cause patterns, shifts, and drifts in a control chart is similar to detecting out-of-the-ordinary behavior in a pair of dice. The probability of rolling a seven with two dice is six in thirty-six, or about 17 percent. That's because there are six possible ways to roll a seven with two dice, out of a total of thirty-six possible outcomes. What is the probability of rolling a seven two times in a row? The combined probability is 17 percent $(0.17) \times 17$ percent (0.17), or 2.8 percent (0.028). The probability of rolling a seven *three* times in a row is $0.17 \times 0.17 \times 0.17$, or about 0.46 percent. So if you see someone roll a seven three times in a row, that probability is small enough that you can safely conclude there must be something out-of-the-ordinary going on (like loaded dice!) This same thinking is used to detect patterns, trends, and shifts in control charts.

Dividing the distance between the control limits and the process average into three equal zones, as shown in Figure 10-7, the following rules can be used to detect special causes of variation:

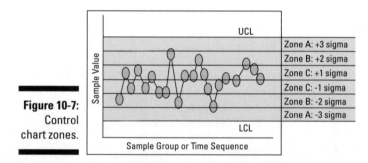

Figure 10-7:
Control chart zones.

 ✔ Any one point beyond either control limit.

 ✔ Two out of any three consecutive points in Zone A, and all three on the same side of the process average.

 ✔ Four out of any five consecutive points in Zone B or A, and all five on the same side of the process average.

 ✔ Fifteen points in a row in Zone C, on either side of the process average.

Table 10-1 shows a handful of additional rules for visually detecting if there are special causes acting on the process characteristic being charted.

Table 10-1		**Tests for Special Causes for Rules One through Six**		
Chart	*Description*	*Example 1*	*Example 2*	*Interpretation*
Stable and predictable	Chart points do not form a particular pattern and they do lie within the upper and lower control limits.			The process is stable, not changing. Only common-cause variation is affecting the process.
Beyond control limits	One or more chart points lie beyond the upper and lower control limits.			Alerts you that a special cause has affected the process. Investigate to determine the source of the special cause.
Run	Chart points are on one side of the center line. The number of consecutive points on one side is the "length" of the run.			Suggests that the process has undergone a permanent change. May require you to compute new control limits for the shifted process.

Chart	Description	Example 1	Example 2	Interpretation
Trend	A continued rise or fall in a series of chart points. (Seven or more consecutive points in the same direction.)			Indicates a special cause with a gradual, cumulative effect. Investigate possible special cause sources.
Cycle	Chart points show the same pattern changes (for example, rise or fall) over equal periods of time.			Indicates a special cause with a cyclical, repetitive effect. Investigate possible special cause sources.
Hugging	Chart points are close to the center line or to a control limit line.			Suggests a possible error in data sub-grouping or selection. Verify validity of sampling plan and/or investigate possible special cause sources.

When you detect any one of these listed patterns, you know that something out-of-the-ordinary has happened in the process input or output you're charting.

Collecting data for control charts

Data for control charts must be collected in such a way that a distorted or inaccurate view — either overly optimistic or too bleak — of the process performance is avoided. Using rational subgroups is a common way to assure that this does not happen.

A rational subgroup is a small set of measurements in which all the items in the subgroup are produced under as similar conditions as possible, typically within a relatively short time period — a time period short enough that special causes are unlikely to occur within the subgroup. It is in this way that rational subgroups enable you to accurately distinguish special cause variation from common cause variation.

Make sure that your subgroup measurements do not unfairly favor any specific operating condition (meaning that your subgroups are instead randomly selected). For example, don't take subgroups only from the first shift's production if you are analyzing performance across multiple shifts. Or don't look at only one vendor's material if you want to know how the overall process, across all vendors, is really running. Finally, don't concentrate on a single time of the day, like just before the lunch break, to collect your subgroup measurements.

Rational subgroups are usually small in size, typically consisting of three to five measurements. It is important that rational subgroups consist of measurements that were produced as closely as possible to each other, especially if you want to detect patterns, shifts, and drifts. For example, if a machine drills 30 holes a minute and you want to create a control chart of hole size, a good rational subgroup may consist of four consecutively drilled holes.

If your process consists of multiple machines, operators, or other process activities that produce streams of the same process characteristic you want to control, it is best to use separate control charts for each of the process streams.

Control Charts for Continuous Data

Continuous control charts refer to control charts that display performance of process input or output measurements that are continuous data — data where decimal subdivisions have meaning (see Chapter 7 for an explanation of data types). When control charts are used to control the input *X*s to a process, it is properly referred to as *statistical process control,* or SPC.

Continuous control charts can also be used to monitor output CTQs, the important process output characteristics. When control charts are used in this way, it is referred to as *statistical process monitoring,* or SPM.

There are two categories of control charts for continuous data: charts for controlling the location of the process average and charts for controlling the width of the process variation. Generally, the two categories are combined in paired, side-by-side charts.

The typical pairing of continuous control charts used in Six Sigma are

- ✔ Individual and moving range *(I – MR)* chart
- ✔ Averages and ranges $(\overline{X} - R)$ chart
- ✔ Averages and standard deviations $(\overline{X} - S)$ chart

Table 10-2 summarizes the important parameters of each type of continuous control chart.

Table 10-2		**Continuous Data Control Chart Summary**	
Control Chart	***Subgroup Size (n)***	***Centerline***	***Control Limits***
Individuals and moving range	1	$\overline{X} = \dfrac{X_1 + X_2 + \cdots + X_k}{k}$	$UCL_x = \overline{X} + E_2\overline{MR}$
			$LCL_x = \overline{X} - E_2\overline{MR}$
I – MR		$MR_i = \lvert X_{i+1} - X_i \rvert$	$UCL_{MR} = D_4\overline{MR}$
		$\overline{MR} = \dfrac{MR_1 + MR_2 + \cdots + MR_{k-1}}{k-1}$	$LCL_{MR} = D_3\overline{MR}$
Average and range	2–10	$\overline{\overline{X}} = \dfrac{\overline{X}_1 + \overline{X}_2 + \cdots + \overline{X}_k}{k}$	$UCL_{\bar{x}} = \overline{\overline{X}} + A_2\overline{R}$
			$LCL_{\bar{x}} = \overline{\overline{X}} - A_2\overline{R}$
$\overline{X} - R$		$\overline{R} = \dfrac{R_1 + R_2 + \cdots + R_k}{k}$	$UCL_R = D_4\overline{R}$
			$LCL_R = D_3\overline{R}$
Average and standard deviation	> 10	$\overline{\overline{X}} = \dfrac{\overline{X}_1 + \overline{X}_2 + \cdots + \overline{X}_k}{k}$	$UCL_{\bar{x}} = \overline{\overline{X}} + A_3\overline{S}$
			$LCL_{\bar{x}} = \overline{\overline{X}} - A_3\overline{S}$
$\overline{X} - S$		$\overline{S} = \dfrac{S_1 + S_2 + \cdots S_k}{k}$	$UCL_S = B_4\overline{S}$
			$LCL_S = B_3\overline{S}$

Where k is the number of subgroups and:

Sample Size (n)	A_2	A_3	B_3	B_4	D_3	D_4	E_2
2	1.880	2.659	0	3.267	0	3.267	2.659
3	1.023	1.954	0	2.568	0	2.574	1.772
4	0.729	1.628	0	2.266	0	2.282	1.457
5	0.577	1.427	0	2.089	0	2.114	1.290
6	0.483	1.287	0.030	1.970	0	2.004	1.184
7	0.419	1.182	0.118	1.882	0.076	1.924	1.109
8	0.373	1.099	0.185	1.815	0.136	1.864	1.054
9	0.337	1.032	0.239	1.761	0.184	1.816	1.010
10	0.308	0.975	0.284	1.716	0.223	1.777	0.975

The use of control charts for SPC and SPM must be carefully planned and managed in order to be successful. The general step-by-step approach for the implementation is as follows:

1. **Define what needs to be controlled or monitored.**
2. **Determine the measurement system that will supply the data.**
3. **Establish the control charts.**
4. **Properly collect data.**
5. **Make appropriate decisions based on control chart information.**

Individuals and moving range chart (I – MR)

The individuals *(I)* and moving range *(MR)* control chart is used when you have continuous data and each subgroup consists of only a single, individual measurement. These charts are very simple to prepare and use. Figure 10-8 shows the individuals chart, where the individual measurement values are plotted, with the centerline being the average of the individual measurements.

The moving range chart shows the range between two subsequent measurements. The centerline is simply the average of these between-point moving ranges.

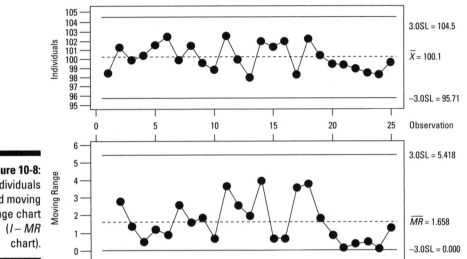

Figure 10-8:
Individuals and moving range chart ($I - MR$ chart).

There are many situations where opportunities to collect data are limited or when gathering the data into subgroups simply doesn't make practical sense. Perhaps the most obvious of these cases is when each individual measurement is already a rational subgroup. This may happen when each measurement represents one batch, when the measurements are widely spaced in time, or when only one measurement is available in evaluating the process. Such situations include destructive testing, inventory turns, monthly revenue figures, and chemical tests of a characteristic in a large container of material. All of these situations indicate a subgroup size of one.

The formula to calculate the control limits is based on the average moving range, which is the variation from one point to the next. The control limits are estimated statistically from these moving ranges.

The $I - MR$ chart in Figure 10-8 shows the individual measurements in the upper chart of the pair and a moving range in the lower half, which allows you to examine the process location and variation width at the same time.

Because the $I - MR$ chart is dealing with individual measurements, it is not as sensitive as the $\overline{X} - R$ or $\overline{X} - S$ chart in detecting process changes (see the two following sections).

Averages and ranges chart ($\overline{X}$ – R chart)

An $\overline{X}$ – R control chart is used when you have continuous data with subgroups of two to ten measurements each. It is used primarily to monitor and control the stability of the process characteristic's average value. The $\overline{X}$ chart plots the average values of each of a number of the small-sized subgroups. The averages of the process subgroups are collected in sequential, or chronological, order from the process. The $\overline{X}$ chart, together with its paired R chart shown in Figure 10-9, is a sensitive method for identifying assignable causes of product and process variation. Because it relies on rational subgroups, it provides great insight into the process characteristic's short-term variation.

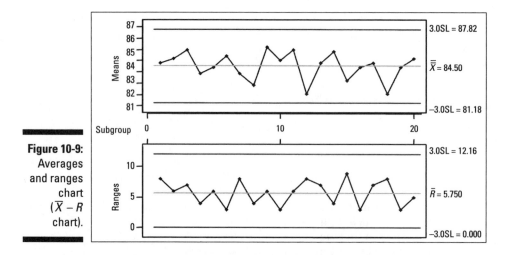

Figure 10-9:
Averages
and ranges
chart
($\overline{X}$ – R
chart).

As with all the paired control charts for continuous data, the $\overline{X}$ and the R charts are most effective when they're used together as a matched pair. That's because each chart individually shows only a portion of the information concerning the process characteristic. The upper chart shows how the process average changes. The lower chart shows how the variation of the process changes.

The R chart must show that the process variation width is stable and in control before you can properly interpret the $\overline{X}$ chart. That's because the control limits for the $\overline{X}$ chart are calculated from the observed variation in the ranges. When the R chart is not in control, the control limits on the $\overline{X}$ chart will be inaccurate and may falsely indicate an out-of-control condition when there really is none.

Averages and standard deviation chart ($\overline{X} - S$)

The $\overline{X} - S$ chart is constructed similarly to the $\overline{X} - R$ chart, but instead of ranges, it plots the standard deviation of each subgroup.

The calculation for the control limits on the $\overline{X} - R$ chart uses only two data points, the highest and lowest value. The calculation for the control limits on the $\overline{X} - S$ chart uses all the data. The $\overline{X} - S$ chart is, therefore, a more accurate indicator of process variation. The $\overline{X} - S$ chart is also very sensitive to small changes in the process average.

Use the $\overline{X} - S$ chart when the size of your subgroups is ten measurements or greater, and the $\overline{X} - R$ when they are less than ten. You should consider using this chart for processes with a high rate of production, when data collection is quick and inexpensive, or when you need increased sensitivity to variation.

An $\overline{X} - S$ chart is less sensitive than the $\overline{X} - R$ chart in detecting special causes of variation that result in only a single value in a subgroup being unusual.

Control Charts for Attribute Data

Attribute data is data that can't fit into a continuous scale, but instead is chunked into distinct *buckets,* like small/medium/large, pass/fail, acceptable/not acceptable, and so on (see Chapter 7 for a detailed discussion of attribute and continuous data). Although it is preferable to monitor and control products, services, and processes with more sensitive continuous data, there are times when continuous data is simply not available, and all you have is less sensitive attribute data. But don't despair, because certain control charts are designed specifically for attribute data to draw out startling information and allow you to control the behavior of your process.

With knowledge of only two attribute control charts, you can monitor and control process characteristics that are made up of attribute data. The two charts are the *p* (proportion nonconforming) and the *u* (non-conformities per unit) charts. Table 10-3 summarizes the important parameters of these charts. Like their continuous counterparts, these attribute control charts help you make control decisions. With their control limits, they can help you capture the true voice of the process.

Table 10-3		Attribute Data Control Chart Summary	
Control Chart	**Subgroup Size (n)**	**Centerline**	**Control Limits**
Proportion defective p chart	Variable (usually > 50)	For individual subgroups: $p_i = \dfrac{\text{number defective}}{n_i}$ Overall: $\bar{p} = \dfrac{\text{total number defective}}{n_1 + n_2 + \cdots + n_k}$	$UCL_i = \bar{p} + 3\sqrt{\dfrac{\bar{p}(1-\bar{p})}{n_i}}$ $LCL_i = \bar{p} - 3\sqrt{\dfrac{\bar{p}(1-\bar{p})}{n_i}}$
Number of defects per unit u chart	Variable	For individual subgroups: $u_i = \dfrac{\text{number defects}}{n_i}$ Overall: $\bar{u} = \dfrac{\text{total number defects}}{n_1 + n_2 + \cdots + n_k}$	$USL_i = \bar{u} + 3\sqrt{\dfrac{\bar{u}}{n_i}}$ $LSL_i = \bar{u} - 3\sqrt{\dfrac{\bar{u}}{n_i}}$

Picture a bowl of soup. If you found a fly in it, you'd deem it unacceptable. What if you found ten flies? You'd still call it unacceptable. Data from cases like this, where something wrong — whether big or small, few or many — causes you to deem the entire item unacceptable, are called *defectives*. It's where any one or more things makes the entire thing bad. If you're charting defectives attribute data (pass/fail, go/no-go, acceptable/unacceptable), you use a *p* chart.

Now picture a bowl of soup with three flies in it. This bowl has three *defects*. Some attribute data for control charts is defect data — the number of scratches on a car door, the number of fields missing information on an application form, and so on. If you're counting and keeping track of the number of defects on an item, you're using defect attribute data, and you use a *u* chart to perform statistical process control.

Although the words sound almost identical, it's critically important to know what type of attribute data you have: whether it's defectives (pass/fail) data, or defect (count) data. If you get this wrong, your subsequent control chart will be completely invalid.

p charts for defectives data are based on a binomial distribution. *u* charts for defects data are based on the Poisson distribution.

The p chart for attribute data

The *p* chart plots the proportion of measured units or process outputs that are defective in each subgroup. The sequential subgroups for *p* charts can be of equal or unequal size. When your subgroups are different sizes, the upper and lower control limits will not be a constant, horizontal value — they will look uneven, as exhibited in Figure 10-10. But the same rules for interpreting the control chart remain — it's just that the control limits move from subgroup to subgroup.

The proportion of defectives for each subgroup is found by dividing the number of defectives observed in the subgroup by the total number of measured in the subgroup.

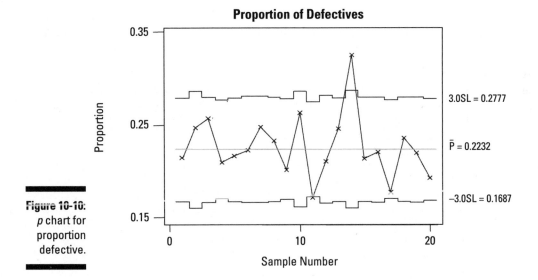

Figure 10-10: *p* chart for proportion defective.

A common application of a *p* chart is when you have percentage data, and the subgroup size for each percentage calculation may be different from one subgroup to the next. For example, the number of patients that arrive late each day for their dental appointment. Or, the number of forms processed each day that have to be reworked due to defects. In both of these examples, the total size of the subgroups measured could vary from day to day.

p charts are generally used where the probability of a defective is low — usually less than ten percent. So to be effective, the subgroup size needs to be large enough to register one or more defectives. It is also important to consider the length of time that a subgroup represents: Long periods of time can make it difficult to pinpoint a specific cause.

Remember, just as with continuous control charts, you need to be alert for other indicators of special cause variation in addition to just exceeding the control limits. The presence of unusual patterns, such as runs or trends, even if all the points are within the control limits, can be evidence of instability or an out-of-the-ordinary change in performance.

The u chart for attribute data

Like with the *p* chart, the *u* chart does not require a constant subgroup size. The control limits on the *u* chart vary with the subgroup size and, therefore, may not be constant.

Counting the number of distinct defects on a form is a common use of the *u* chart. For example, errors and missing information on insurance claim forms (defects) are a problem for hospitals. As a result, every claim form has to be checked and corrected before being sent to the insurance company.

One particular hospital measured its defects per unit performance by calculating the found number of defects per unit for each day's processed forms. Figure 10-11 demonstrates their performance on a *u* chart.

Figure 10-11: *u* chart for insurance claim forms.

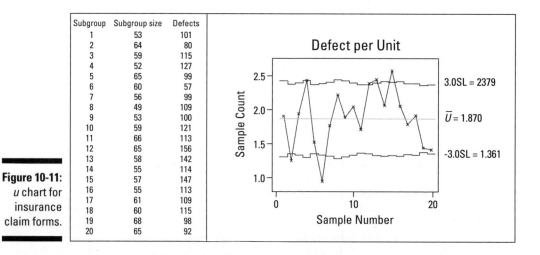

Subgroup	Subgroup size	Defects
1	53	101
2	64	80
3	59	115
4	52	127
5	65	99
6	60	57
7	56	99
8	49	109
9	53	100
10	59	121
11	66	113
12	65	156
13	58	142
14	55	114
15	57	147
16	55	113
17	61	109
18	60	115
19	68	98
20	65	92

Defect per Unit

3.0SL = 2379
$\bar{U}$ = 1.870
-3.0SL = 1.361

Each point on the chart in Figure 10-11 represents the average defects per claim form for that subgroup. Points higher on the chart represent a greater number of defects per unit. The center line, calculated at 1.870, means that there is an overall average process performance of 1.87 defects per form.

Poka-Yoke (Mistake-Proofing)

Mistake-proofing, or Poka-Yoke (pronounced POH kah YOH kay) as it is known in Japan, is an action taken to remove or significantly lower the opportunity for an error or to make the error so obvious that allowing it to reach the customer is almost impossible. These two approaches are depicted in Figure 10-12.

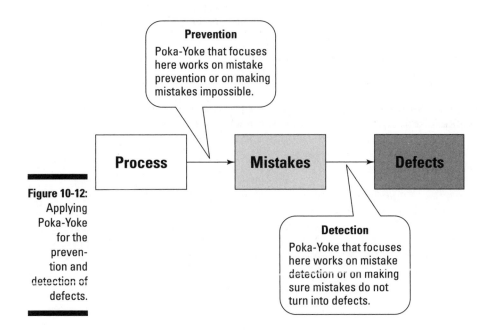

Prevention
Poka-Yoke that focuses here works on mistake prevention or on making mistakes impossible.

Detection
Poka-Yoke that focuses here works on mistake detection or on making sure mistakes do not turn into defects.

Process → Mistakes → Defects

Figure 10-12:
Applying Poka-Yoke for the prevention and detection of defects.

Poka-Yoke is very consistent with the fundamental aims and philosophy of Six Sigma, and it has wide applicability in manufacturing, engineering, and transactional processes. It is one of the simplest tools to master. It involves the creation of actions that are designed to eliminate errors, mistakes, or defects in everyday activities and processes.

Poka-Yoke starts with an understanding of the cause-and-effect relationship of a defect. This is followed by the implementation of a remedy that eliminates the occurrence of the mistakes that lead to that defect. Poka-Yoke solutions can include the addition of a simple physical feature, the creation of a checklist, a change in the sequence of operation, a highlighted field on a form, a software message that reminds the operator to complete a task, or any other way of helping to ensure that mistakes will be either totally eliminated or substantially reduced.

You can find a number of everyday examples of Poka-Yoke. Look at the connector for your computer keyboard or mouse. Its shape prevents it from being connected in the wrong place or turned incorrectly, damaging your computer. Or remove the gas cap and look at the gas filler tube on your car. It is designed so that you can only put the right kind of gas into your car.

Poka-Yoke is also an ideal form of control for transactional processes. Some examples include

- ✔ Computer data entry forms will not let you advance until all the information is input correctly.
- ✔ Checklists are used so items are not inadvertently missed.
- ✔ Process workflow is automatically routed and executed.

In summary, the objective of the control phase is to establish measurement points for the critical Xs and other significant parameters of the process to assure that the CTQs are predictable and meet established requirements. Different levels of control have different levels of effectiveness.

The most effective form of process control is sometimes called a *Type-1 corrective action*. This is a control applied to the process that eliminates the error condition from ever occurring. This is the primary intent of the Poka-Yoke method. The second most effective control is called a *Type-2 corrective action*. This a control that detects when an error occurs and stops the process or shuts down the equipment so that the defect cannot move forward. This is the detection application of the Poka-Yoke method.

Part III
The Six Sigma Tool and Technology Landscape

The 5th Wave   By Rich Tennant

"Look Mitchell, we're working with a strict methodology of cause and effect. I don't think there's any place on that matrix for the term 'co-inky-dink'."

In this part . . .

Simply put, you can't do Six Sigma without tools. This part provides an overview of the technical and managerial tools you can use to apply Six Sigma at your company.

Chapter 11

Identifying the Six Sigma Practitioner Tools

. . . .

In This Chapter

▶ Understanding what process optimization tools do

▶ Knowing about statistical analysis tools

▶ Seeing how these tools are used by the Six Sigma practitioner

▶ Finding out about available software tools and technologies

. . . .

*Y*ou don't have to be a programming whiz or a Ph.D. statistician to apply Six Sigma in even the most rigorous of situations. All the necessary tools are well defined and readily available, and they enable the Six Sigma practitioner to directly connect Six Sigma theory to practice. Each of the strategies and methods discussed in Part II are implemented through these tools.

The Six Sigma tools marketplace has many products available. But fear not — they all sort into just a few categories. Chapter 12 addresses the tools designed for management. This chapter discusses the tools created and honed specifically for Six Sigma practitioners. When applied to Six Sigma projects, these tools help you make the outcomes accurate, presentable, and reusable.

Most Six Sigma tools are implemented in software programs, most of which run directly on a PC. These programs perform the many process and analytical functions for you. Unleashing your Six Sigma genius is just a few clicks away.

As a bonus, this chapter also provides advice on the platform and technology issues involved in tool selection and application.

The Practitioner's Toolkit

To be a successful Six Sigma practitioner, you must be accomplished in the application of the Six Sigma analytical and statistical concepts and formulas defined in this book. In the early days of Six Sigma — that was way back in the 1980s — such analyses and statistical processing were largely a manual and complex effort, confined to the world of the statistical geeks. Unless you were both an accomplished statistician and a computer programmer, the practice of Six Sigma was off-limits.

Today, this has all changed. The methods and tools are now well defined. And the power of desktop computing, combined with several generations of accelerated development in application software, has made all the analysis, including advanced calculations and data display, a relatively easy and simple thing to do. With the wave of a mouse, you can easily execute the most complex functions, run advanced simulations, conduct a Design of Experiments and create impressive charts and plots.

In short, as a Six Sigma practitioner, you are now enabled by a fully capable set of practical application tools. As with all tools, you have to know how to use them properly and interpret what they're telling you, but after you understand the theory and strategy of Six Sigma, you can use these tools to directly apply your new-found knowledge — quickly, comprehensively, and accurately.

Practitioner tools come in many colors and flavors, but they all fall into one of two primary types: process optimization tools and statistical analysis tools. Each plays a critical role in the successful application of Six Sigma.

- ✔ **Process optimization** tools enable you to design, simulate, and optimize work processes. These include tools for creating process and work flow diagrams, building cause-and-effect matrices, constructing fishbone diagrams, developing SIPOC (Suppliers-Inputs-Process-Outputs-Customers) diagrams, assessing process capabilities, and more. The goal of these tools is help you see how work is performed and identify where the source of problems is.

- ✔ **Statistical analysis** tools enable you to analyze data collected either from the real-world performance of a product or process, or as the output of a simulation or experiment. These include basic statistics tools, and tools for analyzing variance, conducting regressions, performing Design of Experiments (DOE), and building control charts, plots, tables, and graphs. The goal of these tools is to help you turn data into knowledge such that you can make informed decisions.

You have choices in selecting and applying these tools. Because each tool is based on fundamental principles or mathematical formulas, you could work them out longhand with pencil and paper. You could use a slide rule, or even a calculator. But in this modern world of personal information technology, we have software programs that implement every tool — quickly, cheaply, and easily. These programs perform every function for you. They also combine multiple tools into kits and present them in a logical order.

Most of these tools run only on a desktop PC under the Microsoft Windows operating system. If you're a Mac or Linux user, or if you wish to deploy these tools via an intranet or through the Internet as Web-based applications, it's improving, but it has been slim pickin's. The last section of this chapter explores this further, but the simple truth is that the Six Sigma toolkit is primarily a Windows environment.

Process Optimization Tools

You practice Six Sigma for one reason, and one reason only: to improve your business processes. Therefore, those tools, directly facilitating efforts to optimize the many types of work processes in a business, are your primary weapons in your battle against ineffectiveness, inefficiency, variation, and waste. All the other tools — be them managerial or analytical — are in a supporting role. It's all about improving the process.

We use the term "process optimization" here as a catch-all to describe both the subject area — processes — and the purpose — optimization. Within this broad category are many supporting tasks, for which sub-categories of tools exist. These are summarized in Table 11-1.

Table 11-1	Process Optimization Tools
Process Tool	*Role*
The SIPOC	Suppliers-Inputs-Process-Outputs-Customers. Create a high-level process map with a few key details about each of the key contributing elements.
CT (critical to) tree	Critical to . . . tree. Identify, organize, and display parts of the process according to areas of critical importance.
Modeling	Define and design processes, including the flow of work or material, the timing of activities, resources consumed, and points of decision, inspection, and delivery.

(continued)

Table 11-1 *(continued)*

Process Tool	Role
Simulation	Simulate the flow of work and material through a process based on the model, and analyze the results of the simulation for overall effectiveness and efficiency. Find defects, errors, bottlenecks, variation, and non value-added elements.
C&E (cause-and-effect) matrix	For the outcomes of any process, define all the contributors, weight their effects, and determine the significant contributors to the outputs.
Fishbone diagram	Create a high-level C&E in the form of a tree structure, with categories for each major type of contributor. A method for capturing potential causes and inputs to a process.
FMEA (failure mode effects analysis)	For any activity or item, define the potential failure modes, including the likelihood of occurrence, and the ability to detect and characterize the effects of those failures.
Capability and complexity analysis	Analyze the tradeoffs between product complexity and process capability, and define the proper configuration of each to achieve desired outcomes.
Plans	Use the outputs of simulation and analysis to define how data will be collected and how the processes will be controlled and audited.

The SIPOC

SIPOC, pronounced sy-pok, is an acronym that stands for Suppliers-Inputs-Process-Outputs-Controls. The SIPOC is one of the most fundamental building blocks in the Six Sigma process. With this tool, you build your first controlled and organized view of your work process and set the foundation for applying the breakthrough DMAIC strategy.

SIPOC is one of those handy reminder acronyms that contains the terms in their proper order, helping you remember not only the five high-level elements of a process map, but the order in which they occur.

Table 11-2	The SIPOC
S: Suppliers	Suppliers are systems, people, organizations, or other sources of the materials, information, or other resources that are consumed or transformed in the process.
I: Inputs	Inputs are materials, information, and other resources provided by the suppliers that are consumed or transformed in the process.
P: Process	The process is the set of actions and activities that transform the inputs into the outputs.
O: Outputs	Outputs are the products or services produced by the process and used by the customer.
C: Customer	Customers are persons, groups of people, companies, systems, and downstream processes that receive the output of the process.

Developing a SIPOC

You build a SIPOC from the inside-out, beginning at the center, with the process — of course! It's a six-step approach:

1. **Identify the process you wish to map and define its scope and boundary points.**

   Using action verbs, describe what the process is supposed to do, and in how much time. Define its starting and ending points.

2. **Identify the outputs.**

   What are the products and the services that will be produced by the process?

3. **Define by name, title, or organizational entity the recipients (the customers) of the outputs.**

4. **Define the customer requirements; what do the customers expect?**

   What will they demand? What will they be entitled to in their fair exchange of value?

5. **Define the inputs to the process.**

   Identify the human, capital, information, materials, and natural resources required by the process to produce the identified outputs.

6. **Identify the sources (suppliers) of the inputs.**

With this information in hand, you now have a fully-contained high-level view of any process. This alone is one of the most powerful tools you can use, because it sets the conditions for the DMAIC of Six Sigma. With the SIPOC, you now have the basis for defining and characterizing the process itself, the context for measurement, and the basis for analysis, identifying areas of improvement, and homing in on your targets of control. SIPOC software tools, like iGrafx, SigmaFlow, and Process Model, help you capture, organize, and display this information.

I hear voices

And who's talking? The loudest voice you hear should be the Voice of the Customer. Known as VOC, Voice of the Customer is a practice within Six Sigma process optimization for ensuring that the customer's requirements, expectations, and entitlements are flowed into the process. But that's not the only "voice" in Six Sigma. Competing with VOC in your mind are two additional voices you need to consider, the voice of the process, VOP, and the voice of the business, VOB.

- ✔ **Voice of the customer (VOC):** This is the voice calling back at your process from beyond the output that offers you compensation in return for satisfaction of its needs and wants. These voices are the needs, wants, and desires of the customer, generally spoken as the customer requirements.

- ✔ **Voice of the process (VOP):** The process must meet the requirements of the customer, and the ability of the process to meet these requirements is called the VOP. This is a construct for examining what the process is telling you about its inputs and outputs and the resources required to complete the functional transformation.

- ✔ **Voice of the business (VOB):** This is the voice of profit and return on investment. At the end of the day, every endeavor has to enable the business to survive, grow, and meet the needs of its employees, investors, and the community.

What's critical? Look in the CT tree

In Six Sigma, you always look for the causes. You want to know what's behind something, what's causing the outcome — find those "critical *X*s." In optimizing a process, you have to understand what's critical to the successful outcome of each step, so you can focus on optimizing the right things. This is what a CT tree is for.

CT stands for "critical to. . . ." Critical to *what*, you may ask? The answer is, simply: critical to whatever matters. Depending on what you are analyzing and optimizing, this could mean anything from the satisfaction of the customer, to the quality and reliability of the product, to the cycle time of manufacture or the cost of the delivered product or service.

The Six Sigma practitioner will often refer to the general CT case as "CTXs," in reference to the many variables that influence a desired outcome. But there are specific cases in process optimization, and the CT tree is a tool that helps you identify and characterize the influencers on specific outcomes.

Most CT trees begin with the output of the SIPOC, customer satisfaction, at the top, and the others are subordinate. And, while the CTXs in Table 11-3 are the most commonly used, you are free to invent and apply any X that fits your need. We've seen everything from CTQ (quality) to CTD (delivery), and even CTC (cost). It all depends on your application.

Table 11-3		Applications of the CT Tree
Critical To . . .	*Title*	*Definition*
Satisfaction	CTS	What contributes to customer success?
Quality	CTQ	What contributes to process or product quality?
Cost	CTC	What contributes to the cost or final price?
Delivery	CTD	What contributes to the cycle time to deliver?

In creating a CT tree, begin by defining your specific area of application, such as customer satisfaction (CTS). This is your trunk. Then, define the branches, by category, of the key contributors to customer satisfaction, which may include availability, price, selection, accuracy, presentation, performance, and so on. These are your subordinate CTXs. Lastly, define the leaf nodes: the causes or influences on those categories of customer satisfaction.

An example CT tree is shown in Figure 11-1. In the main window, you can see that the root node of the tree is labeled as Critical to Satisfaction. The branch nodes for this CTS tree are identified, as selection, price, performance, and availability. The leaf nodes are then identified and defined for each branch. In this example, one leaf node, configuration, has contributing sub-leaves as well, deemed worthy of inclusion as being critical to the configuration.

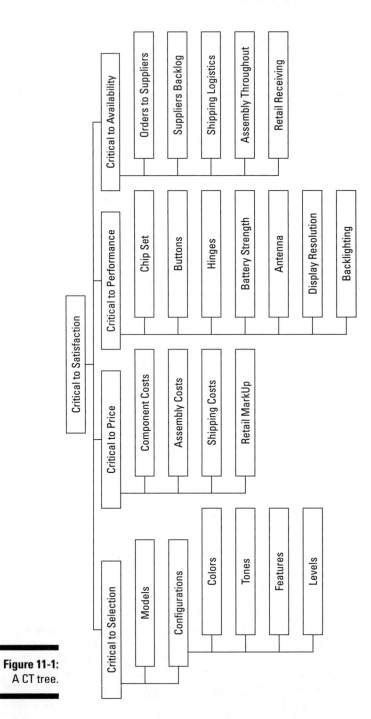

Figure 11-1:
A CT tree.

Modeling a process

A Six Sigma process is defined precisely — *very* precisely — down to the last detail of activity, resource, decision, dependency, and value. Only in this way can a process be sufficiently measured and analyzed, leading to breakthrough improvements and, ultimately, effective controls. The process model is our representation of this precise process definition, and the practice of process modeling is therefore at the very heart of Six Sigma.

Process modeling has been practiced for decades, and the fundamental concepts of process modeling are nothing new. The Six Sigma style of process modeling has a few different wrinkles, however, and as a result, the Six Sigma process model bears only a superficial resemblance to its ancestors. In the world of Six Sigma, the process model is characterized in mathematical terms, permitting us to perform a plethora of statistical analyses on its various parts and pieces. Each node, each function, and each activity is backed by numerical descriptions and quantifiable attributes, enabling us to see the process in this mathematical light.

In Six Sigma process modeling, you are characterizing a practical situation in ways that permit it to be described in statistical terms, allowing you to develop statistical solutions, which you then apply back into your practical environment. On the surface, a Six Sigma process model looks like a flow chart, but underneath, it's a raging mathematical beast.

The 1, 2, 3s of process modeling

Process modeling is rigorous. It requires to you understand the whole of things as well as their detailed intricacies. A process model takes time to build. It crosses boundaries and borders, and sometimes just in the act of creation, you're likely to uncover issues and even step on a few toes.

But don't despair — your process model speaks the truth! It's the basis for understanding and breakthrough improvement. The time you spend building it will reap its rewards in performance and satisfaction.

Six Sigma process modeling begins with the building of process maps. The paths, encounters, decisions, and destinations on these maps are then annotated and defined in quantitative terms, including such measures as value, time, resources, yields, and the statistical distributions around each. The outcome of this process is the statistical basis for simulating the process and analyzing the results.

Drawing a process map

A process map looks like a flow chart, and, at the top level, that's exactly what it is. A process map is a picture of the activities and events in a process. Figure 11-2 is an example process map.

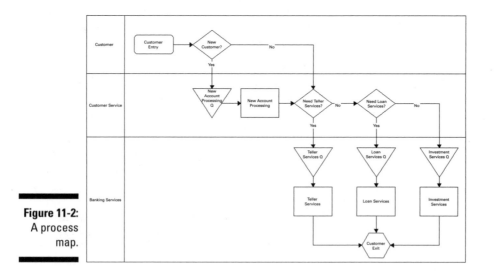

Figure 11-2:
A process
map.

You can draw a process with a pencil and paper, or with a drawing tool like Microsoft Visio. However, only more advanced tools like iGrafX Process, SigmaFlow, and Traxion permit sufficient definition and attributing to enable Six Sigma–class simulation and analysis. It's important to follow a consistent set of conventions when using shapes, connectors, and other drawing elements.

Figure 11-3 is an example set of some drawing conventions used in process mapping. While these icons are typical, the exact shape may vary slightly from one tool to another.

Use standard process mapping shapes across the organization. With the emergence of the Business Process Modeling Notation (BPMN) standard, process modeling is poised to become more routine and effective. In the meantime, your best bet is to adopt the conventions used in one of the software applications, and standardize their set of icons for use across your team or organization. Choose something, and then stick with it.

At this stage, you're not worried about the details of what happens inside each of these boxes. Your goal is to capture each of the steps, identify their basic function, and connect them in the manner that represents the process.

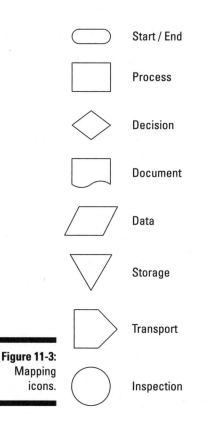

Start / End

Process

Decision

Document

Data

Storage

Transport

Figure 11-3:
Mapping
icons.

Inspection

Defining the process points

Once you've drawn a process map, the next step is to define explicitly each of the map's objects. You must be precise — and quantitative; the accuracy of your process model depends on it. If you are using a process modeling tool, your tool will include prompts for the attributes at each node in the model. These attributes are numerous. The categories of process element definitions include:

- ✔ **Operation cycle time** of the process element, including its average time to complete, the variation in time called the standard deviation, and perhaps a distribution curve to represent all the possible completion times as well.

- ✔ **Resources** used in the process element, including human, capital, and natural resources. The better tools will permit you to identify resources by name and type, and then later track their utilization during simulation.

✔ **Value added** by the process step, in the units of measure that mean the most to your organization. At a minimum, you must be able to define whether the process step is value-added (VA) or non-value added (NVA).

✔ **Costs** of the resources consumed. These include the costs of personnel, facilities, direct material, and can even include indirect costs.

The closer you can come to defining costs in the same terms as your accounting system, the better. Ultimately, you will be reconciling cost and claiming value that will be verified by your accounting department. Get the bean counters involved up front and make them your partner by counting your beans the same way they count theirs.

Swimming in lanes

A recent development in process modeling is a visualization technique called Swim Lanes. Remember how we told you that processes cross boundaries and borders? Imagine you are the customer: You're in Lane 1. Customer Service is in Lane 2. Internal Processes are in Lane 3. And so on. Time flows from left to right. The process crosses lanes as it traverses departments on its journey from start to finish. See Figure 11-4.

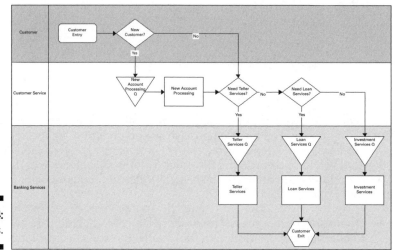

Figure 11-4:
Swim lanes.

The swim lane is an effective visualization technique that enables each functional contributor to a process to understand their role, while at the same time giving everyone a chance to see just how complicated the process may be within your organization. Remember, each time we cross a lane we have in essence created a supplier-customer interaction that implies needs, wants, and desires that must be met.

To be, or not to be

Process modeling is typically an exercise in defining how you envision your process can work sometime in the future, after implementing the changes that would enable your new concepts. It's the *to-be* state of affairs. Modeling the future in this way is powerful, because it provides you the opportunity to examine your plans in detail and consider the options before you implement the changes. Coupled with available simulation capabilities, you wouldn't dream of making changes without first modeling them.

The other application for process modeling is to create a model of today's reality: the so-called *as-is* state. Few organizations do this. They are so eager to dismiss with today's problematic world that they leap-frog straight to the dream of tomorrow's possibilities. Big mistake! The only excuse for not modeling the As-Is process is if you are implementing something brand new and there is no existing process. Otherwise, if a process exists today, model it first. There are compelling reasons for this.

✔ **Set the baseline.** Before you can measure the effects of your sweeping changes, you must first characterize the present conditions. By using the same process modeling techniques to characterize today's as-is state as well as the future to-be state, you have the basis for measuring the effectiveness of your process optimization effort.

✔ **See the process.** There are three conventional views of a process:

  • What you think is going on

  • What is really going on and

  • What should be going on

These are three distinctly different states of a process, and it is precisely what we are trying to do with Six Sigma. The only way to achieve this is by achieving the second view, mapping what is really going on. Then and only then can we move to the third view.

✔ **Stimulate closed-loop behavior.** Your investment in modeling primes the pump for breakthrough performance improvement. To continue the cycle of improvement, your model should be a dynamic, living entity, where at any point in time, your model and reality are in sync. Modeling the as-is condition from the beginning stimulates this closed-loop behavior.

Whither the SIPOC?

A SIPOC is not a process model, and vice-versa. But even if you are rigorously process-modeling your business, there is a role for the SIPOC. The SIPOC is applicable as an early-stage tool, and for high-level views of processes.

Simulating a process

A process map by itself just sits there. The process map is the first half of process modeling. While there is great benefit to the process map, its benefit is further enhanced when we can extend this static view or picture of our work activity into a dynamic view or movie of our work activity.

Simulation is the other half. Once you have mapped a process, simulation is the practice of stimulating your model into action. Simulation tools are advanced computer-based programs that ingest all the parameters of your model and run dozens, hundreds, and even thousands of trials in your computer. By doing this, you generate simulated real-life outcomes without having made a single physical change to the process, and you generate vast amounts of detailed results for statistical analysis.

The more advanced simulation tools animate your process map as the simulations run, tracing for you where your process will operate smoothly and where your bottlenecks are — as they occur. From the act of watching your model in action, and then in analyzing the results of the simulations, you can pursue the goal of process optimization. It is an iterative process.

The simulation environment

Simulation requires both a computer and considerable expertise. The programs are sophisticated. You must set up the simulator precisely, with data generated specifically for the simulator by the modeler. Fortunately for us, the advanced software tools on the market perform this task seamlessly.

Simulators are demanding computational programs that can require advanced understanding as well as capable computers to run swiftly and properly. You will want to check the specifications of your computer against the requirements of your choice of simulator. To accommodate less-capable machines, several of the more advanced simulators also contain switch settings that permit you to operate simulations with selected real-time features disabled. All of the same results are generated, but the simulation will run longer and feature less animation.

Configuring simulations

To run a simulation of your process model, you must set a number of configuration parameters. These will typically include the following:

- ✔ **Number or duration of runs:** You can specify the number of passes through the process that the simulator will perform, or specify the overall elapsed simulation time. The higher the number of runs or the longer the simulation executes, the more statistically representative the results.

✔ **Randomization:** Many simulators permit the specification of random inputs, which better mimics the variability that occurs in real life. For this to be effective, you need to understand the nature of the variability in your process inputs.

✔ **Patterns:** Your process may encounter predictable patterns of variation, such as work shifts, days of the week, month-end effects, batch inputs, time zones, distributions, and the like. These can be specified in the simulation.

✔ **Data storage:** Specify the nature of the data to be stored from the simulation. Also, specify the collection of data snapshots, either from elapsed time or after specified numbers of runs.

✔ **Interactivity:** Some simulators permit you to interact with the simulation as it runs. In this way, you can modify certain parameters and observe the resulting behavior.

Simulation results

The results of simulations can be startling and invigorating! They are almost always full of surprises. Rarely is the outcome just what you expected. More often, simulation results reveal unexpected connections and dependencies that cause you to rethink, redesign, and re-plan your process.

The results of process simulations are usually available in the form of standardized reports generated by the simulator. In rare cases, the simulator stores the simulation data in a relational database, but in most cases, the data are presented as a list output or a set of canned reports. The more advanced tools permit you to specify custom statistics for additional viewing. The report statistics categories are summarized in Table 11-4.

Most simulators produce only rudimentary reports. Sufficient analysis will require you to export the simulator data to an analytical tool, like Minitab.

Table 11-4	Simulation Report Categories
Category	*Purpose*
Time	Show overall transaction times, and times per department, process, or activity.
Cost	Report statistics on costs for all resources, transactions, and activities.
Resources	Report statistics on resource utilization, time, activities, and costs.
Queues	Report on bottlenecked processes or transactions waiting in queues due to resource, inputs, or other constraints.

Cause-and-effect (C&E) matrix

In Six Sigma, $y=f(x)$. All outcomes (Y's) are the result of some inputs (X's) and the transformations that acted upon them: cause and effect. An effective tool for the process analyst is the cause-and-effect matrix, known as the C&E matrix.

The *C&E matrix* is an extension of the C&E diagram or fishbone chart, the brainchild of Kaoru Ishikawa, who pioneered quality management processes in the Kawasaki shipyards, and in the process became one of the founding fathers of modern business management. Cause and effect helps the Six Sigma practitioner to identify and prioritize the relationships between several inputs and the resulting outcomes. With the C&E matrix, you can identify, explore, and graphically display all of the possible causes related to a problem or condition and search for the root cause. An example of the C&E matrix is shown in Figure 11-5.

#					1	2	3	4	5						
Rating of Importance					9	4	9	8	2						
Select	#	Activity Name	Process Inputs	Notes	No Work Order Defects	Billing Accuracy	No Production Defects	Order Completed on-time	Minimum Cost	Total	%	Potential / Vital X	FMEA	CP	DCP
☐	6	Assisted Service	C: Operator/Shift - Production	Individual / shift / performing work activity	1	4	9	9	4	186	8.32	No	☑	☐	☑
☑	7	Assisted Service	C: Materials	Raw material quality	1	1	4	1	4	65	2.91	No	☐	☐	☐
☑	8	Assisted Service	C: Work Type	B/W, Color, Poster, Other	4	4	9	4	4	173	7.74	No	☑	☐	☑
☐	9	Self Service	C: Work Type	B/W, Color, Poster, Other	1	4	4	1	1	71	3.18	No	☐	☐	☐
☐	10	Self Service	S: Equipment Maintenance		1	4	4	1	1	71	3.18	No	☐	☐	☐
☐	11	Payment Service	?: Scrap	Self service often purposely forget to report scrap	1	4	1	1	4	50	2.24	No	☐	☐	☐
☑	12	Payment Service	C: Customer discount	Corporate discount schedule	1	9	1	1	1	64	2.86	No	☐	☐	☐
☐	13	Existing Customer Processing	C: CSR - Greeter	Individual validating customer credit hasn't changed and enters work order	9	4	9	9	1	252	11.27		☑	☐	☑
☐	14	Existing Customer Processing	S: Work Order Accuracy	Accurate recording of work to be performed	9	9	9	9	4	278	12.43	Yes	☐	☑	☐
☐	15	Quality Assurance Service	C: QC person	Individual	9	4	9	9	1	252	11.27		☑	☐	☑
☐	16	Other Inputs	C: Working Conditions		1	1	9	4	1	128	5.72		☐	☐	☑
				Total	540	268	810	544	74	2236					

Figure 11-5: C&E matrix.

You can use a C&E matrix to examine a top-level complex process or system, and you can use it for mid-level, less complex processes and systems. For top-level applications, a C&E is used to relate process outputs to the customer requirements; it focuses your improvement efforts and identifies projects. For mid-level applications, the C&E relates process inputs to process outputs and can be used to prioritize tasks and projects.

The system-level software tools that implement C&E automatically database this information and carry it forward into further activities, including failure mode effects analysis (FMEA), control plans, and data collection plans.

Dem' fishbones

A variation on the C&E matrix is the fishbone diagram, a brainstorming tool used to explore and display sources of variation or influence on a process. With the fishbone diagram, you can quickly create the inputs to a C&E matrix, identifying the key sources that contribute most significantly to the problem or process being addressed. The fishbone diagram also serves as an affinity mechanism for relating and categorizing inputs.

A fishbone diagram is so simple that it can be done on a whiteboard, notepad, or even a lunch napkin. However, the software-based tools will also capture, categorize, and promote the data for you.

To create a fishbone diagram, you identify the major categories of influence on an outcome. Within those categories, you list the causes, as shown in Figure 11-6.

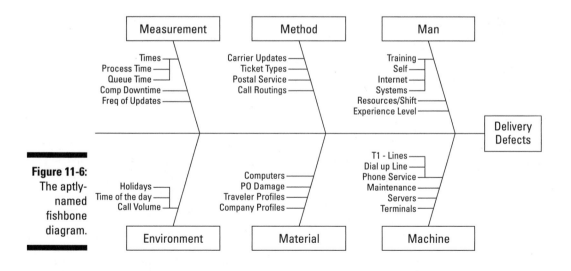

Figure 11-6: The aptly-named fishbone diagram.

FMEA: Failure mode effects analysis

Failure is nasty business. Product failures can mean everything from unhappy customers to harmful outcomes. Process failures result in poor products, lost profits, or both. The failure mode effects analysis is key to reducing or eliminating the risk of failures. The concept was first developed in the aerospace industry. And being from the aerospace industry, it is therefore universally referred to in its acronymic form, *FMEA*.

The FMEA provides you with a structured approach to identifying the potential ways a product or process can fail, how readily you can detect the failure and the effects of those failures, so you can reduce the risk of either their occurrence, or impact, or both. Using the FMEA, you can further prioritize the actions to be taken to reduce failure risk, and you can evaluate your design and control plans for their robustness to failure.

The FMEA is invaluable in applications where processes or products have safety or security implications, but it is equally applicable to any process or product where failures have a material impact on customer satisfaction or measurable business success.

The FMEA is a structured yet simple way of simulating the risk associated with a particular event occurring. It helps us to find and focus our efforts on the more significant contributors to our success or failure. It's an excellent tool to funnel down the most likely contributors or *X*s to process optimization efforts.

Applications of FMEA include

- **Design FMEA,** for analyzing product designs prior to release into production. The DFMEA is conducted early — well in advance of first builds — with a focus on product functionality.

- **Process FMEA,** for analyzing design, manufacturing, assembly, distribution, services, support, and other processes. The process FMEA is directed towards process inputs.

- **Product FMEA,** addresses failure modes possible in products or projects.

- **Software FMEA,** for analyzing failure modes in software applications.

You can build the FMEA from your Process Map, the C&E matrix, or even the fishbone diagram. In any case, the approach is the same: You add three new categories of information to the identified failure outcomes or effects, as listed in Table 11-5.

Table 11-5	Primary Elements of the FMEA
FMEA Element	*Definition*
Severity of impact	Assign a normalized score to the severity of the impact in the event of a failure.
Probability of occurrence	Evaluate and assign a probability score to the likelihood that the failure will occur.
Likelihood of detection	Assign a probability score to the likelihood that the current controls will detect the causes and therefore prevent either the failure itself or its effects from having impact.

Armed with these data, you are positioned to critically analyze the failure modes in your system, process, and products. The analysis phase of the FMEA is the process of determining probabilities and ranking the results. One of the primary indicators is the risk priority number (RPN). The RPN is simply the product of the three elements:

$$\text{RPN} = \text{severity rating} \times \text{probability rating} \times \text{detection rating}$$

Idiot-proofing

A Japanese manufacturing engineer at Toyota named Shigeo Shingo is credited with creating and formalizing an approach to quality management called *Poka-Yoke* (pronounced "PO-kah YO-kay), which loosely means *mistake-proofing* (the literal translation is to avoid inadvertent errors). Poka-Yoke is used to prevent the inadvertent causes that result in defects, mostly using simple, low-cost methods for prevention.

A Poka-Yoke device is any mechanism or procedure that either intercedes to prevent a mistake from being made, or makes the mistake so obvious as to eliminate it. Poka-Yoke efforts or devices make it nearly impossible to make a mistake. They are especially relevant where humans are part of the process effort, because humans sometimes inadvertently forget or are likely to do things differently on occasion.

Examples include such everyday tools as lock-out mechanisms, electrical connectors that are specially shaped to prevent reversed plug-in, and overflow prevention systems. The fact that your car's gas tank has an inlet smaller than the size of the filling nozzle, preventing you from putting leaded gas into your car, which requires unleaded gas, is an example of Poka-Yoke.

For each failure outcome, you can plot the RPN in a Pareto chart, like the one in Figure 11-7. With this, you can see instantly where you should focus your attention.

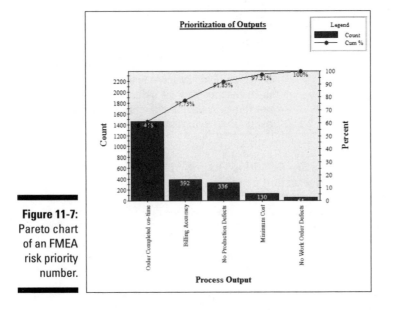

Figure 11-7:
Pareto chart
of an FMEA
risk priority
number.

The RPN is a primary indicator, but it is not the only important output of an FMEA. It's vital for you to consider the relationships between all the elements, including severity, probability, and detection, as well as cause, actions, conditions, and other circumstances. Because failure, by definition, is unwanted, you turn over every stone in your FMEA.

The outcome of the FMEA leads you directly to examine your fundamental designs, funnel reports, control plans, and data collection plans. Once you have updated these, you run the FMEA again — and again — until your failure risk profile is within acceptable tolerances.

KISS and tell: Capability-complexity analysis

Remember KISS? No, not that 1970s rock band, but that elegant acronym of simplicity: *Keep it simple, stupid*. Why do we say that? Because the simpler you keep things, the fewer chances there are for something to go wrong. Everyone knows that.

At the same time, what about those special people who seem to be extra capable and can seemingly handle anything, no matter how much you heap on them? They don't have as much trouble with the extra load. It's obvious that the more capable you are, the more you can handle.

When you put those two concepts together in the context of complex products and processes, it leads you to examine the precise relationship between complexity and capability. In Six Sigma terms, we can define, measure, and control both the complexity of our products and services as well as the capability of our processes. So, where's the point of optimization?

- ✔ How capable must our processes be to handle the complexity in our products and services?

- ✔ How complex can our products and services be in order to handle them with the capability of our processes?

- ✔ If we're going to introduce new complexity into our products, how much must we ratchet up the capability of our processes to handle it?

- ✔ If we introduce new complexity into our products and services and don't ratchet up the capability of our processes, what's the increase in our defect rate?

These are vitally important questions, and, to answer them, the Six Sigma practitioner applies capability-complexity analysis (CCA) in the pursuit of process optimization. Your process mapping and modeling depend on the balance of settings in a CCA, as do the C&E analysis, FMEA, and other tools.

Because the calculations required to compute the quantitative values of a CCA involve the manipulation of multiple variables simultaneously, it is ideally suited for computer-based application software. A CCA program solicits your input for complexity parameters about your product or service as well as capability and control parameters about your sigma capability, static mean offset, and dynamic variation expansion factors. It will then compute your short- and long-term defect rates and yields per-element and per-unit. An example CCA display is shown in Figure 11-8.

The more advanced CCA tools will permit what-if analysis where you can set outcome metrics and determine what changes in process capability or product complexity are required to achieve them.

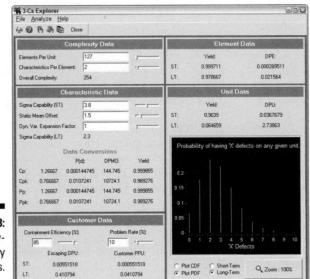

Funnel reports

Six Sigma is all about finding those *critical few* influencers out of the *trivial many* candidates that affect the outcome. The number of possible contributors can be extremely large at the beginning of a process optimization or problem solving effort. In fact, it sometimes seems so overwhelming that we are de-motivated to solve the problem.

Six Sigma to the rescue. Inherent in the Six Sigma methodology is a process called variable reduction. Six Sigma is almost automatically reducing the number of contributors or funneling the *X*s to find the so-called "critical *X*s" or "vital causes." When you have these, you have the basis for obtaining breakthrough performance improvement.

Funnel Reports help you filter through the trivial many, extract the critical few, and manage them. The sources of information for the funnel report come primarily from the CT trees, C&E matrices, and FMEAs. The more advanced software tools will import these automatically. In the Funnel process, each candidate is subjected to a set of analytical and statistical considerations, which serve as tests to qualify if the cause is vital.

The outputs of the funnel report are considered to be the most likely causes of our problem or process deficiency. The next step is to further funnel down this list into the actual root causes using statistical inference and other experimentation tools.

Plans

The Six Sigma practitioner produces and manages a set of plans that affect the MAIC elements of the breakthrough strategy. The data collection plan ensures the measurements. The control plan ensures management of the critical Xs, and the audit plan addresses the ongoing monitoring of the vital causes.

Data collection plan

The data collection plan provides a concise and focused set of directives and actions required to collect all necessary data associated with a process or within a Six Sigma project. The data collection plan can be voluminous, in that it addresses not only the content, but the reliability, availability, and presentation or formatting of the data.

Identifying the information at a high level can come from a number of sources, including the process model, the CT tree, the C&E matrix, the FMEA, and the funnel report. The more sophisticated Six Sigma software applications will populate a data collection plan template directly from these other tools. The data collected feed both the control plan and the audit plan.

The more elusive goal is in the manner by which the data themselves are collected. You will almost certainly need to work with members of your Information Technology team to determine how best to gather the data properly. The issues you need to address here include:

- **Data sources:** You're best off if you can get the data directly from the point of origin, as generated — and verified — by the originator.

- **Data timing:** Transactional data from operations changes regularly. The timing of when you pull the data is as critical as the data itself. Getting the right data at the wrong time leads to bad data.

- **Data stability:** People change the basis of operational measures regularly and without notice. This is a configuration management problem — assuring that the definition of the data you're depending on doesn't change out from under you.

- **Data format:** The physical formatting of data is critical. Be certain to identify how you want the data to be formatted in your collection plan.

- **Data transfer:** Specify how the data is to be shipped to you. By far the best way is for an automatic extract and transfer to occur on a scheduled basis. By far the most common way is for someone to periodically e-mail you some sort of extract. Press hard for the former.

Your plan will include all of the above and should be agreed to formally by all involved parties.

You'd be well served to apply some of these Six Sigma process tools to the process of data collection. The validity of your process optimization effort is only as good as the data upon which your decisions are founded. Data is a slippery beast; don't underestimate the effort required to do it right.

Control plan

Based on the fundamental concept of $Y=f(X)$, if you can control the Xs that dominate the outputs of interest (Y), you will have an improvement that lasts. The control plan directs your focus on the vital cause critical Xs and ensures all participants understand the activities, items, and specification limits required for your process to be in control. The control plan is a proactive effort to assure long-term performance and also a call to action if a triggering event occurs, indicating the process performance is deteriorating.

Your control plan (see an example in Figure 11-9) is a key Six Sigma management tool. It's a one-stop reference view of all the vital contributors to the success of your process, and it contains sufficient detail to exercise sharply-focused management controls.

Figure 11-9:
Control plan.

Select	#	Activity Name	Variable Name	Output	Input	Specification Characteristic	LSL	Target	USL	Measurement Method
☐	1	New Customer Processing	C: CSR - New Customer		☑					
☐	2	New Customer Processing	S: Work Order Accuracy		☑					
☐	3	Need Assistance	N: Job Complexity		☑					
☐	4	Need Assistance	N: Information not getting to the QA person		☑					
☐	5	Assisted Service	C: Operator/Shift - Production		☑	Only 5% errors allowed			5%	Packet checklist.
☐	6	Assisted Service	N: Production Rework		☑					
☐	7	Payment Service	S: Customer discount		☑					
☐	8	Existing Customer Processing	S: CSR - Greeter		☑	Packet complete and accurate.				Pipeline report and packet checklist
☐	9	Existing Customer Processing	N: Electronic File Option		☑					
☐	10	Existing Customer Processing	S: Work Order Accuracy		☑	Any errors are detected before passing packet on to Production				Packet checklist.
☐	11	Other Inputs	S: Equipment Training		☑					
☐	12	Other Outputs	No Work Order Defects	☑		Any errors are detected before passing packet on the Production			1%	Packet checklist.
☐	13	Other Outputs	Billing Accuracy	☑		Accuracy 98% expected	98%			Audit pricing of 20% of corp. accounts
☐	14	Other Outputs	No Production Defects	☑		Process produces a complete and accurate production	98%			Packet checklist.
☐	15	Other Outputs	Order Completed on-time	☑		ensure 98% compliance to service level agreements (SLA)	98%			control chart plotted for each shift
☐	16	Other Outputs	Minimum Cost	☑		Overtime needs to be managed			20 hrs	Time sheets

Manage your control plan closely. Solicit broad support from management and affected contributors, including approvals and signoffs. Manage configuration changes to the plan closely as well, coordinating changes officially. If everyone operates according to this plan, you will be successful. Make it happen!

Audit plan

The audit plan acts as the measurement tool for the control plan. When your control plan is in place, the audit plan is your means for regular measuring and monitoring of the outcomes.

Statistical Analysis Tools

At the heart of Six Sigma are the statistical tools (see Table 11-6). These enable the Six Sigma practitioner to first analyze practical problems statistically, and then to craft statistical answers that enable breakthrough practical solutions. The statisticians who pioneered Six Sigma forged the developmental application of these tools through grit and determination. Today, with the benefit of powerful desktop software applications, we merrily point and click our way through.

This section is an overview of the suite of Six Sigma statistical analysis tools and will show you which tools are applied in practice. These are the tools used traditionally by the Six Sigma Green Belts and Black Belts. Refer to Chapters 5 and 6 for the theory behind the application of these tools.

This section is not a tutorial on the statistical analysis tools of Six Sigma. That's a whole textbook in itself, and you have to invest in Belt training to master the applications! This general overview of the tools will show you where you should use them.

Table 11-6	Six Sigma Statistical Analysis Tools
Stats Tool	*Role*
Basic stats	The basic and descriptive statistics, such as averages, ranges, variance, and so on, used routinely in Six Sigma analysis
Plots and charts	Histograms, Pareto charts, control charts
Time series	Specific tools for analyzing results of data collected over time — trends, decompositions, moving averages
ANOVA (analysis of variance)	Analyze variances, test for equality of variances, and determine whether there is a valid relationship between variables.
Tolerance analysis	The analysis of margins and tolerances to determine optimal design specifications
DOE (Design of Experiments)	Systematically investigate the process or product variables that affect product quality
Process capability analysis	Determination of the capability of a process to perform to expectations. The output is a numerically defined index of capability.

(continued)

Table 11-6 *(continued)*

Stats Tool	Role
Regression	Determining the strength of the relationship between a response variable *(Y)* and one or more predictors (*X*s).
Multivariate analysis	The analysis of data from multiple measurements on various items or subjects. The output is a graphical picture of the various relationships.
Exploratory analysis	Methods used to explore data before applying more traditional statistical analysis tools
Measurement Systems Analysis	The analysis of the measurement system to determine the accuracy and precision of the data obtained from the measurement.
Reliability and survivability	Accelerated life testing, lifetime characteristics analysis, growth curves

The basics

At the root of Six Sigma is a set of statistical tools that drive most of the analytical activity, underlie the higher-level practices, and dominate the walk and talk of the Six Sigma practitioner.

In the practice of the statistical analysis side of Six Sigma, these tools are required fundamentals. You must understand them and be comfortable with what they mean and how to use them. The good news is that you needn't actually perform any of the calculations manually; they're all done for you by application software programs on your computer. Refer to the "Platforms and Protocols" section in this chapter for the overview on the applications software.

A picture's worth a thousand . . . dollars

Time is money. Plots and charts are a fast and powerful way to help you interpret and communicate the data. To get the message, use pictures — and lots of 'em! Plots and charts can turn masses of unintelligible data into coherent information that leaps off the page and smacks you with the message. The most commonly used plots and charts are summarized in Table 11-7.

Table 11-7	Plots and Charts	
Plot or Chart	**Description**	**Example**
Histogram	A bar chart that plots the spread of data into bins according to frequency of occurrence, immediately suggesting the distribution function.	
Dot plot	A type of histogram where data are displayed in a single-point format; used to assess a distribution or compare distributions.	
Pareto chart	A bar chart in which the bars are ordered from highest to lowest, showing the critical contributors.	
Scatter plot	Shows the relationship between two variables, immediately conveying the nature of correlation.	
Matrix plot	A matrix of scatter-plots, showing the relationships between many pairs of variables at the same time.	
3D scatter plot	A three-dimensional scatter plot, useful for evaluating the relationships between three different variables at the same time.	
Interval plot	A two-dimensional plot of data values with added confidence intervals or error bars; useful for showing both the central tendency and the variability.	
Box plot	A side-by-side comparison of sample distributions. By convention, the central line is the mean, the boxes are ±25%, and the lines are the limits.	
CDF (cumulative distribution function) plot	A stepped cumulative histogram (without bars), overlaid with a best-fit normal cumulative distribution function. Used to fit a distribution to your data.	

(continued)

Table 11-7 *(continued)*

Plot or Chart	Description	Example
Probability plot	A scatter plot, overlaid with a CDF cumulative probability line. Used to determine how closely a particular distribution fits your data.	
Time series plot	A plot of data spread over time. Used to evaluate patterns in activity across time. By convention, time is plotted on the x-axis.	
Marginal plot	A scatter plot with an added histogram (or sometimes a box plot), used to assess the relationship between two variables and their distributions.	

As powerful as the software applications are in crunching the statistical data in the first place, they really shine in creating these plots and charts for you. All the application programs on the market today will generate these types of plots and charts from the data automatically, with simple menu selections. They further will provide numerous plotting and charting options, including everything from curve and data fits to labels and legends and even colors and fonts.

The time machine

Most human activity is measured, reported, and valued over time; hence, *Time-Series Analysis* is closely correlated to the management and measures of performance improvement. Numerous Six Sigma statistical analysis tools are dedicated to time-series examination of every phase of a process. These include the following:

- **Trending:** Fit a general model to past data and observe the trends.

- **Forecasting:** Simple forecasting and smoothing methods help you decompose data into its component parts, and then extend the estimates into the future to predict ongoing performance.

- **Decomposition:** Separate seasonal or cyclical trends into groups and profile repetitive performance.

- **Moving average:** Average consecutive observations and observe the trend over time. A pattern recognition tool called ARIMA (AutoRegressive Integrated Moving Average) can help you find patterns that may not be visible in plotted data.

✔ **Exponential smoothing:** Smooth the time-series data using ARIMA and calculate the average level and, optionally, in a Double Exponential Smoothing, both the average level and trend.

✔ **Autocorrelation:** Discover repeating patterns in time-series data.

✔ **Cross-correlation:** Compute, plot, and discover the relationship between two separate time series.

Analysis of variance: ANOVA

Because variance is one of the fundamental principles of Six Sigma (see Chapter 5), the analysis of variance is a major field of Six Sigma application. Analysis of Variance is so significant in both Six Sigma and in general statistics that it warrants its very own acronym: ANOVA.

ANOVA tools include such analytical marvels as: one-way and two-way analyses (variance testing with classification by one or two variables); Analysis of Means (test the equality of population means); balanced ANOVA (accounting for data collected by different designs or procedures), also sometimes referred to as the General Linear Model; fully-nested ANOVA (estimating the variance component for each response variable); MANOVA (multi-variate analysis of variance, for simultaneously testing the equality of means from different responses); and the test for equal variances (determines the variance difference between samples from populations of different means).

All that's a mouthful, but don't despair; once again, software to the rescue! All of these tools are defined and executed in each of the major statistics applications programs on the market. These packages walk you through these tools, holding your hand every step of the way. No sweat.

If the shoe fits . . .

One of the great challenges in this world is getting the right fit. The pen cap doesn't stay on the pen; the lid doesn't close on the jar; the door leaks air; the paint runs across the line. Things are too tight, or too loose, or off the mark. How does this happen? It's not because they were intentionally designed that way. It's because the design didn't take into account the combination of variations in manufacturing the different components.

Tolerance analysis is the statistical analysis tool that helps you determine the right specifications and limits on individual parts and components to ensure that they fit together properly as a system once manufactured. It's treated as an advanced topic, as part of the field of Design for Manufacturability (DFM), and is usually taught in the advanced Design for Six Sigma (DFSS) courses.

Apply Tolerance Analysis in cases where parts or components must come together precisely for the system to function properly in satisfaction of the customer's expectations.

Design of Experiments

Most people know DOE as the Department of Education. Well, in the Six Sigma case, that's just about right, because in Six Sigma, DOE stands for *Design of Experiments*, a highly educational activity. Use DOEs to statistically investigate the variables that influence a process and the resulting quality of products and services in an experimental setting. You are then in position to effectively interpret the results and direct improvement efforts to enhance the process in the production environment.

A DOE also allows the practitioner to simultaneously understand the effects of changing the settings of multiple variables. Without DOE you're reduced to performing what we call OFAT experiments, which stands for one factor at a time. OFATs cannot detect the interactions that occur between variables. Besides, watching one-factor-at-a-time experiments takes forever.

Experiments are vitally important tools. They permit us to prototype, evaluate, and test our hypotheses in controlled settings before unleashing them in the real world. Experiments are critical risk-reducers and confidence-builders. They are a footbridge between models and reality.

Because of this keystone role, experiments must be done right. Time and resources for experiments are always limited, because people are impatient and see an experiment as a hurdle. Therefore, if you're conducting an experiment, it's very important that you get the most out of it. Well-designed experiments will yield much more useful results than tests that are casually thrown together. In fact, poorly defined experiments may yield the wrong results!

Experiments are mini-projects unto themselves. They consume resources, including personnel, equipment, and materials. They cost money and time. And because so much is riding on the results, they deserve the care and attention that any project or program would receive.

1. **Define the problem.**

   Strictly define — in quantitative terms — the nature of the problem that you intend the experiment to clarify or solve.

2. **Define the objectives.**

   Be certain that your experiment is focused on yielding specific, practical, and useful information.

3. **Design the experiment.**

   Using the many available DOE tools, design a robust experiment that will satisfy the objectives.

4. **Develop the plans.**

   Thoroughly analyze the environment, the background, and the conditions that will guide and constrain the experiment, and develop a plan that will meet the objectives with the time and resources allotted. Develop a Data Collection Plan that ensures you have the measurement systems in place to capture all the required information, and a Data Analysis Plan that ensures you have accounted for the work required to properly interpret the results.

Well-honed through years of experience, Six Sigma practitioners have defined a suite of tools to aid you in developing your DOE.

- **Factorial designs:** Factorial designs help you study simultaneously the effects that several different factors may exert on your process or product. This improves experimental efficiency, by enabling you to vary the levels or settings of parameters simultaneously during the experiment.

- **Response surface designs:** Response surface designs help you examine the relationship between one or more response variables and a set of experimental variables. This approach is particularly useful after you've determined which parameters constitute the "vital few," and you want to find the settings that optimize the output.

- **Taguchi designs:** Named after Dr. Genichi Taguchi, who is widely regarded as the foremost authority in robust parameter design, Taguchi experiment designs help you find the settings that permit your product or service to operate consistently over a variety of conditions.

How capable is your process?

Process capability analysis is the next of kin to statistical process control (SPC), and is how you determine if your process, once in control, is also meeting specifications. Process Capability Analysis is a critical component of the Six Sigma methodology, and Six Sigma practitioners calculate a variety of indices and measures and draw numerous plots and charts to assess and optimize process capability.

In summary, capability analysis takes the voice of the process (VOP) and compares it to the voice of the customer (VOC) to see if it is capable of meeting the requirements.

We cover the definition of Process Capability at some length in Chapter 6. The tools for process capability analysis are extensive. We've listed the most commonly applied tools in Table 11-8.

Table 11-8	Process Capability Analysis Tools
Tool	*Application*
Normal analysis	Analyze process capability when the data are from a normal distribution.
Non-normal analysis	Analyze process capability when the data are from a non-normal distribution.
Between/within analysis	Analyze process capability for between-subgroup and within-subgroup variation.
Multi-variable analysis	Analyze the capability of an in-control process when each of multiple continuous variables follow a normal distribution.
Binomial analysis	Analyze the process when the data are from a binomial distribution — when examining the number of defective items out of the total number of items sampled.
Poisson analysis	Analyze the number of defects observed, where the item occupies a specified time or space.
Capability six-pack	An set of six charts, which collectively contain key process capability metrics. An example Six-Pack is shown in Figure 11-10.

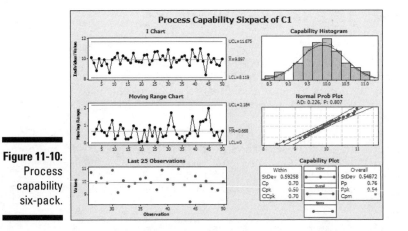

Figure 11-10: Process capability six-pack.

Regression

Regression analysis is used to discover and characterize the relationship between a response and one or more predictors. In regression analysis, you fit models or distribution functions to observed data. And depending on the data, this can lead you to a variety of functions.

The goal of regression analysis is to fit a line and create an equation to explain or predict the way your process output is behaving. As an example, imagine plotting your car's gas mileage for different driving speeds. We all know intuitively that the faster we drive the lower the gas mileage, but could you come up with an equation to predict your car's mileage as a function of its speed? Yes you can. Regression analysis helps you do it.

- **Fitted line:** For when the best fit to the data is linear or logarithmic. Derivatives include second-order (quadratic) and third-order (cubic) fits.

- **Least squares:** When the response variable is continuous.

- **Partial least squares:** When the predictors are highly correlated or if they outnumber our observations.

- **Logistic:** Used with categorical response variables. There are three types: binary (two levels), ordinal (three or more levels), and nominal (no natural ordering of the levels).

- **Stepwise:** A technique of removing or adding variables to the regression model in order to identify a useful subset of the predictors.

- **Best fit:** Examining all the subsets, identify the best-fitting models that can be constructed with the specified predictor variables.

Multivariate analysis

Quite often, you will have multiple measurements on a given item or subject. Multivariate Analysis helps you understand the structure in this mix of data. It helps you assign different observations to statistically-significant groups and visually explore the relationships among the grouped variables.

Multivariate analysis begins with applying tools to understanding the covariance structure in the data. Principal component analysis and factor analysis are two methods for helping you determine structure, alignment, and dimensions of the variables within the data. Grouping tools then help you aggregate data. These tools include data clustering from similar observations, clustering of variables, grouping by known similar averages (called *K-means*), and grouping by comparison to a sample group (known as discriminant analysis).

When you have statistically segmented your variables, multivariate analysis explores the relationships among them.

- **Simple correspondence analysis** explores variation between two variables.
- **Multiple correspondence analysis** extends the process of simple correspondence analysis to the case of three or more variables.

Exploratory analysis

Sometimes, you're not quite sure where to begin or which statistical tools you should apply to a given situation. Sometimes, you're not sure which tools apply — or if any of the traditional tools apply at all. That's okay! A variety of *exploratory analysis* tools let you examine data in nontraditional ways, giving you the ability to work outside traditional boundaries and see your data in a different light. A sampling of these tools is summarized in Table 11-9.

Table 11-9	Exploratory Data Analysis Tools
Tool	**Application**
Stem-and-leaf	A quick way to examine the spread and shape of your data.
Box plots	Assess and compare sample distributions (see example in Table 11-7).
Letter values	Assign data into broad buckets.
Median polish	Analyze variance relative to the median instead of the mean.
Resistant line	Fit a straight line to your data while ignoring the outliers.
Resistant smoothing	Smooth your data, removing random fluctuations, before examining trends.
Rootogram	Plot your data up as a histogram, fit a normal distribution to it, and examine how closely the data fit or deviate from the normal distribution.

Measurement Systems Analysis

All the emphasis on the collection and analysis of data begs the obvious question: How good is your measurement system? If your measurement system is faulty, your data is faulty, in which case your analysis is no good, and you may as well put your plans to better use on the bottom of the bird cage.

Measurement Systems Analysis (MSA) is the practice of determining the extent to which observed process variation is due to variation in your measurement systems. Any time you take measurements, you will encounter variation. The source of this variation is two-fold:

✔ Real variation in the actual process

✔ Imperfections in your measurement system

Measurement system errors are classified into two broad categories: accuracy and precision. With most measurement systems, both errors are present.

Accuracy

Accuracy is the difference between your observed measurement and the true value. Three sources contribute to accuracy error:

✔ **Linearity** is a measure of how the observed error is somehow related to the size of the measurement. If your measurement is accurate in the middle of the measurement range, but not for very large or very small measurements, you have linearity error.

✔ **Bias** is the condition when your measurement system is skewed — like when you dial the zero value on your bathroom scale down a few pounds before stepping on to check your weight!

✔ **Stability** is the tendency of your measurement system to vary over time or some other condition, such as temperature or humidity.

Gauge Linearity, Gauge Bias, and Gauge Stability studies help you analyze measurement systems accuracy issues.

Precision

Precision error is the condition of observing variation from measurement to measurement, or from part to part. The two components of precision error are as follows:

✔ **Repeatability:** Variation in the *measuring device*. All other conditions being equal, there is variation in the measuring device itself.

✔ **Reproducibility:** Variation in the *measurement system*. The device performs properly, but the system of measurement — including the procedures, human error, and support systems — introduce variation.

Gauge R&R (repeatability and reproducibility) studies help you determine the extent to which device and process variation contribute to your overall measurement system variation.

Back to the future

Reliability and survivability analysis helps you use all the measurements and data from the past to predict what is most likely to occur in the future.

- ✔ Develop tests that demonstrate compliance with reliability specifications to specified confidence levels.
- ✔ Determine the number of tests needed to develop precision estimates of percentiles and reliabilities.
- ✔ Define criteria for accelerated life tests to determine the relationship between failure time and key predictors.

Platforms and Protocols

Throughout this chapter, we've been telling you that the many tools and methods of Six Sigma are nicely encapsulated in application software packages, available for your immediate use. It's true. While the statisticians, analysts, and progenitors of Six Sigma were busy refining the methods and tools of Six Sigma, so, too, were the software programmers. The Six Sigma software marketplace is now brimming with well-tuned packages. Every tool we address in this chapter is programmed into a number of nicely designed software products. And what's more, they're relatively inexpensive, and easy to use.

By and large, the software programs follow the tools: process optimization and statistical analysis. As the software matures, the overlap is increasing, but the areas of expertise are well-established.

Software products

It's a crowded field. By our last count, over 120 commercial software programs supporting Six Sigma process and statistical analysis were available on the market. Many of these come from small shops with niche products for specialty purposes. As Pareto would have it, however, the market is led and dominated by the critical few larger and very professional organizations, who bring solid and fully capable commercial-grade application software products to a demanding market.

Statistical analysis software

The leaders in Statistical Analysis software include the following:

- **Minitab:** The undisputed leader. Minitab is taught extensively in colleges and universities, used extensively in major corporations, and fostered universally by Six Sigma consultancies. In its 14th release as of this writing, Minitab is packed full of features and is completely capable of stellar performance for you on every statistics tool discussed earlier in this chapter. It runs only on a PC.

- **JMP:** From the prestigious SAS Institute, JMP (pronounced *jump*) is a professional statistics package that rivals Minitab in its features and capabilities. Its greatest advantage is in its multi-platform support: JMP runs on Windows, Macintosh, and Linux.

- **Excel:** Yes, as in Microsoft Excel. That ubiquitous spreadsheet program that comes on nearly every PC is also a powerful computational and display program, and it's used extensively in Six Sigma statistical analysis applications. Unlike Minitab and JMP, you have to program Excel to perform the calculations, but there are also a plethora of software companies that sell Excel add-ons and extensions for statistics.

Process optimization software

The Process Optimization space is much broader — and younger — than the statistical analysis market, and no one software program does it all. You have to be willing to piece together your solution from several different software vendors. Following is a short list of leading software companies whose products support the core process tools. They all run on the PC platform, with a few exceptions.

Process tools are categorized in two classes:

- **Business Process Analysis (BPA)** tools enable you to model and map processes, simulate how they'll work, and analyze the results.

- **Business Process Management (BPM)** tools enable you to connect with the information systems in your business and provide process measurement and control functions.

The leading tools in the process management arena are:

- **Traxion:** From CommerceQuest. Traxion is a complete BPM tool, with modeling and simulation capability, similar to iGrafx and SigmaFlow. But Traxion has the unique additional capability to collect information out of your operational environment and give you feedback on your performance in real time. This so-called "closed loop" solution integrates your Six Sigma design and simulation with the measurement and control systems in your business. More on this in the "Technology architectures" section.

- ✔ **iGrafx:** The iGrafx mapping and process simulation software is by far the most widely used full-featured process analysis tool in the marketplace. As a company, iGrafx has bounced around, and as of this writing, it's a division of Corel, Inc. But the iGrafx pedigree goes back nearly 20 years, and the product set is well-regarded as the BPA leader.

- ✔ **SigmaFlow:** Although a relative newcomer in the market, SigmaFlow is earning fans through its more business-focused approach to modeling and simulation. It's fully integrated internally and automatically populates one tool with the information and output from another.

- ✔ **Visio:** Surprisingly, a lower-level tool from Microsoft is a major player in the Six Sigma marketplace. Visio has long been used for drawing process maps. No detailed model attributing or simulation, though.

- ✔ **Varyx:** From Savvi International, Varyx is the only Tolerance Analysis software on the market. A niche player, but with a powerful and important product. In the interest of full disclosure, you should know that two of your authors work for Savvi. But we still recommend these tools!

- ✔ **3-Cs Explorer:** Also from Savvi International. Capability-Complexity Analysis is made simple with the 3-Cs Explorer analysis and display.

Technology architectures

Software is complicated stuff. Beneath the covers and underneath all the windows, dialog boxes, drop-down menus, and snazzy reports of commercial application software swims an ocean of program code. Software programs are developed according to an architectural design, and a program's architecture dictates how the code will perform, what types of computing environments it will work in, how it can interact with other programs, and how accessible its functions and data will be to the outside world.

You must be aware of the implications of the architectures in the software products you consider for implementing the tools of Six Sigma. These products have been built to a range of architectural models, and while many may have similar features, underneath they're different and may not suit your application. This section addresses these differences and gives you some guidance to help you choose the right solutions.

PC-Windows

With a few notable exceptions, most of the programs for Six Sigma process optimization and statistical analysis have been developed exclusively for the PC-Windows operating system. They run on PC-Windows computers only. If you have Macs or Linux systems in your environment, these PC programs will not run on them. But that may be okay. If you're operating in a PC-Windows world, these tools may be sufficient.

Few company environments are this monolithic. For this reason, most of the statistical analysis programs have import and export capability, so they can move data into flat files or Excel files. This permits users in other environments to generate or view the results. The Excel file type is used as a universal translator in this manner.

The gotcha with PCs is that many PC programs operate as standalone systems, and provide little by way of connecting or operating with other people or systems. E-mailing data files back and forth gets really old, and file-sharing is cumbersome, error-prone, and difficult to manage. In short, the PC desktop environment by nature often works against your Six Sigma philosophy and goals.

This is what's known as *functional sub-optimization* — the tool may be great for you, but it doesn't help you work well with others. The solution to the sharing problem is in what's known as enterprise technology, addressed later in this section and in Chapter 12.

Mac and Linux platforms

These two main platform alternatives to PC-Windows have been classically under-served by the Six Sigma tools market. Very few providers have offerings for these platforms, with the exceptions of Microsoft Excel and the very capable JMP statistical analysis product. JMP is what's known as a cross-platform tool; it runs on all three desktop platforms — PCs, Macs, and Linux. If you are in a mixed-platform environment, JMP is a viable solution you should strongly consider.

Using a mix of platforms can also present problems when you want to share information and work in a team environment. Typically, the architects of Mac and Linux solutions include more integration and connectivity, but many programs offer you little more than the chance to e-mail your data files around. Remember that you can always run PC programs through emulation software on the Mac. It's not pretty, but it works.

Enterprise platforms

The solution to the challenge of working together with computers is provided by what's known as *enterprise technology*. Enterprise systems are designed for interoperability — permitting people to fulfill their business and functional roles while interacting with a coherent system of information management. Large software systems have been built this way for decades.

The Six Sigma technology and tools industry grew up in the PC era, and as a result, precious few of the process or analysis tools have been crafted to an enterprise architecture. (Note that this is *not* the case for the management tools, which have mostly been developed to an enterprise architecture. This is discussed further in Chapter 12.) All the integration and interoperability in enterprise systems comes at a price, however. It usually also means that each user makes some personal sacrifice, in terms of performance or independence, for the greater good. But if your business environment requires extensive sharing of analytical or process information in a controlled manner, look for enterprise solutions.

The best way to recognize an enterprise software solution is the user interface. Most enterprise systems are accessed via a Web browser like Internet Explorer or Mozilla Firefox. The programming logic and the database of information reside across the network somewhere, rather than on your local machine.

Chapter 12

Mastering Six Sigma Manager Tools

. . . .

In This Chapter

▶ Assessing your Six Sigma management tool requirement

▶ Exploring the different types of Six Sigma Management tools

▶ Understanding where and how Six Sigma Management tools are used

▶ Finding out about available management tools and technologies you can use

. . . .

*T*he only thing more important than practicing Six Sigma is managing Six Sigma. You think it's important to understand all the technical practices and analytical tools? It is, but it's even more important to manage resources (people), schedules, and budgets — and to be accountable for bottom-line results.

Managing Six Sigma projects and programs requires that you understand your area of application as well as the use of process methods and tools. But it also requires you to apply your methods and tools of the management process. These tools support your need to manage the many interactions between multiple contributors, who occupy different roles in the organization at many different levels. The tools must also support the complex technical interactions between information systems. We suppose that's why the managers get the big bucks.

In this chapter, you discover the methods and tools of Six Sigma management. These begin with program leadership tools and include project definition and tracking, as well as business reporting. In addition, this chapter covers the tools you need for accessing reference information. The chapter concludes with a look at knowledge transfer systems and the emerging world of online learning.

The Manager's Toolkit

To be a successful Six Sigma manager, you must not only understand Six Sigma but also be skilled in the methods and tools of project management. A Six Sigma initiative is an endless series of projects — of various sizes and shapes — cascading together in a programmatic fashion, creating an unending stream of breakthrough improvements in business performance. These improvements are made one project at a time, and each project is an encapsulated universe of Six Sigma activity unto itself.

The Six Sigma manager's toolkit is, therefore, a set of project and people management tools in a portfolio. These tools are inspired by leadership, enabled by infrastructure, tailored to the Six Sigma methodology, and implemented through technology. Some of these tools are relatively straightforward, such as tools to help you manage project deliverables and tools to help you remember how to do Six Sigma. Others are more involved, like tools for tracking and communicating critical business indicators, and those for helping you manage cost and schedule.

Unlike the tools used by practitioners, where most are used in an individual, standalone fashion, most management tools have a focus on integration and communication. Management systems must robustly link the daily work products of many individual contributors. As such, Six Sigma management tools are typically built to an enterprise information architecture, with core data repositories and shared access to the application logic, thus minimizing operational error. To be sure, plenty of management tools are integrated via *sneakernet* — the practice of running files back and forth (usually with e-mail) — a practice that begs for error. In any case, management tools provide specialized information access and control to each of the constituents with a stake in the success of the initiative.

The management process is a little different for Six Sigma than it is for most other activities. Managing scope, schedule, and budget is still the manager's job, but there are specific methods and tools in the case of Six Sigma. You want to integrate existing management tools and the knowledge you currently possess with specific management tools you need to make Six Sigma easier and more beneficial.

The gallery

At the management level, everybody's watching and listening. And asking why. Six Sigma management tools support each of these constituents, including both participants and spectators:

- ✔ **Executive management:** Because most Six Sigma initiatives are strongly and directly endorsed by executive management, tools must support the executives and provide them the information and interaction needed to continue their endorsement.

- ✔ **Six Sigma champions and Deployment Leaders:** Champions are steering the overall Six Sigma initiative and are accountable to the executives and the operational business units for the results. They're in the cat-bird seat, must have a direct line of sight on people and projects, and must constantly know the pulse of the Six Sigma activity.

- ✔ **Financial executives:** Because Six Sigma projects contribute directly to the bottom line, their performance is of great interest to financial managers, who want to maintain close touch with their progress and results.

- ✔ **Process Owners:** These managers own the profit and loss (P&L) or the budget and productivity of the processes that either support or deliver the value proposition of the company. Process Owners must have immediate access to the information and rationale behind any changes in order to support and implement those changes.

- ✔ **Black Belts:** Black Belts are the team leaders of major Six Sigma projects. These are the projects with the most complexity, difficulty, and the greatest impact and return to the business. As team leaders, Black Belts use project tracking and management tools as well as the process optimization and statistical analysis tools discussed in Chapter 11.

- ✔ **Green Belts:** Green Belts have traditionally acted as support staff but they also act as project managers within their areas of responsibility. When acting as Six Sigma project managers, Green Belts use similar tools as Black Belts with a lower level of analytical prowess.

- ✔ **Yellow Belts:** Six Sigma initiatives affect everyone in the business, and the successes and performance of these initiatives are communicated to everyone in the company. Training and reporting tools are used by Six Sigma managers to involve and inform the staff, and by the staff to initiate new projects and participate in existing ones.

- ✔ **Suppliers:** As suppliers become more integrated into business processes and enabled by the enterprise architecture in many of the management tools, Six Sigma tools securely enable the management of vertical value chains.

- ✔ **Customers:** The external customer is the customer who pays for the product or service that we deliver. Management is ultimately accountable to the customer and uses the tools and techniques of Six Sigma to direct improvements on behalf of the customer.

Types of management tools

Because the constituencies served in the Six Sigma process are such a broad set, the tools of management are a diverse lot. In total, these are the tools of communication and leadership, project management, reporting, knowledge management, and learning.

- **Communication and leadership:** Communication and leadership tools are both formal and informal: company Intranet sites, video messages, letters and memos, reports, and other messages. And don't forget the most important leadership tool: face-to-face contact.

- **Project management:** Management tools include everything from the capture of ideas into project assignments, staffing, budgets, and performance. The more advanced tools include multi-project and cross-project portfolio management in a shared enterprise architecture.

- **Reporting tools:** These are tools that query data and create reports provide standard and repeatable ways to communicate detailed information. These reports include tables, plots, and charts of analytical and process performance data. These are combined with budgets, schedules, resources, and business-impact information to create comprehensive pictures of project and program status, progress, and trends. When aggregated together, these tools are typically called dashboards.

- **Knowledge management tools:** These tools are extensive collaboration tools, granting individuals and teams access to information repositories. By having access to the right knowledge at the right time, managers and practitioners can expedite their return on improvement investment.

- **Learning tools:** Beyond traditional training, learning tools provide direct, just-in-time, and lower-cost training to individuals, teams, and companies. These tools are critical enablers for the job of training large numbers of people in the concepts, ways, and methods of Six Sigma.

Because these tools integrate people, functions, and systems, utilities known as Application Integration tools help tie together and share the information they generate and use. A class of these utilities, called Enterprise Application Integration (EAI), or *middleware,* helps you move data between and among not only these management tools, but also between and among transaction systems, including customer management, accounting, design, and shop-floor systems.

Through the Looking Glass

After you get the basic concepts of Six Sigma, you're changed forever. You'll have insights and vision that dramatically enhance your abilities. The knowledge and tools of Six Sigma well up in you an emboldened sense of personal empowerment. With Six Sigma, you command the power and have the ability to foster significant positive change in the world. As a result — regardless of your title or official duties — you become a leader!

Your leadership role compels the use of the single most important tool for any leader: communication. Your Six Sigma knowledge and capabilities grant you significant influence, and you apply that influence through all manner of communication. The tools of communication you must use are the broadest set of communication tools possible and they're summarized in Table 12-1.

 We can't overemphasize the power of leadership within every Six Sigma practitioner. Whether you're an analyst, executive, manager, engineer, or administrative assistant — it doesn't matter. When you know how to apply the methods and tools of Six Sigma, there's no turning back. You have this special insight, a new ability, and you're going to use it. With that ability comes the essence and responsibility of leadership.

Table 12-1	The Tools of Leadership Communications
Communication Tool	*Role*
Face-to-face communication	The most powerful leadership tool is your personal communication. Direct interaction is the best way to listen and influence.
Formal presentations	Using a presentation tool like PowerPoint, a formal presentation is a common, effective, and repeatable leadership and communication tool.
Impromptu presentations	White boards and flip charts make ideal platforms for conveying important ideas and information, conducting brainstorming sessions, developing early designs, and troubleshooting.
E-mail	Messages, directives, requests, and reports can all be communicated via e-mail, which communicates directly and by passing along through different audiences. Using attached files, e-mail is a powerful communication conduit. It's poor and inappropriate for resolving issues, however.

(continued)

Table 12-1 *(continued)*

Communication Tool	Role
Shared repositories	Systems like intranets, file servers, groupware, and enterprise application systems help communicate broadly and consistently.
Phone calls	Particularly when there's an issue or problem, there's nothing quite as effective as just picking up the phone and calling them.
Memos and letters	Formal memoranda and letters are most useful for communicating in an official manner, such as a policy directive or formal announcement.
Bullhorn	Hey, whatever it takes! Just make sure you get the message out.

In addition to communication tools, you must use other leadership tools, including motivational tools and the tools of influence.

Project Management

Six Sigma benefits are derived from a series of projects. Lots of projects. Big projects, little projects. Long projects and short projects. Projects within a single department, and projects that cross departments. Projects inside companies, and projects that cross company boundaries. Dozens of projects — and, in big companies, hundreds of projects. Dr. Seuss could write a book on all the Six Sigma projects!

At the business level, Six Sigma projects are the players in the overall game plan of a breakthrough performance improvement initiative. The business perspective is that a Six Sigma project is the agent of action that executes the business strategy and returns the results. Selecting the right projects is, therefore, critical, as is executing them properly. This means that the effective management of projects is core to the success of a Six Sigma initiative.

The skills and tools required to manage a Six Sigma project are similar to those required to manage other types of projects. It's rigorous, but you don't need a certification from the Project Management Institute to do it.

First, you define the fundamental problem or need you intend to solve or address with your project effort. Then, you define the objectives and results you seek to achieve. From this, you define the project plan, which includes scope, schedule, and benefit. Upon gaining approvals, you're off and running. When you're underway, you must track and manage the project to plan, and deliver the results to the Champion or Deployment Leader.

The application domain of the project may be unique to Six Sigma, but the management of the project follows many standard project management rules and guidelines. In Table 12-2 are listed the major categories of project management tools used in the management of Six Sigma projects. Application software packages of various types are available on the market to assist in the execution of these tools.

Table 12-2	Six Sigma Project Management Tools
Project Tool	*Role*
Ideation	Capture ideas for potential Six Sigma projects.
Definition	Establish the project scope, write a problem and objective statement, set a schedule, and assign initial team members.
Selection	Establish priorities for projects, manage the queue of projects, and launch projects.
Tracking	Track and manage project progress. Identify and manage variance to plan. Ensure deliverables to the established objectives and schedule.
Reporting	Communicate the status and results of the project — to the project team members, business owners, Six Sigma Champions, executives, and other constituents.

Eureka!

Projects begin with a problem or a need to improve. Someone, somewhere, realizes that it can be done better. Improve a process. Reduce defects. Eliminate waste. Projects can be motivated in countless ways. (Refer to Chapter 4 for more on sourcing and defining Six Sigma projects.)

The process of discovering the opportunity to perform a Six Sigma project is known as *project ideation*. This funny word, *ideation* — short for idea creation — refers to the process of creativity and insight within the formality of the controls that permit the idea for the project to flourish. Tools for project ideation enable you to capture the essence of the idea, along with supporting information, in a central database to evaluate and consider. An example of a Web-based project ideation portal is shown in Figure 12-1.

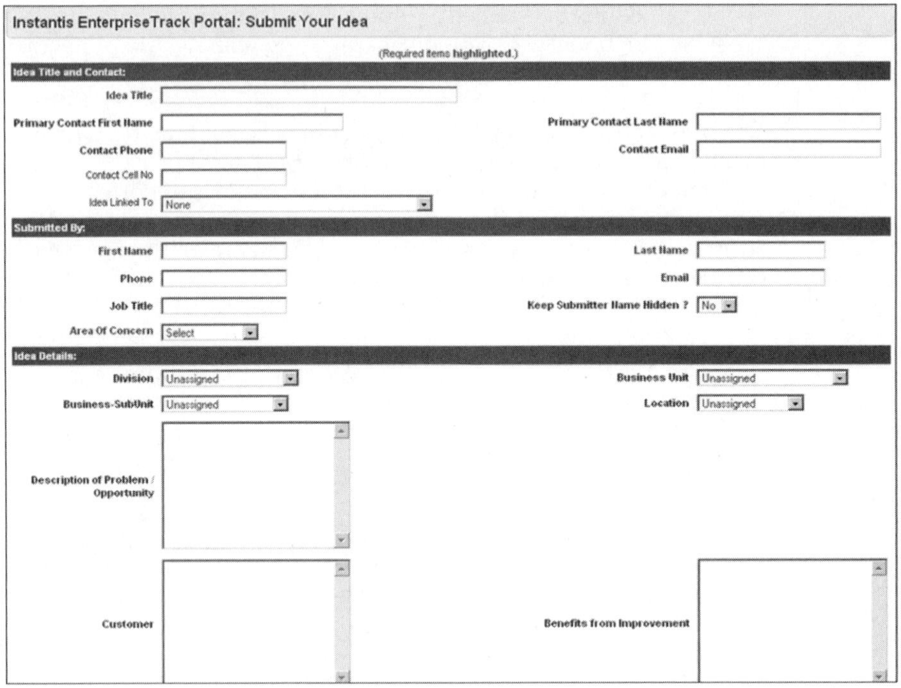

Figure 12-1:
Project
ideation
portal.

Ideation tools like these are powerful ways to enroll everyone in the organization — including customers and suppliers — in the process of identifying potential improvement projects.

Pick a winner

Project selection is a delicate act of evaluation, alignment, and prioritization. Your Six Sigma projects must be of proper value and contribution in their own right, but they must also be set in the context of the improvement of the business and in meeting its stated goals. Rogue Six Sigma projects can solve the wrong problems.

As part of the selection process, a project must first be defined in rough terms — but sufficiently quantified in scope, schedule, difficulty, and expected impacts on the business. Then you can determine if it's worth doing.

Evaluation

First, evaluate any proposed project for its direct contribution to its specific area of business and its alignment to the overall business strategy or objectives. These contributions should include quantifiable measures, such as significant percentage of defect reduction or measured customer satisfaction improvements, as well as the financial contributions to profitability.

> ✓ Quantifiable improvements: 70 percent or greater improvement over baseline performance on key metrics
>
> ✓ Quantifiable returns: Return on investment is less than 1 year

Alignment

Next, evaluate the project in terms of its alignment to the goals and strategies of the business, and for its context relative to core or enabling business processes. The Six Sigma Champion or Deployment Leader should evaluate how the project will contribute to the overall business needs.

> ✓ Categorize the project in terms of hard dollar value or soft contribution. No more than 25 percent of Six Sigma projects should be soft-savings projects.
>
> ✓ Align the project profile to the overall business to ensure its efforts and contributions are placed strategically.
>
> ✓ Consider the learning value and the contributions toward generation of momentum as part of the total Six Sigma improvement initiative.

Priority

As a result of your evaluation and alignment exercise, assign a numerical priority to the project. Typically, use a range of 0 (project disapproved) to 10 (assigned top resources and budget).

Use the priority scheme to identify those projects that have the largest potential impact on the organization, either strategically or financially, and that have the highest probability of success with the lowest level of required resources. A priority matrix is a useful tool in comparing parameters and prioritizing projects.

Project definition

Project definition is the critically important process of transforming a practical business problem into a Six Sigma project. The output is a well-defined problem statement and a well-scoped set of objectives, including approvals from those who are either involved in the project or affected by its results. The Six Sigma management community believes that 50 percent of the success of a project is in the quality of its definition.

The project definition worksheet breaks down the many elements of defining a project into easy-to-handle pieces. Refer to Chapter 4 for more on sourcing and defining Six Sigma projects.

Management — in the form of the Champion, Deployment Leader, and/or Process Owner — is responsible for defining projects. Management must decide which projects will achieve business (VOB) goals and meet customer (VOC) requirements. Six Sigma practitioners are closely involved, assisting management in this effort, contributing input to the evaluation and alignment of candidate projects.

At the highest level, that's really all there is to the essence of project definition. But while it may sound easy, a lot of information and work goes into defining projects, which means you have a lot to track and manage.

You have difficult hurdles in front of you. Resources — budget, people, and equipment — are always in short supply. Schedules are always tight. You have to account for the constraints and risk factors, too. However, if you follow the project management process, you will produce a well-defined project plan and enable your project team to be successful.

Behind the magic trio of a problem statement, an objective statement, and approvals are a number of supporting elements that make up a sound project definition. These are summarized in Table 12-3. Every project definition should contain a concise and accurate description for each of these elements.

Table 12-3	Basic Elements of Project Definition
Element	*Definition*
Purpose	The reason and motivation for doing the project. This includes a precise statement of the problem, and its impacts.
Objectives	The core set of objectives that must be met if the project is to be judged a success. Be quantitative in identifying the anticipated levels of improvement.
Benefits	How everyone will gain from successfully meeting the project objectives. For Six Sigma projects, this specifically includes the bottom-line benefits.
Team members	Identify the team of individuals and skills needed to complete project. The team should be small to remain agile, yet have the sufficient expertise and representation. Typically, a core team of six or fewer are required, with additional help on a part-time basis.
Schedule	The schedule includes the total duration of the project as well as the individual duration of each project phase
Risk and controls	Scope, schedule, and objectives hang in a delicate balance. A change in any one affects at least one of the other two. Estimate the risk and impact of possible and probable changes, and identify the controls you apply to prevent them from occurring and to respond if they do.

Project planning and tracking

The preceding section describes the tools of project definition. In this section, you find out about the tools for Six Sigma project planning and tracking.

Planning the project

After the Six Sigma project definition phase is complete, the next step is to plan the project. Project planning is important, because a project plan is no better than all the effort and consideration that went into it. A project is a process, and the effort to plan a Six Sigma project is just as rigorous as the development of the process you're setting out to improve. As General and two-term U.S. President Dwight D. Eisenhower once said, "Plans are nothing. Planning is everything."

To prepare a project plan, you must first collect and organize the information from your project definition effort.

- **Methodology:** In a Six Sigma project, the project method follows the DMAIC process (see Chapter 3). Any of the project planning and tracking software tools for Six Sigma have built-in templates for DMAIC. The project milestones and subordinate deliverables will follow this approach.

- **Roles:** Choose and assign the people and skills you need to complete the project. This includes Black Belts, Green Belts, and Process Owners. If the project is very complex, spans many organizations, or has been unsolvable in the past, you need a Black Belt to contribute in-depth technical analyses and leadership.

- **Schedule:** Six Sigma projects are short, usually three months or less. To realize the advertised returns, the project team should complete its work in a short timeframe. Project milestones normally coincide with the application methodology, such as DMAIC, with deliverables and checkpoints at each phase boundary.

- **Reporting:** The communication of project status is critical in Six Sigma projects, just as it is in other types of projects. Each stakeholder and participant must be regularly informed as to progress and results. This includes not only the project team members, but the finance group, process owners, and executive leaders. The tools of leadership communications (refer to Table 12-1) facilitate the project-reporting effort.

- **Cost/benefit:** Because the ultimate deliverables and returns on Six Sigma projects are measured in terms of bottom-line contributions, your most important project metrics are the returns you're generating as a result of the project effort. Manage to the return on investment (ROI), and use methods of valuation that are consistent across your business.

The output of the project planning process — the *project plan* — is a specific and controlled set of information. The project plan includes text documents, supporting spreadsheets for financials, and a Gantt or similar type of project schedule, with milestones, resource information, and reporting mechanisms. Collectively, this information set is reviewed and, after it's approved, is set down as what is known as the *baseline* project plan. This baseline plan is what everyone works to. Any changes to the baseline plan must be reviewed with the Champion or Deployment Leader as well as other stakeholders to determine if or how the project should continue.

The supporting application software tools to complete the project plan include:

- **Word processor:** A tool like Microsoft Word captures all textual information, and stores it in files. You want to print one or more copies for physical reference and include signature authority to allocate resources to perform the project.

- **Financial calculator:** Typically, a spreadsheet tool like Microsoft Excel supports financial planning information. However, in more sophisticated environments, this may be replaced by built-in capabilities in your company's ERP system or managed from within an integrated project planning tool like Instantis or SixNet.

- **Scheduler:** Project schedulers are like process mappers for projects. They enable you to capture all planned work tasks, resources, costs, and risks and place them in a scheduling format according to a formal organization of work. Numerous project management software tools are on the market; tools specifically designed to support Six Sigma projects include Instantis and SixNet. These are powerful, and they perform project scheduling for Six Sigma-specific projects from an Internet-based architecture. There are many others; the most commonly used generic project scheduling tool is Microsoft Project. Refer to Figure 12-2 for an example of a project schedule.

- **Reporting:** Project status reports are typically generated directly by the project planning and scheduling tools. You may need to extract information from your project scheduling tool to generate the precise type of reports you need. The following section addresses this in more detail.

- **Document manager:** Often overlooked but of critical importance are the tools for managing the plethora of project documentation. Document management is the practice of securing a set of data files in a repository with strict access and revision controls. These systems are invaluable for controlling updates to official or reference documentation.

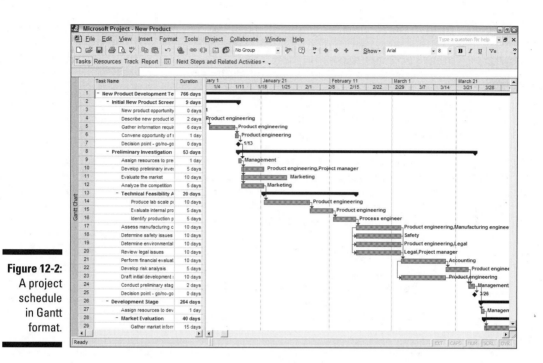

Figure 12-2:
A project
schedule
in Gantt
format.

Tracking the project

Project plans are really great — until the day the project begins. Tracking and managing the project to plan is critically facilitated by the tools, and this is where they really shine. These tools help you track and report project status; make changes to resources, budgets, and schedules; and redefine work and deliverables. In many cases, the tools will also manage changes to the plan, and compare the real results, called *actuals,* to the original baseline to produce variance-to-plan information.

The saving grace for Six Sigma projects is that they're short. While longer projects become increasingly complicated to manage, Six Sigma projects typically last only a few months. This way, projects — and their models — can't get into too much trouble, because they don't last long enough to be overly complicated.

Just the Facts, Ma'am

Reports communicate results. They are the trailing indicators, demonstrating the outcomes of your initiatives. Reporting tools are communication tools that tell everyone how well your initiatives are performing. These tools are vitally important, because they provide visibility into the bottom-line results of your projects and programs.

As key communicators, you must pay close attention to your project reports. Without them, your constituents have no way of knowing all the great things you've accomplished and, therefore, have no way of supporting you or your project team. After all the work and all the achievements, you want to ensure that everyone gets the good news.

Reporting tools for Six Sigma projects and programs are available in many flavors.

- **Generic reporting tools:** The information management marketplace has a category for what is known as *business intelligence tools.* These tools are useful for culling information from databases and presenting nicely formatted reports on a repeating basis. This class of tools is not specific to Six Sigma, but because they are generic, they are adaptable to the application. Among this group are tools like Cognos, BusinessObjects, and even Microsoft Office.

- **Integrated tools:** The enterprise integrated tools used for project planning and tracking also include a suite of reporting tools. If you've used these tools on the planning and tracking side of your management effort, they are efficient and effective as reporting tools. See Figure 12-3 for an example.

- **Balanced scorecard:** A specialized system of reporting specific business measures and performance in a proscribed manner, known as the *balanced scorecard,* has emerged in recent years. The balanced scorecard is an entire field of study unto itself, and its methodology is specified by the members of the Balanced Scorecard Institute, which include both corporations and governments. In some cases, Six Sigma results must be presented in this manner. Figure 12-4 shows an example of a balanced scorecard.

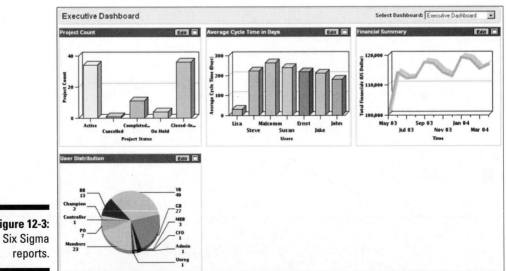

Figure 12-3:
Six Sigma reports.

BSC: Internal

Per	YTD		Var Per	Var YTD
●	●	Cycle Time	4.55	3.52
●	●	Returns %	-1.07	-1.02
●	●	Status	-0.16	-0.09
●	●	TeamEfficiency	1.10	0.87
●	●	Timeliness	-0.75	-0.97
●	●	Wastage %	-2.35	-1.48

BSC: Finance

Per	YTD		Var Per	Var YTD
◄	◄	Asset Growth %	-14.29	-23.81
★	★	Net Profit %	20.60	18.83
●	●	Revenue	1.89	1.60
●	●	Status	4.41	-1.03
●	●	TROCE	9.44	9.44

BSC: Learning + Growth

Per	YTD		Var Per	Var YTD
●	●	EmployeeSat'n	1.27	-1.56
●	●	RecruitmentCost	-0.63	-0.72
●	●	Skill Change	10.00	1.67
●	●	Staff Devt	0.70	1.30
●	●	Status	3.15	0.37

BSC: Customer

Per	YTD		Var Per	Var YTD
◄	◄	Complaints %	14.99	13.04
●	●	Cust Retention	8.67	2.67
●	●	CustomerSat'n	1.58	-1.47
●	●	Market Share %	-8.47	-4.66
★	★	New Customers	150.00	91.67
★	★	Status	27.36	15.05

Figure 12-4:
Balanced
scorecard.

Knowledge Management

Knowledge Management (KM) tools are extensive collaboration vehicles that help you transfer and share knowledge and information across your organization. These are by no means specific to Six Sigma, but the savvy Six Sigma manager employs these tools to ensure a widespread effect of the behaviors and results of a Six Sigma initiative.

KM tools are almost exclusively enterprise-class applications that operate across networks. They work together with learning tools to provide effective and efficient mechanisms for sharing intellectual capital and creating an environment of responsiveness and furthering innovation. KM tools are an informal, bottom-up way to bring together and share information.

The marketplace for Knowledge Management tools is quite broad, and in the broadest sense it includes all information, reporting, and content management technologies. More specifically, KM tools enable people to collect, access, manage, and share all relevant information on a variety of topics. This includes

- Six Sigma methodologies
- Statistical analysis methods and tools
- Process optimization methods and tools
- Results of past statistical analyses
- Past process management activities and results
- Project definitions and charters
- Project plans
- Project results

The field of Knowledge Management considers this list a treasure trove of intellectual value within a business. All manner of tools and technologies, from Internet and intranet access tools to structured access and control tools to library management systems are fair game for your consideration relative to how you choose to integrate this information into the regular daily lives of your staff and co-workers.

Knowledge Management is not an esoteric field of academic ballyhoo about life in the electronically-enabled information age. Six Sigma initiatives produce a wealth of vital information that contribute significantly to the intellectual capital of your business. KM is the technology that releases this capital into your organization to generate sustained growth and performance improvement.

An Apple for Your Apple

A key tool of Six Sigma management is training. Corporate training in the principles and practices of Six Sigma is traditionally delivered by consultants or internal Master Black Belts. This training follows a prescriptive training regimen, whereby executives, Champions, Deployment Leaders, "Belt" staff, and functional support staff receive the training necessary to conduct themselves in their respective Six Sigma roles.

More and more, instruction and learning are taking place through the computer. This is called online learning, or *e-learning*. The field of online learning has been growing and maturing dramatically in recent years, and represents an increasingly larger piece of formalized instruction and corporate training. Chances are you've experienced some form of e-learning.

Online learning for Six Sigma is an attractive management tool for several reasons:

- ✔ On a per-student basis, e-learning is far less expensive than conventional stand-up training.

- ✔ E-learning eliminates most of the time and expense of travel — either for the student or for the instructor.

- ✔ With e-learning, students are often able to take classes during off-times, reducing work interruptions.

- ✔ E-learning reduces instructor time, permitting companies to deploy more Master Black Belt trainers back into the workforce.

- ✔ Because e-learning is conducted within information technology environments, it directly facilitates understanding of technology tools.

- ✔ E-learning is a natural companion to knowledge management, and the materials for e-learning quickly translate to reference knowledge.

You can see how attractive e-learning for Six Sigma can be. E-learning technologies and platforms do not replace conventional Six Sigma training in one key area, however: Students must still complete workplace projects and be mentored closely through the project process. The Master Black Belt is an important mentoring component of the student's knowledge development process. Automation has not fully replaced the instructor — at least not yet!

Several methods of e-learning for Six Sigma are available as discussed in the following sections.

Computer-based training (CBT)

This is the most famous and common of all e-learning techniques. In this approach, the training is delivered either via a compact disk (CD) or through the Internet on the Web. Students receive the training by clicking through pages of material and, once completed, they usually verify their knowledge by taking online examinations.

This approach is common in lower-level types of training, but has fallen short of delivering value with the higher-level constructs and learning required in a Six Sigma environment. The timing and interaction of the mentor is also difficult to schedule through this approach.

Synchronous mentored learning

This approach, often referred to as "the instructor in a box," is more intimate than CBT. With synchronous learning, the student attends class online at a fixed time of day, during which the instructor presents the materials. The student usually has a real-time link and can interact with the instructor and other students with questions and discussions.

This approach is favored by several universities, and we have observed it in several corporate training environments. The benefit includes a certain spontaneity in the instructor's lecture materials, but the intimacy of the real-time online interaction comes at the price of high network bandwidth.

Asynchronous mentored learning (ALN)

The Asynchronous Learning Network approach is a hybrid of the preceding two. With ALNs, students follow the lectures independently, and yet interact with the classes and their classmates on a fixed routine. ALNs are increasing in popularity in corporate and government training applications because of this duality.

Part IV
The Part of Tens

The 5th Wave   By Rich Tennant

"Okay — let's play the statistical probabilities of this situation. There are 4 of us and 1 of him. Phillip will probably start screaming, Nora will probably faint, you'll probably yell at me for leaving the truck open, and there's a good probability I'll run like a weenie if he comes toward us."

In this part . . .

We give you short lists of best practices, common mistakes, and where to go for help.

Chapter 13

Ten Best Practices of Six Sigma

In This Chapter

▶ Setting ambitious goals and achieving quantifiable results

▶ Living by some important principles

▶ Selecting the right projects and people

▶ Changing the culture through exposure and training

Successful Six Sigma efforts have several practices and characteristics in common. This chapter lists ten of the best. As you launch into your own Six Sigma journey, use these as landmarks to set your course and bearing. Even after you've been doing Six Sigma for a while, it's a good idea to periodically compare what you do with what others have found to be most effective, so revisit this chapter from time to time.

Set Stretch Goals

Six Sigma isn't for the mildly ambitious manager or the person who wants to incrementally improve the output of a process. Instead, Six Sigma is for people who want to improve by leaps and bounds.

Six Sigma has repeatedly proven that it produces breakthrough improvement. But to achieve this, you have to combine the power of the Six Sigma method and tools with *stretch goals,* goals that almost seem too aggressive, too optimistic.

Specifically, a stretch goal represents a 70 percent improvement over current performance. For example, if your company's profit margin is seven percent, you want to aim for 11.9 percent (a 70 percent increase). Or if a certain process or product is producing ten defects per 100 units, you want to reduce that number to three defects per 100 units (a 70 percent improvement).

Another common way to set the right stretch target is to benchmark yourself against your competition. A *benchmark* is the level of performance achieved by the best companies, organizations, functions, or processes in your industry. If someone else is doing it, you should be able to do it, too, right? Toyota, for example, is a company that is benchmarked for the time it takes them to introduce a brand-new vehicle design. Most companies take 36 to 48 months to bring a new vehicle to market; Toyota did it in about 24 for its hybrid car, the Prius, which also presented a technical challenge far beyond those of traditional gasoline-only cars.

Target Tangible Results

Typically, Six Sigma leads organizations to reduce their costs by as much as 20 to 30 percent of revenue. At the same time, these organizations increase their revenues by 10 percent or more.

To realize these returns, however, each Six Sigma project must be tied to a tangible financial measure of return — dollars saved, new revenue gained, specific costs avoided, and so on (see Chapter 4 for details). These measured financial returns must be formally measured, tracked, and rolled up if you want to achieve the startling financial return that is a hallmark of Six Sigma. Without tying projects to tangible financial measures and tracking their financial impact, Six Sigma efforts naturally drift away from their financial potential.

In isolated cases, a Six Sigma project is not directly focused on cost reduction or revenue enhancement. Instead, it is targeted on a strategic objective of the organization. If you complete a project with an object of increasing brand awareness, for example, you'll have difficulty quantifying how much that project improves the company's bottom line. But if it enables the company's key business strategies, the project is still worth the effort.

Determine Outcomes

Every output or result is determined by a set of inputs. This is the idea of determinism discussed in Chapter 2. The natural outgrowth of this principle is that you actively go out and adjust and control the inputs in a way that enables you to reach your desired outcomes with certainty and consistency.

Think Before You Act

Too often, people jump into action and do something — anything — to solve a problem. They confuse action with effectiveness. Undoubtedly, this approach showcases activity, but it usually ends in a continuation of the problem or, at best, a suboptimal solution.

Six sigma's DMAIC methodology (see Chapter 3 for details) forces you to shift the bulk of the activity of solving a problem into defining, measuring, and planning a solution. Each project starts with a detailed, in-depth definition of what the problem really is and what the objectives of the solution are. Next, extensive measurements are taken to verify the current performance of the process or system. This is followed by in-depth analysis of inputs, outputs, conditions, and causes-and-effects. Only after completion of all of these steps is an improvement solution attempted. The result of this upfront rigor is, almost always, an optimal solution that can be quickly and efficiently put in place. In the long-run, the front-loaded DMAIC approach solves the problem more quickly and with better, more consistent results than other approaches.

Businesses and organizations have a vested interest in getting optimal results quickly and consistently. This is the emancipating power of Six Sigma.

Put Your Faith in Data

There is an admonition among Six Sigma practitioners: "In God we trust; all others bring data." Without data, decisions are based on supposition, estimation, opinion, and sometimes wishful thinking. Data allows you to objectively identify and select the truly best ideas and solutions from among the many alternatives.

Making decisions based on data, however, is not easy. Data require you to suspend judgment and personal bias, to confront sometimes brutal and undesirable facts. You have to believe that, in the long-run, trusting data will consistently lead you to better and more rapid solutions.

If you listen to it, the data will tell you what you need to do to improve by leaps and bounds. Common sense, opinion, and "trying harder" are not guaranteed to get you there.

Minimize Variation

Most people think of excellence in terms of averages or single numbers — the average yield on a production line, the monthly cost to run a department, the rate of return on an investment. But the reality is that variation around these averages or single numbers — even when they are at acceptable levels — can often cause more damage than their level itself.

For example, having a high average number of orders is great. But if the day-to-day number of orders varies widely, it requires the company to have excess equipment and staff always on hand, just in case. When the number of orders varies to the low side, equipment and staff sit idle. The company would actually come out ahead if its average number of orders were lower but its day-to-day variation were smaller. That way equipment and staff needs would be steady and costs would be reduced.

Variation will always be present in the plans you design, the products you make, the transactions you conduct, the services you deliver. Even in the environment outside your control, events and circumstances change and vary in ways beyond your control.

Six Sigma does two important things. One, it narrows the range of variation in any process, product, service, or transaction. Two, it enables you to configure your work so that you can meet your performance targets in spite of the variation you can't control.

Align Projects with Key Goals

One of the most important Six Sigma success factors is selecting projects that are aligned with the key goals and objectives of your organization (see Chapter 4 for details). Six Sigma efforts that are successful and lasting are always made up of projects that are each specifically focused on moving an organization towards its stated objectives.

Celebrate Success!

A Six Sigma initiative may start small with a single pilot project, or a deployment within a lone department. Others grow to include an entire global organization or accumulate staggering financial returns. Regardless, celebrate success.

Success is contagious. When the first, small victories are showcased and lauded — with recognition, rewards, praise, and publicity — people develop real interest. They build confidence and trust. They begin to believe in the power and potential of the method. Each successive victory becomes that much easier.

Involve the Owner

Six Sigma projects require change. Black Belts and Green Belts develop improvements to systems and processes for which they are not accountable. And when these participants are done with their project, they ask the real system or process owner to implement and sustain their solution.

Put yourself in the owner's shoes. Does the idea of tinkering with the process you own without knowing the future results sound exciting?

Successful Six Sigma practitioners communicate with and involve the owner of the process or system they are working in. They solicit their input and provide feedback through all the stages of DMAIC. Then, when the time for change arrives, the owner jumps at the chance to implement the awaited improvements.

Unleash Everyone's Potential

The best Six Sigma efforts extend beyond full-time Black Belts. When an organization broadens its Six Sigma knowledge and participation to Green Belts and Yellow Belts, it unleashes the vast potential of a greater number of its employees. What an advantage! Instead of relying on a handful of isolated, specialized experts to drive organization-wide improvement, an entire army is enlisted to contribute to the effort.

Chapter 14

Ten Pitfalls to Avoid

. . . .

In This Chapter
▶ Dispelling common Six Sigma myths
▶ Knowing what to watch for
▶ Avoiding common mistakes

. . . .

Navigating through Six Sigma can be treacherous. There are storms and hidden reefs. This chapter gives you ten common mistakes and perceptions that can hinder your success.

Not Allowing Enough Time

An organization breaking through to a new level of performance requires an engine of project activity. That's why a small portion of an organization — the Black Belts — are asked to dedicate all their time and efforts toward completing Six Sigma projects. They set aside their usual job duties and concentrate full time on completing assigned project(s).

A common mistake is to assume that an organization can get the same magnitude and speed of change by having Black Belts work on projects on the side, as a part-time assignment, between the tasks and duties of their regular work. This approach simply doesn't generate the force necessary to sustain organizational change. Project completion drags out and resulting savings languish. Ultimately, momentum and interest wane.

Who's the Leader?

Some organizations have tried to deploy Six Sigma without a designated, empowered deployment leader. They train Belts, they assign projects, they infuse tools, they track results. They believe breakthrough change will occur by the sum of the individual, independent efforts. But a Six Sigma deployment without a leader is like a ship without a captain — individual crew members may know what to do in their own areas, but there is no direction or overall progress.

Taking Too Big a Bite

Almost invariably, the failure of any Six Sigma project can be traced to a scope that was too broad. Trying to minimize variation in an entire product, for example, is so defocused that little improvement can happen on any part of the product. Concentrating on minimizing the variation in a single critical characteristic of a product, however, allows you to dig deep enough to discover the real source of improvement.

Always err on the side of scoping your projects too small.

Focusing On Isolated Areas

A mistake companies can make with Six Sigma is to implement it in isolated pockets, rather than as a uniform and pervasive campaign. Sometimes, an organization will allow a couple of Black Belts or Green Belts to be trained and to work a few projects. The problem with this approach is that the Belts don't get the needed support from management, and they run into political and organizational roadblocks that impede their success.

Organizations are living, connected organisms. When you make an improvement in one area or in one process, you have to make other improvements in other areas to receive the full benefits. What sense does it make, for example, to improve the design of a product but not improve your ability to manufacture that product?

"But We're Different"

It's natural to consider yourself or your organization to be unique — so unique that you may even think that what's worked for others couldn't possibly work for you. This is one of the most common myths people have about Six Sigma.

Six Sigma is a general methodology. It has proven itself in every arena where it's been applied — manufacturing, operations, logistics, design, supply chains, services, transactions, processing, legal, human resources, software, sales, marketing, management, healthcare, the public sector, defense contracting — the list literally goes on and on! Don't fall into the trap of thinking you're the lone exception to the rule.

Overtraining

Not every officer of the peace needs to be trained as an elite Special Forces commando. Likewise, not everyone doing Six Sigma needs to know the details of every advanced statistical tool and method.

The amount of information in Six Sigma courses has ratcheted up, as consultants and trainers have competed against each other in their marketing efforts. But the use of the tools tells the real story. Only a handful of the taught Six Sigma tools are used regularly. The majority are brought out only occasionally for rare Sunday drives.

Don't get fooled into thinking that more and more knowledge is always better. And don't think you have to use every tool on every project. Expediency in learning and in application is the key! The best system gets the right knowledge to the right person at the right time.

Blindly Believing Your Measurement System

Data and measurements are the foundation of Six Sigma. All too often, however, Six Sigma practitioners neglect to check the validity of their measurements. Unknowingly relying on a faulty measurement system is like building a house with a crooked ruler — you won't get what you thought you were going to get, and you won't know why.

Always take the time to perform a measurement systems analysis at the beginning of your project. Taking this step saves you from many potential headaches.

"Remind Me Again, Is It CLs or SLs?"

Control limits (CLs) are a critical part of every control chart. They capture and represent the true voice of the process. The problem is that they are often confused with specification limits — which represent only the voice of the customer. It's critically important to know when to use which limit in which situation — control limits for the voice of the process and specification limits for the voice of the customer. See Chapter 10 for details.

Exaggerated Opportunity Counts

The definition of Six Sigma performance is no more than 3.4 defects per million opportunities for defects — counting every single opportunity for defects in a given system. But one way to achieve a high capability is to offset the discovered number of defects with a falsely inflated assessment of the number of opportunities. Some practitioners erroneously inflate the number of opportunities in a system to make their performance look better than it really is. What you want is performance that looks and *is* great.

Not Leveraging Technology

Technology and software are inseparable from Six Sigma. Yet many people try to segment technology into its own, isolated corner. Others dismiss its contribution outright, because they don't understand how to leverage its potential.

The right technology can help any person in Six Sigma do his or her work better and faster — and that's a goal everyone desires.

Chapter 15

Ten Places to Go for Help

In This Chapter

▶ Using a Web portal

▶ Perusing publications

▶ Joining associations and societies

▶ Using the services of trainers and consultants

*W*hether it's the statistics, the projects, the deployment planning, applications, leadership, management, or support — Six Sigma is hard. No doubt about it. It's big and it's complicated, and you need lots of smarts (or, at the very least, this book) to pull it off. But while you may be blazing new trails through your own life and organization, thousands of people have forged similar trails before you. You can trod merrily on the bleached bones of those who have gone before.

There are many, many places to go for all kinds of help on every subject. Academics, corporations, societies, associations, practitioners, consultants, and authors — they're all out there and available to assist you, with knowledge, education, training, consulting, tools, technologies, and publications. We've organized them into ten groups.

Colleagues

Chances are, you know someone who has been involved in Six Sigma, perhaps even a specialist of some type. If you're working in a company that's deployed Six Sigma, you have Champions, Master Black Belts, and Black Belts all around you. You then also have reference material at your fingertips.

Even if you don't know of anyone personally, you may be surprised by just how few degrees of separation lie between your interest and a Six Sigma expert. Ask your friends and associates, at your church or at the ballgame. Try shouting "Six Sigma" in a crowded movie theater! You know people who know Six Sigma; you just have to ask around.

Six Sigma Corporations

Hundreds of corporations have deployed Six Sigma, including corporations in every industry and every corner of the world. Many of them will openly meet with you to discuss their experiences and offer advice. Several, like pioneer Motorola, have consulting groups that offer this advice as a service. Don't hesitate to consider calling on a company that's been through the process and ask them about it.

Associations and Professional Societies

Several associations and professional societies cater to the Six Sigma industry and audience. These associations offer a variety of services to members, including access to knowledge and information, such as white papers and case studies, special events, contacts, and discounts on materials and services. If you're entering the Six Sigma world, membership to one of these is highly recommended.

- ✔ **The International Society of Six Sigma Professionals (ISSSP):** ISSSP is the premier industry organization that caters to the professional.

- ✔ **American Society for Quality (ASQ):** ASQ is the largest quality association in the United State, with over 100,000 members.

- ✔ **Six Sigma Benchmarking Association:** This association conducts benchmarking studies, shares best practices, and facilitates process improvement and total quality.

- ✔ **American Statistical Association (ASA):** ASA is a scientific and educational society that promotes statistical practice, applications, and research; publishes statistical journals; and improves statistical education.

- ✔ **The Royal Statistical Society (RSS):** RSS, based in the U.K., is the world's oldest quality association. RSS publishes a journal, organizes meetings, sets and maintains professional standards, accredits university courses, and administers examinations.

Conferences and Symposia

Numerous organizations regularly sponsor conferences and symposia around the United States and the world on topics in Six Sigma, quality, and Business Process Improvement. These conferences are outstanding forums for meeting with peers, surveying product and service providers, and attending seminars on current topics of interest.

Major Six Sigma conferences include the following:

- ✓ **ISSSP Conferences:** ISSSP holds several conferences annually.
- ✓ **The International Quality and Productivity Center (IQPC):** IQPC provides tailored conferences and hosts numerous Six Sigma conferences worldwide.
- ✓ **American Society for Quality (ASQ):** ASQ hosts a large annual conference.
- ✓ **Worldwide Conventions and Business Forums (WCBF):** A conference organization that hosts topical Six Sigma conferences.
- ✓ **Ixperion:** This group hosts focused conferences, primarily in Europe.

Check the Internet for more information about these groups.

In addition to these major industry events, many minor events of topical interest occur regularly. These events are hosted by associations, consultancies, and tool vendors. You wouldn't want to miss the International Conference on Axiomatic Design, for example!

Publications

At last count, we place the number of books on Six Sigma at over 200 titles. You can find them easily through iSixSigma or directly on Amazon. The authors of these tomes are usually consultants and practitioners who have published works based directly on industry experience. The works in general are grouped by topic; choose the ones that best suit your needs:

- ✓ **Guide books:** How to implement Six Sigma in your company
- ✓ **Pocket guides:** Handy little reference books that you can literally stick in your pocket
- ✓ **Management books:** Stories and advice on how to manage Six Sigma initiatives
- ✓ **Handbooks to be used as tools:** Detailed, mathematically rich volumes on every statistical tool and topic
- ✓ **Technology books:** Books about the technical and management tools

Web Portals

The fastest access information is right at your fingertips. Web portals aggregate vast sums of information and whisk you directly to the source with the click of your computer mouse. We recommend the Web as the starting point for outside help.

- ✔ **Google:** There's no bigger access point to the world's information. We mentioned in Chapter 1 that the term "Six Sigma" returns over 2 million hits on Google. But that's only the starting point. Try entering **ANOVA,** and Google returns 2 million hits on that! How about something more esoteric? **Six Sigma Black Belt** yields 9,000 places to go. How about **Run charts?** 1,200 responses. Or **Six Sigma online training:** 700 hits. Google is a portal of awesome power.

- ✔ **iSixSigma:** The Six Sigma industry has its own commercial portal, www.isixsigma.com. iSixSigma provides extensive free information on almost any Six Sigma topic. Content on the site focuses on three primary areas: information, community, and supplemental services. You can find products, tools, hire a Black Belt, and even find a job. The site also includes chat rooms, forums, and libraries.

Periodicals

Several publications support the Six Sigma industry. The larger and more significant journals include the following:

- ✔ *iSixSigma Magazine:* The publishing end of the Web portal

- ✔ *Six Sigma Forum:* The magazine of the American Society for Quality (ASQ); directed at the Six Sigma audience

- ✔ *International Journal of Six Sigma and Competitive Advantage:* A practical and research-oriented journal that addresses new Six Sigma developments, thinking, tools, techniques, and methodologies that improve business and organizational performance

- ✔ *Quality Progress:* The quality publication of the ASQ

- ✔ *Quality Digest:* An independent magazine about the business of quality

Technology Vendors

An increasing number of software and technology products related to Six Sigma (see Chapters 11 and 12) are on the market. These tools are powerful and enable your initiatives. These vendors sell the software, provide product training, and assist with implementation and integration in your environment.

Technology vendor products and services come in several categories:

- ✔ Process modeling and simulation
- ✔ Statistical analysis
- ✔ Process management and execution
- ✔ Program portfolio and project management

Consultants

Help is on the way. Numerous consultancies cater to supporting Six Sigma initiatives. These consultancies can help you with every aspect of your interest — everything from "Should I consider a Six Sigma initiative?" to "How do I run a process simulation?" and everything in between.

The consultancies fall primarily into three categories:

- ✔ **Large scale consultancies from Big-6-type firms:** These firms have Six Sigma expertise but also tend to provide enterprise-class coverage of topics in business process management and information technology systems integration.
- ✔ **Six Sigma consultancies:** The industry boasts several dozen firms who cater specifically to Six Sigma implementation and support.
- ✔ **Boutiques:** Numerous highly focused one-person firms dot the landscape; these consultants provide specialized assistance in specific topics and areas.

Six Sigma consulting is expensive. Don't be surprised to pay $3,000 or more per day for experienced senior consulting. It's worth it — if you can afford it.

Six Sigma Trainers

Training in the principles and practices of Six Sigma is a commodity industry with numerous providers. Training is available on every conceivable topic and through multiple modes, including traditional classroom, computer-based training, and asynchronous learning networks. Several firms license training materials and train a company's trainers.

Training providers come in three flavors:

- **Academics:** More and more colleges and universities offer Six Sigma training. This is usually offered through the College of Engineering or the Business School, and is either part of the regular undergraduate or graduate curriculum or offered as an outreach through a professional development center. Contact your local college or university for more information.

- **Training consultancies:** Most of the Six Sigma consulting firms also offer training. Unlike many academic sources, consultancies train on both technical and non-technical topics. In addition, they often tailor the training curriculum to the needs of a particular business.

- **Online training:** Growing in popularity, online training is increasingly available on topics in Six Sigma. Online courses are available through universities and several of the training consultancies, and is also offered by firms that specialize in online curriculum.

Appendix

Glossary

● ●

affinity diagram: An organization of individual pieces of information into groups or broader categories.

ANOVA (analysis of variance): A statistical test for identifying significant differences between process or system treatments or conditions, performed by comparing the variances around the means of the conditions being compared.

attribute data: Data that has a set of discrete values such as pass or fail, yes or no.

average: Also called the mean, it is the arithmetic average of all of the sample values. It is calculated by adding all of the sample values together and dividing by the number of elements (n) in the sample.

bar chart: A graphical method depicting data grouped by category.

Black Belt: An individual who receives approximately four weeks of training in the Six Sigma DMAIC methodology, analytical problem solving, and change management methods and who leads a project of significant value to completion. A Black Belt is a full time Six Sigma team leader solving problems under the direction of a Six Sigma Champion.

breakthrough improvement: A rate of improvement at or near 70 percent over baseline performance of the as-is process characteristic.

capability: A comparison of the required operation width of a process or system to its actual performance width. Expressed as a percentage (yield), a defect rate $(DPM, DPMO)$, an index (Cp, Cpk, Pp, Ppk), or as a sigma score (Z).

cause-and-effect diagram: *See* fishbone diagram.

central tendency: A measure of the point about which a group of values is clustered; two measures of central tendency are the mean and the median.

Champion: A Six Sigma leader, who recognizes, defines, assigns, and supports the successful completion of Six Sigma projects; a Six Sigma Champion is accountable for the results of projects and the business roadmap to achieve Six Sigma results within their span of control.

characteristic: A process input or output that can be measured and monitored.

common causes of variation: Those sources of variability in a process that are truly random; that is, inherent in the process itself.

complexity: The level of difficulty to build, solve, or understand something based on the number of inputs, interactions, and uncertainties involved.

control chart: The most powerful tool of statistical process control. It consists of a run chart, statistically determined upper and lower control limits, and a centerline.

control limits: Upper and lower bounds in a control chart that are determined by the process itself. They can be used to detect special or common causes of variation. They are usually set at ±3 standard deviations from the central tendency.

correlation coefficient: A measure of the linear relationship between two variables.

cost of poor quality (COPQ): The costs associated with any activity that is not done right the first time. It is the financial qualification of any waste that is not integral to the product or service that your company provides.

C_P: A capability measure defined as the ratio of the specification width to short-term process performance width.

C_{Pk}: An adjusted short-term capability index that reduces the capability score in proportion to the offset of the process center from the specification target.

critical-to-quality (CTQ): Any characteristic that is critical to the perceived quality of the product, process, or system. *See also* significant *Y.*

critical *X*: An input to a process or system that exerts a significant influence on any one or all of the key outputs of a process.

customer: Anyone who uses or consumes the output of a process, whether internal or external to the providing organization or provider.

cycle time: The total amount of elapsed time from the time a task, product, or service is started until it is completed.

defect: An output of a process that fails to meet a defined specification or requirement, such as time, length, color, finish, quantity, temperature, and so on.

defective: A unit of product or service that contains *at least one defect.*

deployment: The planning, launch, training, implementation, and management of a Six Sigma initiative within a company.

Design for Six Sigma (DFSS): The use of Six Sigma thinking, tools, and methods applied to the design of products and services to improve manufacturability initial release performance, ongoing reliability, and life-cycle cost.

Design of Experiments (DOE): An efficient, structured, and proven approach to investigating a process or system to understand and optimize its performance.

DMAIC: The acronym for the five core phases of the Six Sigma methodology: Define, Measure, Analyze, Improve, and Control; used to solve process and business problems through data and analytical methods.

DPMO (defects per million opportunities): The total number of defects observed divided by the total number of opportunities, expressed in events per million. Sometimes called Defects per Million (DPM)

DPU (defects per unit): The total number of defects detected in some number of units divided by the total number of those units.

entitlement: The best demonstrated performance for an existing configuration of a process or system. It is an empirical demonstration of the level of improvement that can potentially be reached.

epsilon (ϵ): Greek symbol used to represent uncertainty or residual error.

experimental design: *See* Design of Experiments (DOE).

Failure Mode Effects Analysis (FMEA): A procedure used to identify, assess, and mitigate risks associated with potential failure modes in a product, system, or process.

finance representative: An individual who provides an independent evaluation of a Six Sigma project in terms of hard and/or soft savings. They are a project support resource to both Champions and project leaders.

fishbone diagram: A pictorial diagram in the shape of a fishbone showing all possible variables that could affect a given process output measure.

flowchart: A graphic model of the flow of activities, material, and/or information that occurs during a process.

gauge R&R: The quantitative assessment of how much variation (repeatability and reproducibility) is in a measurement system compared to the total variation of the process or system.

Green Belt: An individual who receives approximately two weeks of training in the Six Sigma DMAIC methodology, analytical problem solving, and change management methods. A Green Belt is a part time Six Sigma practitioner who applies Six Sigma techniques to their local area, performing smaller-scoped projects and providing support to Black Belt projects.

hidden factory or operation: Corrective and non-value-added work applied to produce a unit of output generally not properly recognized as unnecessary and a form of waste of time, resources, materials, and cost.

histogram: A bar chart that depicts the frequency of occurrence (by the height of the plotted bars) of numerical or measurement categories of data.

implementation team: A cross-functional executive or management team representing multidisciplinary areas of the company, whose charter is to drive the implementation of Six Sigma by defining, documenting, and leading practices, methods, and operating policies.

input: A resource consumed, utilized, or added to a process or system. Synonymous with the terms X, characteristic, and input variable.

lshikawa diagram: *See* fishbone diagram.

least squares: A method of curve-fitting that defines the best fit as the one that minimizes the sum of the squared deviations of the data points from the fitted curve.

long-term variation: The observed variation of an input or output characteristic that has had the opportunity to experience the majority of the variation effects that influence it.

lower control limit (LCL): For control charts: the limit above which the subgroup statistics must remain for the process to be in control; typically three standard deviations below the central tendency.

lower specification limit (LSL): The lowest value of a characteristic that is acceptable.

Master Black Belt (MBB): An individual who has received additional training beyond Black Belt. The MBB is a technical, go-to expert for technical and project issues in Six Sigma. Master Black Belts are qualified to teach and mentor other Six Sigma Belts and support Champions.

mean: *See* average.

measurement: The act of obtaining knowledge about an event or characteristic through measured quantification or assignment to categories.

measurement accuracy: For a repeated measurement, it is a comparison of the average of the measurements compared to some known standard.

measurement precision: For a repeated measurement, it is the amount of variation that exists in the measured values.

Measurement Systems Analysis (MSA): The assessment of the accuracy and precision of a method for obtaining measurements. *See also* gauge R&R.

median: The middle value of a data set when the values are arranged in either ascending or descending order.

metric: A measure that is considered to be a key indicator of performance. It should be linked to goals or objectives and carefully monitored.

natural tolerances of a process: *See* control limits.

nominal group technique: A structured method used by a team to generate and rank a list of ideas or items.

non-value-added (NVA): Any activity performed in producing a product or delivering a service that does not add value, where value is defined as changing the form, fit, or function of the product or service and is something for which the customer is willing to pay.

normal distribution: The distribution characterized by the smooth, bell-shaped curve; synonymous with Gaussian distribution.

objective statement: A succinct statement of the goals, timing, and expectations of a Six Sigma improvement project.

opportunities: The number of characteristics, parameters, or features of a product or service that can be classified as acceptable or unacceptable.

out of control: A process is out of control if it exhibits variations larger than its control limits or shows a pattern of variation.

output: A resource, item, or characteristic that is the product of a process or system. *See also* Y and CTQ.

Pareto chart: A bar chart for attribute (or categorical) data where the categories are presented in descending order of frequency.

Pareto Principle: The general principle originally proposed by Vilfredo Pareto (1848–1923) that the majority of influence on an outcome is exerted by a minority of input factors.

Poka-Yoke: A transliteration of a Japanese term meaning "to mistake-proof."

probability: The likelihood of an event or circumstance occurring.

problem statement: A succinct statement of a business situation used to bound and describe the problem that a Six Sigma project is destined to solve.

process: A set of activities, material, and/or information flow that transforms a set of inputs into outputs for the purpose of producing a product, providing a service, or performing a task.

process certification: The act of establishing documented evidence that a process will consistently produce its required outcome or meet its required specifications.

process characterization: The act of quantitatively understanding a process, including the specific relationship(s) between its outputs and the inputs, and its performance and capability.

process flow diagram: *See* flowchart.

process member: An individual who performs activities within a process to deliver an output, product, or service to a customer.

process owner: The individual who has responsibility for process performance and resources, and who provides support, resources, and functional expertise to Six Sigma projects. The process owner is accountable for implementing Six Sigma solutions in processes.

quality function deployment (QFD): A systematic process for integrating customer requirements into every aspect of the design and delivery of products and services.

range: A measure of the variability in a data set; the difference between the largest and smallest values in a data set.

regression analysis: A statistical technique for determining the mathematical relation between a measured quantity and the variables upon which it depends; includes simple and multiple linear regression.

repeatability: The extent to which repeated measurements of a particular object with a particular instrument produce the same value. *See also* gauge R&R.

reproducibility: The extent to which repeated measurements of a particular object with a particular individual produce the same value. *See also* gauge R&R.

rework: Activities required to correct defects produced by a process.

risk priority number (RPN): In failure mode effects analysis, the aggregate score of a failure mode including its severity, frequency of occurrence, and ability to be detected.

rolled throughput yield (RTY): The probability of a unit going through all process steps or system characteristics with zero defects.

RUMBA: An acronym for Reasonable, Understandable, Measurable, Believable, and Achievable, used to describe a method for determining the validity of customer requirements.

run chart: A graphical tool for charting the performance of a characteristic over time.

scatter plot: A chart in which one variable is plotted against another to observe or determine the relationship, if any, between the two.

screening experiment: A type of experiment used to identify the subset of significant factors from among a large group of potential factors.

short-term variation: The amount of variation observed in a characteristic that has not had the opportunity to experience all the sources of variation from the inputs acting on it.

sigma score: A commonly used measure of process capability that represents the number of short-term standard deviations between the center of a process and the closest specification limit. Sometimes referred to as sigma level, or simply Sigma. Also called the Z score.

significant Y: The output of a process that exerts a significant influence on the success of the process or customer satisfaction.

SIPOC (Suppliers-Inputs-Process-Outputs-Customers): A visual representation of a process or system where inputs are represented by input arrows to a box (representing the process or system) and outputs are shown using arrows emanating out of the box.

Six Sigma: A proven and proscriptive set of analytical tools, project control techniques, reporting methods, and management techniques that combine to form breakthrough improvements in problem solving and business performance.

Six Sigma leader: An individual who leads the implementation of Six Sigma, coordinating all of the necessary activities, and who assures optimal results are obtained and keeps everyone informed of progress.

Six Sigma project: A specifically-defined effort that states a business problem in quantifiable terms and with known improvement expectations.

special cause variation: Those non-random causes of variation that can be detected by the use of control charts and good process documentation.

specification limits: The bounds of acceptable performance for a characteristic.

stability: A process with no recognizable pattern of change and no special causes of variation.

standard deviation: One of the most common measures of variability in a data set or in a population; the square root of the variance.

statistical problem: A problem that is addressed with facts and data analysis methods.

statistical process control (SPC): The use of basic graphical and statistical methods for measuring, analyzing, and controlling the variation of a process for the purpose of continuously improving the process. A process is said to be in a state of statistical control when it exhibits only random variation.

statistical solution: A data-driven solution with known confidence/risk levels; as opposed to a qualitative, or "I think," solution.

supplier: An individual or entity that provides an input to a process in the form of resources or information.

trend: A gradual, systematic change over time (or some other variable).

TSSW (thinking the Six Sigma way): A mental model for improvement that perceives outcomes through a cause-and-effect relationship combined with Six Sigma concepts to solve everyday and business problems.

two-level design: An experiment where all factors are set at one of two levels, denoted as low and high (–1 and +1).

upper control limit (UCL): The upper limit below which a process statistic must remain to be in control. Typically, this value is 3 standard deviations above the central tendency.

upper specification limit (USL): The highest value of a characteristic that is acceptable.

variability: The property of a characteristic, process, or system to take on different values when it is repeated.

variable data: Data where values are continuous, and can be meaningfully measured and subdivided; that is, can have decimal subdivisions.

variables: Quantities that are subject to change or variability.

variance: A specifically defined mathematical measure of variability in a data set or population. It is the square of the standard deviation.

variation: *See* variability.

VOB (voice of the business): The representation of the needs of the business and the key stakeholders of the business; usually including profitability, revenue, growth, market share, employee satisfaction, and so on.

VOC (voice of the customer): The representation of the expressed and non-expressed needs, wants, and desires of the recipient of a process output, a product, or a service; usually expressed as specifications, requirements, or expectations.

VOP (voice of the process): The performance and capability of a process to achieve both business and customer needs; usually expressed in some form of an efficiency and/or effectiveness metric.

waste: Material, effort, and time that does not add value in the eyes of key stakeholders (customers, employees, investors).

X: An input characteristic to a process or system. In Six Sigma, it is usually used in the expression of $Y = f(X)$, where the output (Y) is a function of the inputs (X).

Y: An output characteristic of a process. In Six Sigma, it is usually used in the expression of $Y = f(X)$, where the output (Y) is a function of the inputs (X).

Yellow Belt: An individual who receives approximately one week of training in Six Sigma problem solving and process optimization methods. Yellow Belts participate in Process Management activities, participate in Green and Black Belt projects and apply concepts to their work area and their job.

Z score: *See* sigma score.

Afterword

You hold in your hands *the* Six Sigma book for everyone! Perhaps you're a business owner, a manager, or even an executive. Or you may be an engineer or administrator. Maybe you're an employee in a Six Sigma company, or you're considering employment with one. Perhaps you're a student, and you want to improve your employment opportunities. Or maybe you're pondering a Six Sigma deployment in your company. Whether compelled or just curious, there is something in this book for everyone, just as there is something in Six Sigma for everyone.

Six Sigma is now found across the world and throughout all of business. It's not just for manufacturing anymore; in service and transactional businesses, not-for-profits, religious organizations, and governments, Six Sigma has improved thousands of organizations. Six Sigma is everywhere.

As the leader of the Six Sigma industry's professional society, I've seen businesses of all sizes and types use Six Sigma as a means to effect robust change and create extraordinary value. I've also seen professionals apply these tools to change their thinking, fuel significant contributions to their organizations, and gain personal opportunities beyond their dreams.

Written with a hands-on focus, *Six Sigma For Dummies* is a unique book in the world of Six Sigma. Unlike the story-telling, parable books or the advanced statistics tomes, in this book, you find clear explanations as well as practical insights. The authors still give you the statistical understanding, but with a unique emphasis on the how and the why.

Two dramatic things happen to people who read this book. First, they see their world very differently. They see cause-and-effect connections; recognize inputs, process flow, and outputs; and understand variation. Second, with this newfound understanding and great problem-solving knowledge, readers make improvements in their personal lives and work environments. This change in mindset alone eliminates countless frustrating problems and adds value worth thousands or even millions of dollars.

The power to make change for the better is now available to everyone. With the stakes higher than ever, *Six Sigma For Dummies* gives you the tools to improve and to prosper.

Roxanne O'Brasky
President, International Society of Six Sigma Professionals

Index

• *Numerics* •

2^k factorial experiments
  analysis, 207–215
  ANOVA (analysis of variance), 216
  blocking in, 206
  curvature, 216
  design matrix, 204–205
  equation general form, 214
  experimental codes, 204–205
  factor selection, 202–203
  fractional factorial experiments, 216
  interaction effects, 210–211
  level setting, 203–204
  main effects, 207–209
  randomization, 206
  replications, 216
  robustness, 216
  RSM (response surface methods) and
    optimization, 216
  Xs, 203
80-20 rule, 39–40
3-Cs Explorer, 280
Σ (sigma), sums in equations, 89

• *A* •

accountability, managerial perspective and, 13
accuracy in measurement, 155–156, 277
adjusted short-term capability index, 145–146
affinity diagram, business case writer and, 70
ALN (asynchronous learning network), 300
alpha risk, 173
analyze (DMAIC Analyze phase)
  description, 42
  project responsibilities and, 66
ANOVA (analysis of variance)
  2^k factorial experiments, 216
  statistical analysis, 267, 271
architecture of software, 280–282
as-is state, modeling, 255
ASA (American Statistical Association), 314
ASQ (American Society of Quality), 314
assignable cause variation, 100

associations, 314
asynchronous mentored learning, 300
attainable (RUMBA), 126
attribute data, 150–151
attribute data control charts
  defectives, 235
  introduction, 221
  p charts, 235, 237–238
  u charts, 235, 238–239
attribute measurement system studies,
    158–160
audit plan, data collection, 266
audits, MSA and, 156–158
autocorrelation, statistical analysis, 271
average. *See* mean

• *B* •

Bank of America, Six Sigma and, 12
basic stats, statistical analysis tool, 267
behavior charts, 117
believable (RUMBA), 126
belts, 71. *See also* Green Belt; Yellow Belt
benchmarks, stretch goals, 304
benefits, project definition and, 292
best fit, regression and, 275
best practices, 303–307
between/within analysis, process capability
    analysis, 274
binomial analysis, process capability
    analysis, 274
Black Belt
  characteristics, 53
  description, 51
  initiative roles, 55
  manager tools and, 285
  Master Black Belt, 52
blocking in experiments, 206
boil-the-ocean experiments, 200–201
box and whisker plots, 108–111
  exploratory analysis and, 276
  statistical analysis, 269
BPA (business process analysis) software, 279
BPM (business process management)
    software, 279

BPMN (business process modeling notation), 252
breakthrough
designing for, 44–45
improvement, 80
leverage for, 52
managing for, 45
processing for, 44
thinking for, 43–44
breakthrough equation ($Y = f(X) + \varepsilon$), 27–29
bullhorn, as tools, 288
business case writer
exercise, 70–71
projects and, 69–71
business metrics, managerial perspective and, 14
business unit leaders, core team, 49

• C •

capability. *See also* CCA (capability-complexity analysis)
improvement plan, 147–148
indices, 144–147
introduction, 123
KISS and, 262–263
yield, 128–133
capability and complexity analysis, process optimization tool, overview, 246
capability six-pack, process capability analysis, 274
casting a big net, 162–163
category data, 150–151
causation
connections, 32
correlation and, 31–32
cause and effect, inputs, 29
CBT (computer-based training), 299–300
CCA (capability-complexity analysis), 263
CDF (cumulative distribution function) plots, statistical analysis, 269
C&E (cause-and-effect) matrix, process optimization tool
fishbone chart and, 258–259
overview, 246
celebration, best practices and, 306
central limit theorem
introduction, 170
sampling distribution and, 171

Champions
characteristics, 48
deployment and, 57
project definition and, 71
tools and, 285
change, managerial perspective and, 15–16
characteristic charts
creating, 118
runs, 120
shifts, 121
trends, 120
variation beyond expected limits, 119–120
characterizing experiments, 201
CLs (control limits)
histograms and, 224
probability and, 224
coaching, Black Belts and, 53
coded design matrix, 2^k factorial experiments, 205
coincidence, correlation and, 32
Collins, Jim *(Good to Great),* 11
commitment, managerial perspective and, 13
common cause variation, processes and, 225
common-cause variation, 34, 97
communication and leadership tools, 286–288
communications, plan, initialization and, 56
communications representative, core team, 49, 50
compensation plans, change and, 15
competency models, change and, 15
conditions, experiments, 197
conferences, 314–315
confidence intervals
averages, 174–175
χ^2, 176–177
differences between items, 174–176
introduction, 172
mean and, 172–176
proportions, 178–180
risk, 173
standard deviation, 176–178
summary table, 178–180
t values, 174
variation, 177–178
confounding, correlation and, 32
consultants, 317
continuous control charts
$\overline{X} - R$ (averages and ranges) chart, 231, 234
$\overline{X} - S$ (averages and standard deviation) chart, 235

I – MR (individual and moving range) chart, 231, 232–233
  pairs, 231
  SPC, 230
continuous data, 151–152
continuous data control charts, 221
continuous variable measurement system studies, 160–161
control chart, SPC
  attribute data control charts, 221, 235–239
  attributes, 223
  continuous data control charts, 221
  control limits, 223
  data collection, 229–230
  distribution, 222
  drifts and, 227
  LCL (lower control limit), 223
  limits, 226
  patterns and, 227
  rational subgroups, 230
  sample data, 226
  shifts and, 227
  subgroup data, 226
  trending, 222
  UCL (upper control limit), 223
  zones, 227
control limits. *See* CLs (control limits)
Control phase, 42, 66
  emphasis on, 217
  plan aspects, 218
  process control of inputs, 218
  process control plan, 219–221
  process monitoring of outputs, 218
control plan
  data collection, 266
  projects, 65
core team
  characteristics, 49
  description, 48–49
  members, 49
correlation
  causation and, 31–32
  description, 30–32
  relationships, 180–183
  scatter plots, 113
  superstitious delusions, 31–32
correlation coefficient, calculating, 182
cross-correlation, statistical analysis, 271
CT (critical to) tree, 245, 249

CTQs (critical-to-quality outputs)
  continuous control charts, 230
  process management summary and, 219
CTXs (critical-to-X characteristics)
  distributions and, 88
  introduction, 17
  performance, 18–19
  statistics and, 85
culture change, managerial perspective and, 16
curvature, 2^k factorial experiments, 216
curve fitting
  multiple linear regression, 193–194
  relationships and, 183–194
customers
  manager tools and, 286
  managerial perspective and, 13

● *D* ●

3D scatter plots, statistical analysis, 269
data, best practices and, 305
data collection, control charts, 229–230
data collection plan
  audit plan, 266
  control plan, 266
  format, 265
  sources, 265
  stability, 265
  timing, 265
  transfer, 265
data types
  attribute data, 150–151
  category data, 150–151
  continuous data, 151–152
  ordinal data, 151
  rank order, 151
  variable data, 151–152
decomposition, time-series analysis, 270
defect rate
  DPMO (defects per million opportunities), 134–137
  DPO (defects per opportunity), 134–137
  DPU (defects per ubiquitous unit), 134
  failure and, 133–134
  metrics summary, 137
  Poka-Yoke, 239
  yield and, 138
defectives, attribute data control charts, 235–239

Define phase
  description, 42
  focus, 63
  project responsibilities and, 66
deployment
  Champion selection, 57
  expansion and, 58
  initialization and, 56
  sustain phase, 59
deployment leader
  core team, 49
  responsibilities, 47
  tools and, 285
Design FMEA, 260
design matrix, 2^k factorial experiments, 204–205
designing domain
  description, 43
  designing for breakthrough, 44–45
  DFSS (Design for Six Sigma), 44–45
determinism
  breakthrough equation and, 28
  proactivity, 31
deviation, variation spread and, 95
DFM (design for manufacturability), 271
DFSS (Design for Six Sigma), design and, 44–45
distribution (statistics)
  control charts, 222
  CTXs and, 88
  definition, 88
  degree of dispersion, 92
  mode, 89
  object statements and, 88
  range, 91–92
  sampling distribution, 171
  squaring, 93
  SSE (summed squared error), 93
  variance, 94
DMAIC (Define-Measure-Analyze-Improve-Control)
  analyze, 42
  control, 42
  define, 42
  improve, 42
  improvement methodology, 42
  introduction, 41
  measure, 42
  recognize, 43
  tollgates, 42

DOE (Design of Experiments), statistical analysis
  factorial designs, 273
  introduction, 267
  response surface designs, 273
  steps, 272–273
  Taguchi designs, 273
domains of activity
  designing, 43
  managing, 43
  processing, 43
  thinking, 43
dot plots
  creating, 103–104
  interpreting, 104–108
  statistical analysis, 269
  variation mode, 104–107
  variation shape, 104
DPMO (defects per million opportunities), 134–137
DPO (defects per opportunity), 134–137
DPU (defects per ubiquitous unit), 134
drifts, control charts, detecting, 227
Dupont, Six Sigma and, 12

• E •

e-learning Six Sigma, 299–300
e-mail presentations, 287
enterprise platforms for software, 281–282
entitlement level
  definition, 101
  processing for breakthrough, 44
equation. *See* breakthrough equation
errors, Poka-Yoke, 101
Excel, 279
executive representatives
  core team, 49
  tools and, 285
expansion, deployment and, 58
expectation, variation and, 33
experiments
  analysis, 207–215
  ANOVA (analysis of variance), 216
  blocking, 206
  boil-the-ocean experiments, 200–201
  characterizing, 201
  codes, 204–205
  conditions, 197

curvature, 216
fractional factorial experiments, 216
inputs, 197
interaction effects, 210–211
introduction, 195–196
2^k factorial experiments, 202–215
levels, 197
main effects, 207–209
observational studies and, 196
one-factor-at-a-time approach, 199
optimization, 201
Pareto Principle and, 203
Plackett-Burman designs, 203
planning, 200
progressive, iterative approach, 201–202
purpose, 196
randomization, 206
replications, 197, 216
response and, 197
robustness, 216
RSM (response surface methods) and
    optimization, 216
runs, 197
runs, minimizing number, 200
screening, 201
significant effects, 212–214
Six Sigma approach, 200
super-experiments, 200–201
trial-and-error approach, 198–199
variables, 197
variables, multiple, 200
*X*s and, 196
Y, 198
exploratory analysis, statistical analysis,
    268, 276
exponential smoothing, statistical
    analysis, 271

• *F* •

face-to-face communication, tools, 287
factorial designs, DOE, 273
factors, 2^k factorial experiments
    levels, setting, 203–204
    selecting, 202–203
failure, defects and, 133–134
fat pencil test, scatter plots, 115
finance representative
    core team, 49, 50
    tools and, 285

finances guidelines, initialization, 56
fishbone diagram process optimization tool
    C&E and, 259
    overview, 246
fitted line, regression and, 275
FMEA (failure mode effects analysis) process
        optimization tool
    applications, 260
    likelihood of detection, 261
    overview, 246
    probability of occurrence, 261
    severity of impact, 261
forecasting, time-series analysis, 270
formal presentations, tools, 287
format, data collection, 265
fractional factorials, 2^k factorial experiments,
    203, 216
FTY (first time yield), 129–130
functional representatives
    core team, 49
    project definition and, 71
functional sub-optimzation, software, 281
funnel analogy, measurement, 161–163
funnel reports, 264

• *G* •

gauge variable measurement system studies,
    160–161
General Electric, Six Sigma and, 12
goals
    best practices and, 306
    stretch goals, 303–304
Good to Great, 11
grade, quality comparison, 17
graphical analysis, observational studies and,
    165–167
Green Belt
    characteristics, 53
    description, 51
    initiative roles, 55
    manager tools and, 285
    training, 52

• *H* •

hard savings, 76
hidden factory, 21, 130–131
hierarchy of roles, 52

histograms
  control limits and, 224
  creating, 103–104
  interpreting, 104–108
  multi-modal, 106
  statistical analysis, 269
  variation mode, 104–107
  variation shape, 104
history of Six Sigma, 15
Honeywell, Six Sigma and, 12
human resources, guidelines, initialization
    and, 56
human resources representative, core team,
    49, 50

• *I* •

I – MR (individual and moving range) chart,
    231, 232–233
iGrafx, 280
implementation, successes, 57
impromptu presentations, tools, 287
improve phase
  breakthrough improvement, 80
  description, 42
  how much, 78–80
  project responsibilities, 66
information technology representative
  core team, 49, 50
  initialization, 56
initialization
  communications plan, 56
  deployment process and, 56
  elements, 56
  finance guidelines, 56
  HR guidelines, 56
  information technology and, 56
  launch planning, 56
  management dashboard, 56
  project reporting, 56
  project selection, 56
  project tracking, 56
initiatives
  lifecycle, 55–59
  overview, 46–47
  stages, 55
inputs
  cause and effect, 29
  experiments, 197
  measurement and, 36

interaction effects
  experiments, 210–211
  multiple linear regression, 193
interaction effects plots, observational
    studies and, 167
interval plots, statistical analysis, 269
IQPC (International Quality and Productivity
    Center), 315
ISSSP (International Society of Six Sigma
    Professionals), 314
iterative approach to experiments, 201–202
Ixperion, 315

• *J* •

JMP, 279
job roles, change and, 15

• *K* •

key executive representatives, core team, 49
KISS, capability-complexity and, 262–263
KM (knowledge management) tools, 298
knowledge management tools, 286

• *L* •

launch
  planning, initialization and, 56
  process, 83–84
LCL (lower control limit), 223
leadership
  hierarchy of roles, 54
  managing for breakthrough and, 45
leadership system, change and, 15
learning tools, 286
least squares, regression and, 275
letter values, exploratory analysis and, 276
letters, as tools, 288
levels
  experiments, 197
  factors, experiments, 203–204
leverage, overview, 38–40
line fitting, relationships and, 191–192
Linux platforms for software, 281
logistics, regression and, 275
long-term capability indices, 146–147

long-term sigma score, 140–141
long-term variation. *See* LT (long-term variation)
Lord Kelvin, 36
LSL (lower specification limit), 125
LT (long-term variation)
  formulas, 100
  introduction, 35
  overview, 99–101
  ST (short-term) variation, 102

• *M* •

Macintosh platforms for software, 281
main effects, experiments, 207–209
main effects plots
  multiple linear regression, 193
  observational studies and, 167
management dashboard, initialization and, 56
management tools
  Black Belts, 285
  Champions, 285
  communication and leadership tools, 286
  communications, 287–288
  customers, 286
  deployment leaders, 285
  executive management, 285
  financial executives, 285
  Green Belts, 285
  introduction, 283
  knowledge management tools, 286
  learning tools, 286
  Process Owners, 285
  project management, 286, 288–295
  reporting tools, 286
  suppliers, 285
  Yellow Belts, 285
managerial perspective of Six Sigma
  accountability and, 13
  change and, 15–16
  commitment and, 13
  connected business metrics and, 14
  customers and, 13
  introduction, 11
  process orientation, 14
  project focus, 14
  ROI (return on investment), 13
  science and leadership bridge, 12–13
  successful companies, 12
  technology and, 14

  tools, 14
  VOC (voice of the customer) and, 13
managing domain, 43, 45
marginal plots, statistical analysis, 270
Master Black Belt. *See* MBB
matrix plots, statistical analysis, 269
MBB (Master Black Belts), overview, 52–53
mean
  calculating, 89–90
  confidence intervals, 172–176, 174–175
  time-series analysis, 270
  variation and, 33, 89
  variation location and, 91
measurable (RUMBA), 126
Measure phase
  description, 42
  project responsibilities and, 66
measurement
  confidence, 171
  funnel analogy, 161–163
  Lord Kelvin and, 36
  observational studies, 163–165
  output values, 88
  pitfalls, 311
  statistics and, 87–88
  variation, 87
  variation, location, 88–91
  visual inspection, 157–158
measurement system
  accuracy, 154–155
  attribute measurement system studies, 158–160
  capability analysis, 152–161
  continuous variable measurement system studies, 160–161
  gauge variable measurement system studies, 160–161
  graphical analysis, 165–167
  MSA, 156–161
  precision, 155–156
  precision, repeatability, 155
  precision, reproducibility, 155
  resolution, 154
  variation sources, 154–156
measurement systems analysis, statistical analysis, 268, 276–278
median, 90, 91
median polish, exploratory analysis and, 276
memos, as tools, 288
mentoring, Black Belts and, 53
methodology, applications, 13

metrics summaries
  defect rate, 137
  yield, 133
Minitab, 279
mistake-proofing. *See* Poka-Yoke
mode
  distribution and, 89
  variation location and, 91
modeling, process optimization tool
  as-is state, 255
  baseline setting, 255
  BPMN (business process modeling
    notation), 252
  closed-loop behavior simulation, 255
  overview, 245
  process maps, 251
  process maps, drawing, 252–253
  process points, 253–254
  process setting, 255
  SIPOC and, 255
  swim lanes, 254
  to-be state, 255
Motorola, Six Sigma and, 12
moving averages, time-series analysis, 270
MSA (measurement system analysis), audits,
  156–158
multi-modal histograms
  definition, 106
  outliers, 107
  variation average, 107
  variation range, 107
multi-variable analysis, process capability
  analysis, 274
multi-variable studies, observational studies
  and, 167
multiple linear regression, 184, 193–194
multivariate analysis, statistical analysis,
  268, 275–276

• *N* •

n, data sets in equations, 89
needs assessment
  project focus and, 66–67
  strategies, 67–68
  VOB (voice of the business) and, 68
  VOC (voice of the constomer) and, 68

non-normal analysis, process capability
  analysis, 274
normal analysis, process capability
  analysis, 274

• *O* •

objective statements
  distributions and, 88
  overview, 80
  writing, 82–83
objectives, project definition and, 292
observational studies
  description, 163–165
  experiments and, 196
  graphical analysis and, 165–167
  interaction effects plots, 167
  main effects plots, 167
  multi-variable studies, 167
obsession, variation obsession, 33
one-factor-at-a-time approach to
  experiments, 199
one-sided specifications, 124
operation cycle time, process maps, 253
opportunities, 135, 312
optimization experiments, 201, 216
ordinal data, 151
outcome
  determining, 304
  measurement and, 36
outliers
  multi-modal histograms, 107
  variation, 90
output, continuous control charts, 230
output values, statistics and, 88
output variation, special cause factors, 100
overall effect, multiple linear regression, 193

• *P* •

p charts (attribute data), 235, 237–238
pairing continuous control charts, 231
Pareto diagrams
  experiments and, 203
  measurement systems and, 158
  RPN (risk priority number), 262
  statistical analysis, 269
partial least squares, regression and, 275
patterns in control charts, detecting, 227

PC-Windows, 280–281
performance, CTX, 18–19
periodicals, 316
phone calls as tools, 288
pitfalls, 309–312
Plackett-Burman experiment designs, 203
planning experiments, 200
plans, process optimization tool, overview, 246
platforms and protocols, software, 278–280
plots and charts, statistical analysis tool
  box and whisker plots, 108–111, 269
  CDF plots, 269
  3D scatter plots, 269
  dot plots, 103, 269
  histograms, 103, 269
  interval plots, 269
  introduction, 267
  matrix plots, 269
  Pareto charts, 269
  scatter plots, 111–113, 269
Poisson analysis, process capability analysis, 274
Poka-Yoke
  errors and, 101
  examples, 261
  overview, 239
  transactional processes and, 240
  Type-1 corrective action and, 240
  Type-2 corrective action and, 240
practical solution, projects, 65
precision in measurement, 155–156, 277
probability density function (statistics), 88
probability distribution (statistics), 88
probability plots, statistical analysis, 270
problem statements
  examples, 77–78
  introduction, 76
  structure, 76
problems
  improvements, 78–80
  objective statements, 80, 82–83
  themes, 68
  transformation, 65
process behavior charts
  creating, 118
  runs, 120
  shifts, 121
  trends, 120
  variation beyond expected limits, 119–120

process capability analysis, statistical analysis
  between/within analysis, 274
  binomial analysis, 274
  capability six-pack, 274
  introduction, 267
  multi-variable analysis, 274
  non-normal analysis, 274
  normal analysis, 274
  Poisson analysis, 274
  VOC (voice of the customer) and, 273
  VOP (voice of the process) and, 273
process control plan
  administrative section, 220
  introduction, 219
  method of control, 220
  SOPs, 220–221
  Type-1 corrective action, 240
  Type-2 corrective action, 240
process FMEA, 260
process leaders, project definition and, 71
process management summary, 219
process maps
  BPMN (business process modeling notation), 252
  costs, 254
  drawing, 252–253
  process points, 253–254
  value added, 254
process modeling. *See* modeling, process optimization tool
process optimization tools
  capability and complexity analysis, 246
  C&E (cause-and-effect) matrix, 246
  CT (critical to) tree, 245, 248–251
  description, 244
  fishbone diagram, 246
  FMEA (failure mode effects analysis), 246
  modeling, 245, 251–255
  plans, 246
  simulation, 246, 256–257
  SIPOC (Suppliers-Input-Process-Outputs-Customers), 245
  software, 279–280
process orientation
  managerial perspective and, 14
  processing for breakthrough, 44
Process Owners, tools and, 285
process problems, Green Belts, 53

processes
    common cause variation and, 225
    in control, 226
    control of inputs, 218
    description, 218
    monitoring of outputs, 218
    special-cause variation, 225, 228
    stable, 226
    tampering with the process, 218
    transactional, Poka-Yoke and, 240
processing domain, 43
product FMEA, 260
products, quality, 17–20
professional societies, 314
progressive approach to experiments, 201–202
project definition
    elements, 292
    improvements, 72–73
    mistakes, 71
    persons involved, 71
    steps in process, 72
    worksheet, 73
project focus
    characteristics, 64
    managerial perspective and, 14
    needs assessment and, 66–67
project management tools
    definition, 289–290, 291–292
    description, 286
    ideation, 289–290
    reporting, 295–297
    selection, 290–291
    tracking, 293–295
project reporting, initialization and, 56
project selection
    change and, 16
    guidelines, initialization, 56
project tracking, initialization and, 56
projects
    business case writer function, 69–71
    characteristics, 64
    launching, 83–84
    life cycle, 64–65
    problem themes, 68
    problem transformation, 65
    responsibilities of those involved, 65–66
    savings, 76
    strategies, 67–68
proportions, confidence intervals, 178–180
publications, 315
purpose, project definition and, 292

• Q •

quality
    grade comparison, 17
    technical perspective and, 17–20

• R •

$\overline{X} - R$ (averages and ranges) chart, 231, 234
randomization in experiments, 206
range of distribution
    definition, 91–92
    variation spread and, 95
rank order data, 151
rational subgroups, control charts, 230
RDMAIC, 43
reasonable (RUMBA), 126
Recognize phase, 43
regression, statistical analysis, 268, 275
relationships
    correlation, 180–183
    curve fitting, 183–194
    fitting lines, 191–192
    multiple linear regression, 184
    residuals, 186–187
    scatter plots, 180–181
    simple linear regression, 184
reliability and survivability, statistical
        analysis, 268, 278
repeatability of precision in
        measurement, 155
replications
    experiments, 197
    2^k factorial experiments, 216
reporting
    funnel reports, 264
    project management tools and, 295–297
    simulations, 257
    tools, 286
reproducibility of precision in
        measurement, 155
residuals, 186–187, 189
resistant line, exploratory analysis and, 276
resistant smoothing, exploratory analysis
        and, 276
resolution, measurement, 154
resources
    associations, 314
    colleagues, 313
    conferences, 314–315

consultants, 317
periodicals, 316
process maps, 253
professional societies, 314
publications, 315
Six Sigma corporations, 314
symposia, 314–315
technology vendors, 317
Web portals, 316
response, experiments and, 197
response surface designs, DOE, 273
results
process simulations, 257
projects, 65
targeting, 304
rise to run, line slope, 116
risk
alpha risk, 173
confidence intervals, 173
risk and controls, project definition and, 292
robustness, 2^k factorial experiments, 216
ROI (return on investment), value and, 13
Rootogram, exploratory analysis and, 276
RPN (risk priority number)
FMEA (failure effects mode analysis) and, 261–262
Pareto charts, 262
RSM (response surface methods), 2^k factorial experiments, 216
RSS (Royal Statistical Society), 314
RTY (rolled throughput yield), 131–133
RUMBA, 125
runs, experiments, 197, 200

• S •

$\overline{X} - S$ (averages and standard deviations) chart, 231, 235
sample data, control charts, 226
sampling distribution, 171
savings
hard savings, 76
soft savings, 76
scatter plots
correlation amount, 113
correlation direction, 115
creating, 111–113
fat pencil test, 115
relationships, 180–181
slope of line, 116–117
statistical analysis, 269
strength of effect, 115
schedule, project definition and, 292
science and leadership, managerial perspective, 12–13
screening
experiments, 201
measurement and, 157–158
second-order effects, multiple linear regression, 193
self-healing culture, sustain phase, 59
service, quality, 17–20
shared repositories, as tools, 288
shifts, control charts, detecting, 227
short-term capability index, 144–145
short-term sigma score, 140–141
short-term variation. *See* ST (short-term variation)
sigma scale, 23–24
sigma shift, 141–143
Sigma (Z) score
changing, 140
deviations, 138–140
score table, 142–143
short-term vs. long-term, 140–141
sigma shift, 141–143
SigmaFlow, 280
simple linear regression, 184
simulation, process optimization tool
configuration, 256–257
overview, 246
reports, 257
results, 257
simulation environment, 256
SIPOC (Suppliers-Input-Process-Outputs-Customers), 245
developing, 247–248
process modeling and, 255
VOC (voice of the customer) and, 248
Six Sigma
Bank of America and, 12
breakthrough equation, 27–29
description, 9
Dupont and, 12
General Electric and, 12
history, 15
Honeywell and, 12
management system orientation, 13–16
managerial perspective, 11–16

Six Sigma *(continued)*
  Motorola and, 12
  overview, 9–11
  sigma scale, 23
  technical perspective, 16–25
  terminology origins, 23
Six Sigma deployment. *See* deployment
Six Sigma improvement. *See* improvement
Six Sigma organization. *See* organization
Six Sigma performance. *See* performance
skewed distribution, dot plots/
    histograms, 104
skill levels
  Black Belt (*See* Black Belt)
  Green Belt (*See* Green Belt)
  Yellow Belt (*See* Yellow Belt)
SL (specification limit), 124
slope, scatter plot lines, 116–117
soft savings, 76
software
  enterprise platforms, 281–282
  introduction, 278
  Linux, 281
  Macintosh, 281
  PC-Windows, 280–281
  process optimization, 279–280
  statistical analysis, 279
software FMEA, 260
SOPs (standard operating procedures),
    process control plan and, 220–221
sources, data collection, 265
SPC (statistical process control)
  continuous control charts, 230–235
  control chart, 221
special-cause variation, 35, 225, 228
specifications
  exceeding, 126–128
  limits, 226
  LSL (lower specification limit), 125
  one-sided, 124
  reasons for, 124
  RUMBA, 125–126
  SL (specification limit), 124
  T (target), 125
  two-sided, 124
  USL (upper specification limit), 125
  voice of the customer (VOC), 123
square root, 94

squared effects, multiple linear regression, 193
squaring, distribution and, 93
SSBI (Six Sigma Benchmarking
    Association), 314
SSE (summed squared error), 93, 190
SSR (squared regression error), 189–190
SSTO (total sum of the squared error),
    residuals and, 189
ST (short-term variation)
  common-cause variation and, 97
  formulas, 100
  introduction, 35
  LT (long-term) comparison, 102
  overview, 96
  standard deviation calculation, 98
stability, data collection, 265
standard deviation
  confidence intervals, 176–178
  ST calculation, 98
  variation spread and, 95
statistical analysis tools
  ANOVA, 267, 271
  basic stats, 267
  description, 244
  DOE (Design of Experiments), 267
  exploratory analysis, 268, 276
  marginal plots, 270
  measurement systems analysis, 268
  multivariate analysis, 268, 275–276
  plots and charts, 267
  probability plots, 270
  process capability analysis, 267, 273–274
  regression, 268, 275
  reliability and survivability, 268, 278
  software, 279
  time series, 267
  time series plots, 270
  tolerance analysis, 267, 271–272
statistical problem, projects, 65
statistical process control. *See* SPC
    (statistical process control)
statistical solution, projects, 65
statistics
  distribution, 88
  introduction, 85
  measurement and, 87–88
  reason for, 86
  variation, 86

stem-and-leaf, exploratory analysis and, 276
stepwise, regression and, 275
strategies, needs assessment and, 67–68
strength of effect, scatter plots, 115
stretch goals, 303–304
subgroup data, control charts
  collecting, 226
  rational subgroups, 230
successful companies, 12
super-experiments, 200–201
superstitious delusions, correlation and, 31–32
suppliers, manager tools and, 286
sustain phase, deployment and, 58–59
swim lanes, process modeling, 254
symposia, 314–315
synchronous mentored learning, 300

• T •

T (target), 125
t values, confidence intervals, 174
Taguchi designs, DOE, 273
tampering with the process, 218
team members, project definition and, 292
technical perspective
  introduction, 16
  product quality, 17–20
  service quality, 17–20
  transactional quality, 17–20
technology
  leveraging, 312
  managerial perspective and, 14
  vendors, 317
thinking domain
  description, 43
  thinking for breakthrough, 43–44
time series, statistical analysis tool
  introduction, 267
  time-series analysis tools, 270
time-series analysis
  autocorrelation, 271
  cross-correlation, 271
  decomposition, 270
  exponential smoothing, 271
  forecasting, 270
  moving averages, 270
  trending, 270
time series plots, statistical analysis, 270

timing, data collection, 265
to-be state, modeling, 255
tolerance analysis, statistical analysis, 267, 271–272
tollgates (DMAIC), 42
tools
  knowledge management, 298
  management tool types, 286
  manager tools, 283
  managerial perspective and, 14
  overview, 243
  process optimization tools, 244–266
  project management, 288–295
  statistical analysis tools, 244, 267–278
trainers in Six Sigma, 318
training representative, core team, 49, 50
transactions
  processes, Poka-Yoke and, 240
  quality, 17–20
transfer, data collection, 265
transformations, problem transformations, 65
Traxion, 279
trending
  control charts, 222
  time-series analysis, 270
trial-and-error approach to experiments, 198–199
two-sided specifications, 124
Type-1 corrective action, process control and, 240
Type-2 corrective action, process control and, 240

• U •

u charts (attribute data), 235, 238–239
UCL (upper control limit), 223
understandable (RUMBA), 126
USL (upper specification limit), 125

• V •

variable data, 151–152
variables, experiments, 197, 200
variance
  beyond expected limits, 119–120
  definition, 94
  variation spread and, 95

variation
  assignable cause variation, 100
  best practices, 306
  causes, 34–35
  common-cause, 34, 97
  confidence intervals, 177–178
  description, 33
  distribution, range, 91–92
  expectation and, 33
  introduction, 32–33
  location, measures, 88–91
  long-term, 35
  LT (long-term variation), 99
  mean, 33, 89
  measurement and, 87
  measurement system sources, 154–156
  median, 90
  outliers, 90
  output, 100
  short-term, 35
  special-cause, 35, 100
  spread, 95
  statistics and, 86
  variance, 94
  variation obsession, 33
  wiggle, bump, and jitter, 22–23
variation average, multi-modal
    histograms, 107
variation mode, dot plots/histograms,
    104–107
variation range, multi-modal histograms, 107
variation shape
  dot plots, 104
  histograms, 104
Varyx, 280
Visio, 280
visual inspection system, scenario, 157
visualization, experiments' main effects,
    207–209
vital few versus the trivial many, 39–40
VOB (voice of the business)
  needs assessment and, 68
  SIPOC and, 248

VOC (voice of the customer)
  managerial perspective and, 13
  needs assessment and, 68
  process and, 128–148
  SIPOC and, 248
  specifications and, 125
VOP (voice of the process), SIPOC and, 248

• W •

WCBF (worldwide conventions and business
    forums), 315
Web portals, 316
whiskers (box and whisker plots), 108

• X–Y–Z •

x_i, measurement values in equations, 89
Xs
  experiments and, 196
  2^k factorial experiments, 203
  χ^2, 176–177

Y, experiments, 198
Yellow Belt
  characteristics, 53
  description, 51
  initiative roles, 55
  manager tools and, 285
  training, 52
$Y = f(X) + \varepsilon$, 27–29
yield
  defect rate and, 138
  FTY (first time yield), 129–130
  hidden factory, 130–131
  measuring, 128–133
  metrics summary, 133
  output versus input, 128–129
  RTY (rolled throughput yield), 131–133
  traditional, 128–129

Z score. *See* Sigma (Z) score